11.25

CBoama

ALSO BY PAUL HOFMANN

That Fine Italian Hand
Cento Città
The Viennese
O Vatican! A Slightly Wicked View of the Holy See
Rome: The Sweet, Tempestuous Life

Vaticano

Porta Angelica

Porta Castello

Castello S.ᵗᵒ Angelo

A

Fabrica
Porta Cavallegiere

C

Villa Barberini

M.ᵗᵉ Gianicolo

Giardino Botanico

R O M
(ROMA)

N

48

Villa Corsini

Porta S. Pancrazio
Aquaduct.   *Villa Spada*

Masstäbe.

Pariser Fuss

500   1000   2000   3000

Römische Palmen

ROMA

*The Smart Traveler's Guide
to the Eternal City*

PAUL HOFMANN

HENRY HOLT AND COMPANY
NEW YORK

Henry Holt and Company, Inc.
Publishers since 1866
115 West 18th Street
New York, New York 10011

Henry Holt® is a registered
trademark of Henry Holt and Company, Inc.

Published in Canada by Fitzhenry and Whiteside Ltd.,
91 Granton Drive, Richmond Hill, Ontario L4B 2N5.

Library of Congress Cataloging-in-Publication Data
Hofmann, Paul.
Roma: the smart traveler's guide to the Eternal City / Paul
Hofmann.—1st ed.
      p.   cm.
      1. Rome (Italy)—Guidebooks.
DG804.H64   1993
914.5'63204929—dc20   92-20991
                                                 CIP

ISBN 0-8050-1906-5

First Edition—1993

Designed by Katy Riegel

Printed in the United States of America
All first editions are printed
on acid-free paper.∞

1 3 5 7 9 10 8 6 4 2

Contents

ROMA

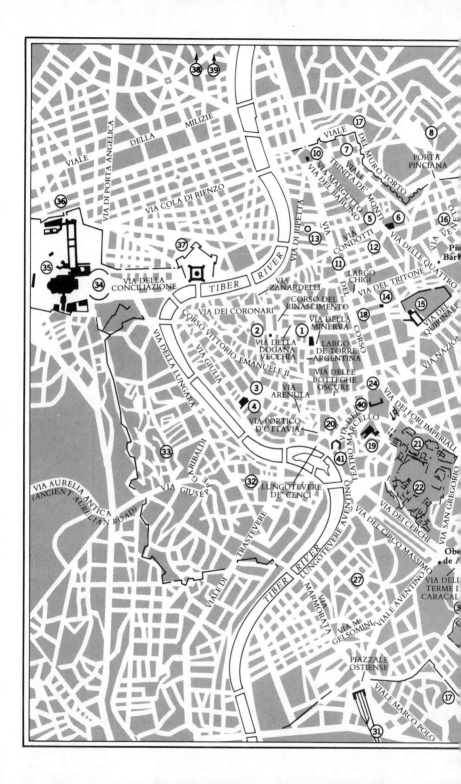

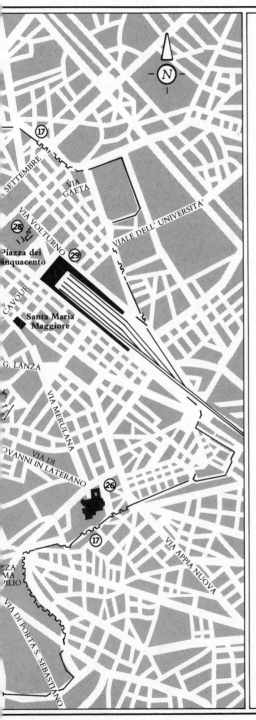

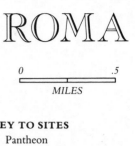

ROMA

0   .5

MILES

KEY TO SITES

1. Pantheon
2. Piazza Navona
3. Campo de' Fiori
4. Farnese Palace
5. Spanish Square
6. Trinità de' Monti
7. Pincio Gardens
8. Villa Borghese Gardens
9. Borghese Gallery
10. Piazza del Popolo
11. Via del Corso
12. Via Condotti
13. Mausoleum of Augustus
14. Trevi Fountain
15. Quirinal Palace
16. Via Veneto
17. Aurelian Walls
18. Piazza Colonna
19. Capitol
20. Former Jewish Ghetto
21. Roman Forum
22. Palatine
23. Colosseum
24. Piazza Venezia
25. San Pietro in Vincoli ("Moses")
26. Lateran
27. Aventine Hill
28. Baths of Diocletian
29. Stazione Termini
30. Baths of Caracalla
31. City Air Terminal
32. Trastevere Section
33. Janiculum
34. St. Peter's Square
35. Vatican City
36. Entrance to Vatican Museums
37. Castel Sant'Angelo
38. Olympic Stadium
39. Italic Forum
40. Mon. to Victor Emanuel II
41. Theater of Marcellus

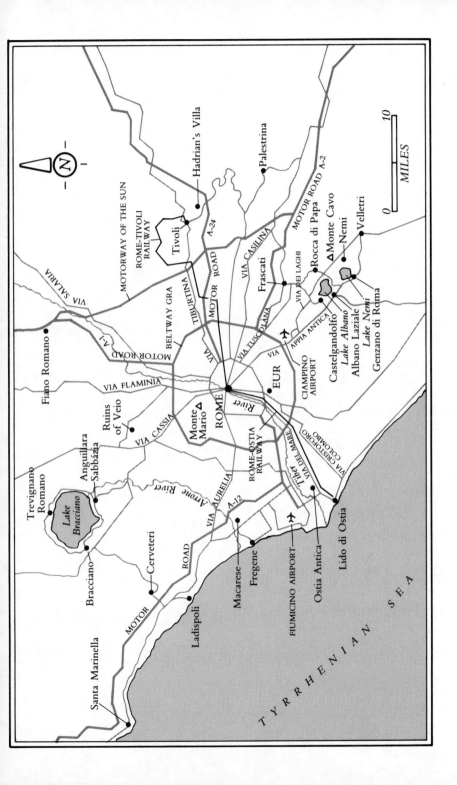

1.

First Impact

THE NEWCOMER TO a foreign place needs a while to get oriented, but first-time visitors to Rome may feel bewildered outright. On their way to the heart of the city from the airport, the railroad terminal, or the motorway they will be assailed by conflicting sensations, noise, and confusion. They glimpse solemn cypresses and umbrella pines as well as tacky houses festooned with laundry, arches, and truncated columns from antiquity near crowded and littered sidewalks. Suddenly a majestic panorama may become visible, with the dome of St. Peter's on the horizon or the sullen hulk of the Colosseum as backdrop to an avenue. It takes at least a few days to sort out one's initial impressions: this is a unique and multifaceted metropolis.

First, the Eternal Rome. Among its innumerable memorials are the 2,500-year-old she-wolf on the Capitol, the triumphal arches, the Egyptian obelisks, the walls that failed to stem the invading barbarians, the basilicas and tower strongholds from the Middle Ages, the Renaissance architecture and art, the exuberant baroque facades.

Another aspect is the grandeur of the Vatican, the center of one of the world's great faiths, with its prelates, priests, and nuns and with pilgrims from many countries flocking to the city of the popes and of more than five hundred churches.

At the same time, Rome is the capital of a major industrial democracy, housing a sprawling government apparatus. The dark blue limousines of its top politicians and high bureaucrats plow through traffic jams, escorted by police vehicles with sirens screaming and roof lights flashing. Including senators, deputies, journalists, and lobbyists, more than ten thousand persons are directly involved in the nation's politics and the making of its laws. An army of Roman men and women are employed in the government departments and semiofficial agencies that dot the city; many thousands rush home between 1 and 2 P.M. any working day for a late lunch.

Still lingering are the remnants of la dolce vita, the (in part imaginary) Eden of languorous hedonism that Federico Fellini projected in his 1960 film classic. Sultry beauties and tanned, relaxed men in stylishly casual attire still sit around café tables in lovely piazzas. Many Romans and quite a few foreign expatriates are still populating the local movie sets, television studios, and fashion houses; they mingle at parties in roof gardens and on terraces.

Immense are the cultural treasures of Rome, inexhaustible its historical memories, deeply stirring—to believers—its blessings. Talking to Romans, the guest will often hear that their city, so enjoyable only a few decades ago, has, alas, become *invivibile* (unlivable) because of the sclerotic traffic, the high-decibel sound level, the dirty streets and scruffy parks, the long lines in banks and post offices, the frequent strikes, the drug addicts and the purse snatchers.

Nineteen centuries ago the satirist Juvenal (a southerner) bitingly complained in Latin hexameters about the disorder, discomfort, and dangers of the imperial city. Today, if you stay on for some time you will discover that few of the contemporary grumblers really want to move elsewhere, and that, if they have to relocate, they will forever miss Rome's balmy climate, the tender artichokes, the quick trips to the espresso shop at the street corner two or three times a day, the gelato in the piazza, the easy way of dealing with people, the feeling that most difficulties can be smoothed over and that solutions to problems can be arranged somehow.

Romans generally go out of their way to be helpful to strangers, and warmly respond to a friendly, smiling face. It helps of course if the traveler has taken the trouble to learn a few basic Italian words and phrases and to memorize the numbers.

LANGUAGE

Unlike many Parisians, the Romans (and Italians in general) don't insist that a foreigner speak their language either to perfection or not at all. If Italian is mangled by a stranger, the natives won't show impatience or contempt but will probably applaud the try.

Keeping in mind a few pronunciation rules will be useful: *C* before *e* and *i* is pronounced like the English "ch," *g* before *e* and *i* like "j," and a double *gg* before *e* and *i* like "dj." *C* and *g* before the other vowels, and *ch* and *gh* before *e* and *i*, are pronounced as in the English "can" and "get." *Sc* before *e* and *i* is pronounced like the English "sh"; *gn* and *gl* between vowels are pronounced "nyi" and "lyi." *H* is always mute, *qu* is pronounced "kw," and the Italian *r* is rolled in a trill.

The stress is regularly on the penultimate syllable unless an accent indicates otherwise (*ia* is considered one syllable). Examples: *scheggia* (splinter), SKED-jah; *cicogna* (stork), chi-CON-yah; *sceglio* (I choose), SHEL-yoh; *biancheria* (linen), byan-ke-REE-ah; *quanto?* (how much?), KWAN-toh; *vedró* (I shall see), ved-ROH.

Mille means thousand, and the plural of this numeral is *mila*. You will hear it all the time when prices are quoted, because the Italian lira (plural: lire, symbol: L) is worth less than one-thousandth of a dollar, and you will have to spend thousands, hundreds of thousands, and maybe millions of lire during your sojourn. A project to introduce a new lira, equal to one thousand old ones, has long been debated, but even if it is eventually adopted most people inevitably will cling for years to the old lira figures.

If you want directions and don't feel like plunging into an Italian conversation, boldly ask any passerby, especially a younger one, your question in English. More and more Italians know at least a few English words from school, television, rock lyrics, sports, video games, and advertising and are proud to show off their linguistic skills, particularly if other local people can hear them too.

Americans of Italian background ought to be warned that it may be better for them to stick to English if they aren't familiar with idiomatic modern Italian. Romans, so tolerant of guests who don't speak their language well or don't speak it at all, are likely to snicker at the Italian-American who genially tries on them grandfather's archaic Sicilian or Friuli dialect and maybe addresses them as *paisà* (southern vernacular for *paesano*, "compatriot," also meaning "pal" or simply "hey, you!").

When trying to get the attention of a waiter or some-body behind a counter, or when requesting a piece of information of somebody, preface what you have to say with *senta, scusi!* (listen, excuse me!). Any request should be introduced with *per favore, per piacere* or—more formal—*per cortesía,* which all mean "please" but are more polite than a simple *prego,* which also means "please." Be lavish with *grazie* (thanks), or push courtesy to *molte grazie, grazie mille,* or *grazie infinite* ("many," "thousand," or "infinite thanks"). The correct response to a *grazie* is *prego,* in this context meaning "you are welcome." On entering or leaving a place or on meeting some person, say *buon giorno* (good day) from morning to about 5 P.M., later *buona sera* (good evening). A "good night" is *buona notte.* On being introduced to somebody, say *piacere* (it's a pleasure).

The Italian all-purpose greeting *ciao* (pronounced "chow"), which may mean "hi" or "so long," has lately become international. One should use it correctly only to address a person one knows well, if not intimately, and is on easy terms with. Recently, it is true, ciao is being heard also as a greeting to a group of people, but it still doesn't sound right. Address good friends or any child with ciao, but don't say it to a customs inspector, police officer, taxi driver, hotel concierge, waiter, or salesperson.

Gestures are an age-old means of interpersonal communication, especially around the Mediterranean Sea, and some are understood everywhere. Romans too gesticulate a lot, but not necessarily to indicate excitement. If someone joins the thumb, forefinger, and middle finger of the right hand and shakes them under your nose with little jerks from the wrist, there is no aggressive intent; the meaning is, "What do you want? I don't understand you." It's also sign language to give vent to frustration in general.

AIRPORTS AND AIR SERVICE

Some eighty airlines operate scheduled flights to Rome in addition to the charter services, especially during the main travel season in summer. Fiumicino, officially called **Leonardo da Vinci Airport**, near the old fishing town of Fiumicino on the seaside 17.5 miles (28 kilometers) southwest of the city center, normally handles all scheduled international and many domestic flights. There are separate international and domestic terminal buildings, linked by passageways and a courtesy bus. For flight information call 60121. **Ciampino Airport**, 9 miles (14.5 kilometers) southeast of the city center, shares its runways with the Italian air force and has a passenger terminal for charters and some domestic flights. In case of unfavorable weather or congestion, incoming international airliners may occasionally be rerouted from Fiumicino to Ciampino. For Ciampino flight information call 4694.

One of the European continent's major aerial gateways, Fiumicino counted sixteen million passengers (almost one-half of them on domestic flights) in 1992 and is being enlarged to an annual capacity of thirty million passengers by the year 2000. Fog is rare, but the airport has chronically suffered disruption from strikes by air traffic controllers, pilots, flight attendants, ground personnel, and fire fighters. If there is no work stoppage or peak holiday period, passengers don't have to wait long for their luggage, and passport and customs controls are ordinarily fast. However, occasional spot checks to catch drug smugglers are very thorough. The international and domestic terminals are patrolled by heavily armed police and soldiers, although actual security controls at embarkation gates often seem spotty.

Hotel information is available, and reservations can be

made at counters in the arrival lounges. Departing passengers will do well to be at the airport early, because at times only a few check-in positions are staffed, and lines are long. In addition to duty-free shops in the departure and transit lounges, airport boutiques offer Italian and imported designer articles; much of the merchandise is overpriced.

Yellow cabs are normally plentiful at Fiumicino, less so at Ciampino Airport. A cab ride from Fiumicino to the center of Rome or vice versa cost around $60 in 1992, depending on the traffic situation; from or to Ciampino Airport the fare was $30 to $35. Drivers of unlicensed cabs demand twice or three times the legal fare; if no yellow taxi is around and you decide to hire a gypsy cab to get to town quickly, negotiate the fare beforehand.

Like other international civil aviation hubs, Fiumicino Airport is connected with a satellite facility, the **City Air Terminal**, an outpost closer to the urban center—but, in Rome's case, not all that close. It is locally and officially called City Air Terminal, a reflection of how current Italian idiom is loaded with terms borrowed from English.

Railroad trains for the City Air Terminal leave from a station in front of the international terminal at Fiumicino Airport every twenty minutes from 5 A.M. to midnight. The trip takes twenty-five to thirty minutes, and in 1992 cost $5. If the ticket counter at Fiumicino Airport happens to be closed, rail tickets can be bought from vending machines. In this case you will need lira coins or small-denomination lira bills; they can be obtained from the money exchange in the arrivals lobby, where long lines are no rarity. It is a good idea to purchase a small quantity of lire before departure.

From 2:15 A.M. to 6 A.M. a bus shuttles four times between Fiumicino Airport and the City Air Terminal, the fare being the same as for the airport train. The spacious, glittering City Air Terminal, opened in 1990, is located in the outlying Ostiense section, a mile (1.6 kilometers) southwest of the Colosseum and considerably farther than that from most hotels. Arriving air passengers may find themselves stranded because of the frequent scarcity or absence of cabs at the City Air Terminal. Any time before 9 P.M. travelers looking for public transport should cross the Ostiense station of the Italian State Railways, which adjoins the City Air Terminal, by a system of escalators, underpasses, and people movers, and proceed to Line B of the Metropolitana, the Roman subway. To reach the subway the traveler will have to negotiate another escalator from Platform 1 of the Ostiense rail station and a long moving sidewalk in an underpass to the Piramide station of Line B.

If this sounds complicated, it is, especially for travelers encumbered by much luggage or those with children, and for disabled persons.

The subway's Line B stops running at 9 P.M. After that hour the No. 176 municipal bus will depart, at intervals, from outside the City Air Terminal; it shuttles between that facility and Rome's railroad terminal (Stazione Termini) without intermediate stops, taking about fifteen minutes for the trip. The subway's Line B also takes arriving air passengers to Stazione Termini.

At Stazione Termini cabs are usually to be found, although air passengers will have to line up together with arriving railroad travelers at a dispatcher's stand. The subway's Line A, which intersects with Line B beneath the Stazione Termini, runs until about midnight. Departing air travelers who take a cab to reach the City Air Terminal from their accommodation at the center of Rome will have to pay a fare of $10 to $12.

From Ciampino Airport a blue ACOTRAL bus leaves

at intervals of about an hour from 6:30 A.M. to 10 P.M. for the Anagnina terminal of the subway's Line A. The subway ride to Stazione Termini takes about twenty minutes.

Travel organizations arrange for coaches to meet tour groups at the airport. Many hotels will on request provide limousine service to or from the airport. Alitalia, the Italian national airline, operates a coach service between Fiumicino Airport and about two dozen hotels in Rome. Alitalia's Intermezzo Bus leaves the airport from a signposted stop outside the international arrivals lounge every hour or every two hours between 6 A.M. and 11 P.M.

The town offices of most airlines cluster in the Via Barberini, Via Bissolati, and Via Veneto area near major hotels. Request airport assistance for disabled passengers from the airline involved.

RAILROAD HUB ROME

The fast, comfortable EuroCity trains from various countries on the Continent, international night expresses with sleepers and bunk-compartment coaches (*couchettes*), and other long-distance trains, as well as regional rail traffic, all converge on **Stazione Termini**. This large terminal complex, completed in 1950, handles almost five hundred trains every day.

Travelers may check luggage in two halls, marked *Deposito Bagagli*, off Platform 1 and Platform 22, but there are no self-service lockers. The rail terminal houses shopping arcades on two levels, coffee shops, espresso bars, a first-aid station, a pharmacy, a "day hotel" with showers (see page 225), a Roman Catholic chapel, a police station, a post and telephone office, plenty of pay telephones, computer screens displaying train information in Italian, English, and other languages, a tourist information office, and bank branches.

The Termini subway station where lines A and B cross is reached from the railroad terminal's front arcade over stairways and escalators. Look for the white letter *M* (standing for *Metropolitana*) on a red field.

Municipal and regional buses (see page 229) depart from platforms in the Piazza dei Cinquecento facing the Stazione Termini. At the taxi rank outside the terminal's front gallery the yellow cabs tend to become rare in the evening. Travelers arriving on late trains are usually met by touts for gypsy cabs.

Delays of incoming trains are frequent, and outgoing trains too occasionally depart belatedly. Schedule changes are announced over a public address system and on electronic signboards.

In the front hall of the Stazione Termini, 390 feet (119 meters) in length, there are almost always long lines at the ticket windows. Many international and long-distance domestic trains require special supplements to the basic tariff. Ticket vending machines are lined up on the wall of the front hall opposite the ticket windows. The computerized touch-screen machines can be used to buy rail tickets to any station in Italy as well as supplements for trains requiring them. Youngsters brought up on video games like to work the machines, but some travelers give up after the message OPERATION CANCELED appears on the screen because they were too slow in answering the computer's questions or gave the wrong command. Travelers to faraway destinations are advised to reserve seats in advance at a small additional fee, as trains in Italy are frequently crowded.

Licensed private agencies throughout the city also sell

railroad tickets and are able to reserve seats, sleeper accommodation, or space in coaches with four to six bunks to each compartment (*couchette*). These agencies usually carry the "FS" (*Ferrovie dello Stato*) logo of the Italian State Railways on their storefront signs and operate terminals of the rail reservation computer system. Addresses of nearly two hundred such agencies can be found under the heading *Ferrovie dello Stato* in the Rome telephone directory. They all sell railroad tickets at the official tariff without any surcharge.

Assistance for disabled travelers at Stazione Termini can be arranged if a request is made by phone (461726) one day before it is needed.

As happens in other cities, the Rome railroad terminal attracts homeless persons and drifters. The Stazione Termini is adequately policed, but be on your guard nevertheless. The neighborhoods surrounding the railroad terminal are a high-risk area, teeming with drug addicts and prostitutes. The park between Piazza dei Cinquecento and Piazza della Repubblica is best shunned after dark.

Some long-distance trains running between northern Italy and the deep south stop not at Stazione Termini but only at the suburban Tiburtina station in Rome's east. Cabs are scarce there, but municipal buses and the subway's Line B link it with Stazione Termini and other neighborhoods. Some trains between Genoa, Rome, and Naples stop not only at Stazione Termini but also at the Ostiense station adjoining the City Air Terminal and at the Trastevere station in the city's southwest.

The state railways' official timetable is issued in spring and fall and can be bought at news vendors. One of its eight-hundred-odd pages explains its symbols in English.

QUEEN OF THE ROADS

A look at a map or satellite photo of Rome reveals the city
as a junction of some thirty major traffic arteries. Four of
them—to the north, east, south, and to the seaside in the
west—are modern multilane tollgate motor roads (*auto-
strade*). Others are national highways, mostly with undi-
vided lanes, for long stretches following the layout of the
roads that ancient Rome's consuls and other high officials
built, the so-called consular roads. The Roman legions
marched on them for hundreds of years; ancient flagstones
in a few sites where the original pavement is preserved
show the ruts worn by the wheels of military and civilian
chariots.

The oldest consular road, the Via Appia, was built by
Appius Claudius in 312 B.C. Leading originally to Capua,
north of Naples, it was later extended to what is now
Brindisi in the heel of the Italian boot, and beyond the sea
across Greece to Asia Minor. On Italian soil, National
Highway No. 7 is today the modern version of the Appian
Way, which the ancients called the Queen of the Roads.

Other consular roads radiating from Rome are the Via
Aurelia (now National Highway No. 1) to Pisa, Genoa,
and France; the Via Cassia (No. 2) to Siena; the Via Flaminia (No. 3) to Fano and Rimini on the upper Adriatic Sea;
the Via Salaria (No. 4) to Ascoli Piceno and the Adriatic;
the Via Tiburtina (No. 5) to Tivoli and Pescara; and the
Via Casilina (No. 6) to Cassino and Caserta.

The ancient names are still in everyday use. Ask a Roman how to drive to, say, Viterbo, and you will be told:
"Just take the Cassia."

All motor roads and major highways converging on
Rome are connected by a beltway surrounding the city at
7 to 9 miles (11 to 14.5 kilometers) from the center, the

Grande Raccordo Anulare (GRA). Traffic on this ring road often backs up for miles. Motorists driving between Florence and Naples on Autostrada A-1, the principal north-south motor road that is known also as the Highway of the Sun, can avoid the traffic of the capital and the GRA beltway by taking a bypass east of the city—not all roads lead to Rome nowadays.

A newcomer, perhaps in a rented car, who gets off the motor road and attempts to reach central Rome may have trouble finding it. The traffic signs are confusing even to local drivers; it is useful to have studied the street map beforehand. It also helps if the trip is timed so that the traveler arrives at the outskirts of Rome between 2 and 4 P.M. on weekdays and avoids Sunday afternoons, when major soccer matches cause traffic jams in a large area around the Olympic Stadium. During the siesta hours traffic slackens. On working days Rome has four rush periods—7:30 to 9 A.M., 1 to 2 P.M., 4 to 5 P.M., and 7 to 9 P.M. At midday many people scramble home for lunch and possibly a nap before going back to their jobs.

The foreign motorist who is sucked into Rome's traffic will quickly realize that it is a free-for-all with almost everybody fighting for every inch of street space. If the Appian Way (and Rome itself) is Queen of the Roads, every Roman driver seems to feel he, and he alone, is king of the street. Female motorists are as a rule more considerate than men, but this does not apply to the swarms of young women on mopeds and motor scooters. These light two-wheel conveyances roam the streets in packs, respecting no traffic rules. Scooters and mopeds are tolerated in areas where most cars are banned, and are parked on sidewalks, chained to some grate or utility pole.

For thousands of Romans, especially younger ones,

their two wheels are a way of beating the traffic by squeez-
ing between jammed cars and crossing intersections when
the light is red. If you feel up to such acrobatics you can rent
a scooter from Motonoleggio Scoot-A-Long, 302–304 Via
Cavour (6780206), not far from the Colosseum, or Scooters for Rent, 66 Via della Purificazione (465485), off the
central Piazza Barberini. For car rental, choose among the
many listings under *Autonoleggio* in the Rome telephone
directory or Yellow Pages.

If your car breaks down and you need assistance, call
4212, or 44595, the emergency phone numbers of the
Italian Automobile Club (ACI).

Parking in Rome's center and in a broad belt around it
is difficult most of the time. ACI operates a few open-air
parking lots (for instance, in a section of the Piazza del
Popolo), but they are usually filled to capacity. Two vast
underground parking garages are below the southern part
of the Villa Borghese gardens, accessible from the Via
Veneto by way of the Via del Muro Torto, and in the Via
Ludovisi, off the Via Veneto (entrance opposite the Eden
Hotel).

Double-parking along sidewalks and in other public
spaces is common, and the furious honking by motorists
who find their curbside car trapped behind others is a habit-
ual Roman sound. Self-appointed guardians make a living
outside restaurants, movie theaters, office buildings, and
in other much-frequented areas by packing every available
space with autos and extricating them again. They expect
a consideration for their services, usually a L1,000 note
(around 83¢). If after two or three appearances you
are known as a good tipper, the *posteggiatore* (roughly:
space finder) will always be able to accommodate your car
somehow.

If your car has vanished from where you left it, it

has not necessarily been stolen (although auto thefts are frequent). It may have been towed away by the municipal police. To find out in which of the storage areas the vehicle is waiting to be ransomed, call 6792495; waste no time, for every additional day costs money. Leave no objects, even of small value, in a parked car.

Although a large segment of the historic city center is closed to commercial traffic and to most autos during certain hours, it is often choked with official limousines, cars, and trucks covered by special permits, the cars of the various police forces, ambulances, and city buses. The narrow, frequently winding streets in the core district, laid out centuries ago for horsemen, litter carriers, and the carriages of the powerful and the wealthy, are ill adapted to the motor age.

Visitors should not only drive defensively but also walk defensively in Rome, especially in the many streets and lanes in the city core that lack sidewalks. Don't expect to get a break from local motorists at an intersection with the green light in your favor or at a crosswalk marked by zebra stripes: drivers coming out of a side street (usually without turn signals on) expect you to yield, and in order to make this clear they will often step on the gas pedal instead of the brake if they see a pedestrian in their way. Elderly people at times threaten inconsiderate motorists with their cane or umbrella, and everybody around laughs. An intrepid way of getting to the other side of the street is to walk with determined steps, ignoring oncoming traffic— but such defiance requires nerves of steel. It doesn't help to gaze boldly at aggressive drivers: they will stare back and drive right at you. Fortunately, the Romans, who often seem inert, have quick reflexes in fact, and fewer accidents occur than one might expect during these daily games of chicken.

Cabs are not supposed to cruise but are to drive to the nearest taxi rank when they are free; they will not necessarily stop when hailed. For radio-dispatched cabs call 3570, 4157, 6645, 8433, or 88177. Most of the time service is efficient and reliable, although during rush hours or when it rains the dispatcher may tell you that all cabs are engaged. Licensed (yellow) taxis have electronic meters, but meter tampering is not unknown. Supplements for trips to one of the airports, for trips at night, or for bulky luggage are legal. Cabbies expect a tip of between 5 and 10 percent of the fare on the meter. An increasing number of taxis have No Smoking signs.

A few licensed horse-drawn cabs can still be found in the Spanish Square, near the Colosseum, in St. Peter's Square, and in some other spots much frequented by tourists. The drivers won't mind posing with their horses for snapshots or films, but hiring them will be expensive. Always negotiate the fare beforehand! The ride, especially during the daytime, may turn out to be less than a romantic experience, because horse-drawn cabs should keep to the taxi lanes indicated on the major thoroughfares, are barred from many narrow streets, and all too often get stuck in traffic.

TRANSIT

The network of the Municipal Tram and Bus Enterprise (ATAC) covers all districts and reaches into distant suburbs. The few surviving trams are being phased out. For information on bus and tram routes and schedules, call 46954444.

Watch out for pickpockets on crowded buses, especially on the notorious No. 64, which runs between the railroad terminal (Stazione Termini) and St. Peter's Square; it is often packed with unwary tourists and is therefore a favorite hunting ground of local and visiting thieves.

The fare on city buses and trams was L800 in 1992 and due to be raised to at least L1,000 (83¢) in 1993. Tickets are bought at green booths near major stops or at some tobacconists and espresso bars. Validate them by inserting them in a machine inside each vehicle when boarding. Tickets entitle holders to travel for ninety minutes with any number of transfers. A day ticket, costing approximately $1.50, entitles the bearer to any number of bus and tram rides.

There is no free transfer between the bus and tram network on one hand and the subway on the other. Subway tickets (83¢ in 1992) are bought from machines in all stations and at windows in some, as well as from some tobacconists and espresso bars.

Warning: whoever is found without a valid ticket on a bus, streetcar, or subway is fined around $40 on the spot.

Subway Line A functions from 5 A.M. to about midnight, Line B from 5 A.M. to 9 P.M. on weekdays and until 11:30 P.M. on Sunday. Line A runs from Via Anagnina at the approaches to the Alban Hills in Rome's southeast to Via Ottaviano, two-fifths of a mile (650 meters) north of St. Peter's Square. It traverses the center with stops at Piazza Barberini, Piazza di Spagna (Spanish Square), and Piazza del Popolo. Line B, crossing Line A at the Stazione Termini stop, connects the northeastern outskirts at Rebibbia prison with the World's Fair district and the Laurentina station near sprawling army barracks in the city's far south. Line B connects with the railroad to Lido di Ostia, the seaside district that administratively is a part of the city of Rome.

Though regular transit service stops before midnight,

some municipal bus lines operate at intervals of between
one and two hours until 5 A.M., linking various parts of
the city.

Periodic attempts are made to relieve the city's traffic
woes by Tiber transit. The latest experiment is the *acquabus*
(water bus). Motorboats sail from the Ponte Duca d'Aosta,
a bridge near the Olympic Stadium on Rome's northern
outskirts, to the Garibaldi Bridge near the center and vice
versa at twenty-five-minute intervals, with one intermediate stop, from 8 A.M. to 8 P.M. daily except Monday.
Another *acquabus* service operates between the Trastevere
section and the archeological park of Ostia Antica, 14 miles
(22.5 kilometers) downstream.

Rome's river, revered by the ancients as a minor divin-
ity, may seem something of a letdown to the newcomer
who has boned up on history. Is this the waterway that
got such top billing in fluvial lore? The river on which
Queen Cleopatra sailed upstream from the sea in 46 B.C.
to visit Julius Caesar and dazzle the Romans with oriental
pomp? When Mark Twain first saw the Tiber, he asked
his Roman hosts why they didn't put a little water in it.
Later, in *The Innocents Abroad*, the former Big River pilot
sneered that the celebrated Tiber "is not so long, nor yet
so wide, as the American Mississippi."

The Tiber often seems a puny stream indeed, its dull
gray color betraying heavy pollution. Only after downpours in Tuscany and Umbria may the river rise overnight
by 10 or 15 feet (3 to 5 meters) and roar under Rome's
twenty-four bridges, carrying small uprooted trees and a
few drowned sheep from flooded areas upstream.

There are still a few floating boat houses and bathing
establishments tied up at the Tiber embankments close to
Rome's center, but swimming in the river has long been

declared hazardous. The floats now serve hard-bitten river enthusiasts for sunbathing and alfresco dining.

PHONES AND MAIL

As elsewhere, hotels in Rome are permitted to add substantial surcharges to tolls for phone calls made from their premises. Public telephones in street booths, subway stations, espresso bars, restaurants, and other places are operated with Italian coins or with the stubbornly surviving phone tokens (*gettoni*). The copper-colored tokens, available from tobacconists, coffee shops, diverse businesses, and automatic dispensers, are also accepted by everybody as money if you have run out of small change. In 1992 a phone token was worth L200 (about 15¢).

An increasing number of public telephones are equipped with a device for processing magnetized, prepaid telephone cards as substitutes for coins or tokens. Buy cards of various denominations from tobacconists. The telephone apparatus automatically deducts the toll for each call from the credit recorded on the card.

Local phone calls cost one *gettone* or the equivalent in coins for three minutes. For longer calls or for long distance, put an adequate number of tokens or coins in the slot unless you are using a telephone card. The button on the phone releases unused tokens or coins.

If you place long-distance or international calls from a post office you may—and should—ask for a receipt. The central telephone office adjoining the central post office in the Piazza San Silvestro is open 8 A.M. to 9 P.M. Monday to Friday, 8 A.M. to noon Saturday. Most post office branches also have telephone service but are open only from 9 A.M. to 1 or 2 P.M. Monday to Friday, although some major outlying post offices will also handle long-distance and international calls afternoons, Monday to Friday.

Telephone numbers in Rome change often, as the tele-communications network is expanding. If you find that some number indicated in this guidebook is out of service or assigned to another subscriber, dial 12 for directory information.

The area code for Rome is 06. Omit the zero if you call from abroad, adding the 6 to the country code for Italy, 39, and proceeding with the number you want to reach in Rome. For instance, to call number 6782651 in Rome from the United States, dial 011-39-6-6782651 (011 is the inter-national access code from the United States). Most Roman telephone numbers have six, seven, or eight digits, but some offices or big hotels have only four or five.

Following is the Italian spelling code for telephoning, dictating telegrams, and giving correct names:

A—Ancona
  (ahn-CO-nah)
B—Bologna
  (bo-LOWN-yah)
C—Como
  (CO-moh)
D—Domodossola
  (domo-DOSS-oh-lah)
E—Empoli
  (AYM-po-lee)
F—Firenze
  (fee-RAIN-dsay)
G—Genova
  (JAY-no-vah)

H—Hotel
  (oh-TEL)
I—Italia
  (ee-TAHL-yah)
J—I lunga
  (ee LOON-gah)
K—Kappa
  (KAHP-ah)
L—Livorno
  (lee-VOR-noh)
M—Milano
  (mee-LAH-noh)
N—Napoli
  (NAH-po-lee)

O—Otranto
  (OH-trahn-toh)

P—Perugia
  (pay-ROO-jah)

Q—Quarto
  (KWAR-toh)

R—Roma
  (ROH-mah)

S—Savona
  (sah-VOH-nah)

T—Torino
  (to-REE-noh)

U—Udine
  (OO-dee-nay)

V—Venezia
  (veh-NAY-dsee-ah)

W—Washington
  (WASH-ing-ton)

X—Ics
  (EEKS)

Y—I greca
  (EE GRAY-cah)

Z—Zara
  (DSAH-rah)

If you want to talk to an American telephone operator in order to place a credit-card or collect call, the cost is one *gettone* or the equivalent in coins or on a phone card; dial 172-1011 (AT&T), 172-1022 (MCI), 172-1001 (Canada), or 172-1877 (Sprint Express).

Postal service in Rome is slow and unreliable. To send mail to foreign countries, many residents turn to the Vatican's post offices to the left and right behind the colonnades enclosing St. Peter's Square; the right-hand office moves into a trailer on the right side of the square during the hot months. Office hours are 8:30 A.M. to 7 P.M. Monday to Friday, 8:30 A.M. to 6 P.M. Saturday; closed on Sundays and church holidays.

Vatican mail stamps, like the pontifical state's coins, come in lira denominations, and the Vatican mail tariff is the same as Italy's. Postcards, letters, and packages carrying Vatican stamps and mailed in the Vatican (including St. Peter's Square) are taken daily to the airport or rail terminal in Vatican mail bags by Vatican vehicles and are usually delivered to their addresses earlier than mail handled by Italian post offices. Don't put letters or postcards with Vatican stamps into Italian mailboxes. Only persons who legally reside in Vatican City can receive incoming mail through Vatican postal channels.

For urgent written communications use the fax machines at your hotel or at one of the many storefront copy shops all over the city. The major international express delivery organizations are represented in Rome and handle shipments. Consult the Rome Yellow Pages under *Copisterie* (for fax) and *Spedizioni Internazionali* (for courier services).

MONEY

Italy's (and the Vatican State's) currency unit is the lira (plural: lire), historically subdivided into 100 centesimi. At present coins of 10, 20, 50, 100, 200, and 500 lire are in circulation, although the 10 and 20 lire pieces are becoming increasingly rare and useless. Banknotes come in denominations of 1,000, 2,000, 5,000, 10,000, 50,000, and 100,000 lire. To do away with the large figures Italians have to deal with in everyday money matters, plans have been under discussion for years to create a "new" or "heavy" lira equivalent to 1,000 current lire. Pending such a long-overdue currency reform Italians and their guests must continue coping with sums of hundreds of thousands and millions of lire every day.

Romans, at any rate, like cash. Payment for merchandise or services by check is much less common in Italy than it is in the United States and other western countries. Hotels, restaurants, and stores in Rome will accept a personal check only from someone who is very well known to the management. Businesses that don't have much experience with foreign customers will even show diffidence toward traveler's checks and credit cards.

CLIMATE AND WINDS

The best periods for visiting Rome, in regard to the weather, are from the end of April to late June and from the end of September to (maybe) mid-November. Winters are usually mild, often rainy, with an occasional cold snap, but the temperature rarely drops below the freezing point. Even January and February will bring a few sunny days when one can sit outside at midday. Snow is rare, and years may pass before it blankets Rome again. Whenever this happens, the City of the Seven Hills slows down to a crawl, because it is hardly equipped for clearing its many sloping streets.

A visitor during the off-season—from mid-November to Easter—finds hotels and the sights less crowded with tourists than during the rest of the year, although guests from Latin America and Australia have lately discovered Rome in growing numbers during their summer, the northern hemisphere's winter. There may be the bonus of a night at the opera, as the season of the Teatro dell'Opera usually lasts from December to June.

The Roman spring is regularly short, and in one day can give way to a long, hot summer. Romans, who like to dress informally all year long, will from July to the end of September wear the lightest of clothing, as if they were living in a seaside resort. The bathing beaches are close. In August the city is all but left to the tourists while a sizable portion of the Romans are vacationing elsewhere. Even parking space is abundant. Rome sinks into complete torpor around August 15, the midsummer festival known as Ferragosto in memory of Emperor Augustus, who gave the Roman populace a few days off at that time of the year. Ferragosto means that most stores and eating places are closed for days or even weeks. Foreign guests will have to search hard for an open restaurant if they don't want to take their meals at their hotel.

The capital does not fully come to life again before the middle of September. Rome's October days, the *ottobrate romane*, are justly famous for the glorious but no longer hot sunshine bathing the city in mellow light. During the pleasant evenings Romans and foreigners linger in the piazzas.

Many building facades in the city core are in hues ranging from a deep yellow to ocher to rust brown; they are repainted in the same color or a riper one whenever the owners get around to having restoration work done. Ocher, which soothingly absorbs bright light and takes on a golden glow at sunset and in the delightful October days, is the characteristic color of old Rome, mightily contributing to its charm. In contrast, the garish monument to Victor Emanuel II and the concrete suburban housing developments glare in their whiteness, while the marble and travertine of the ancient ruins have through the ages taken on shades of gray and brown. Many new buildings on the outskirts have been painted in brown hues.

During eight months Rome is an outdoor city. In the cool period, rare are the places outside private homes, restaurants at mealtime, and hotel bars where people can meet comfortably for any length of time. Many espresso bars do have a few tables inside at which patrons sit, often without taking off their overcoats, but cozy tearooms, coffeehouses, and barrooms are scarce (see pages 75–77).

A discussion of the Roman climate would be incom-

plete without mention of the winds that in the life of the
city play a remarkable role. The ancient Romans paid tribute to the wind gods in a temple built before the third
century B.C. (it has long since disappeared); ever since then
the city has been very much aware of the frequently blowing air currents from all directions and their effects on
people. Winds are listed by their old names on a wind rose
of oval stone slabs set into the pavement of St. Peter's
Square, around the central obelisk.

The ancients liked best the west wind (*favonius* or, in
Italian, *vento di ponente*); today's Romans praise its gentle
form, the *ponentino*, or "little west wind," as one of their
city's delights. It is the breeze that springs up fairly regularly during summer evenings: after a torrid day the *ponentino*, wafting from the seaside up the Tiber, brings fresh
air to the city and vivifies its inhabitants.

The cold north wind, which the ancient Romans compared to an eagle (*aquilo*), is now known as *tramontana*
because it comes from "beyond the mountains." It sweeps
the sky clear, cleans the air, and is invigorating.

Romans loathe the hot, humid, and squally south wind,
the sirocco (spelled *scirocco* in Italian). It is a frequent in-
vader from Africa, and for two or three days dumps many
tons of Sahara sand on the city, causing all cars outside
garages to break out in reddish brown spots. The sky looks
leaden, and many Romans suffer from migraines or are
short-tempered—conditions attributed to electricity gen-
erated by myriads of wind-borne sand particles rubbing
against one another. When at last the oppressive sirocco
dissolves in rain, everybody feels better. Romans don't
mind the east wind blowing in from the Balkans and
Greece, called *grecale*.

Although there are very few smokestack industries in
and around Rome, the air quality, especially in the crowded

center, is poor most of the time. The culprit is motoriza-
tion. Early risers and visitors who set out at or before 7
A.M. for jogging or sightseeing strolls are rewarded by
purer-than-usual air, light traffic, and an absence of much
of the din that during later hours will drown out the rus-
tling of the pines in the breeze and the murmur of the many
fountains (see page 147).

Rome slows and quiets down again during the siesta
period. The natives think, with Noel Coward, that only
"mad dogs and Englishmen go out in the midday sun."
Romans who do have to get out during the siesta hours
always walk on the shady side of the streets and squares,
and foreigners will quickly follow their example. An early-
nineteenth-century churchman is known to have offered
advice in a booklet on how to traverse the entire city on
foot, always in the shade. His itineraries, now lost, might
also have been useful for summer strolls in the historical
core today.

After the siesta, between 4 and 5 P.M., traffic noises
swell again. In summer they mix in residential neighborhoods during the evening hours with the blare of television
from open windows. At the city center it may be 2 A.M.
before the street noises at last abate.

NEWCOMERS TO AN OLD CITY

A foreigner arriving in Rome is required by law to request
a residence permit (*permesso di soggiorno*) from the police
within three days. Registration at a hotel or pension is a
valid substitute for this formality—the management will
forward the newcomer's statement to the police. Foreigners living in private homes or intending to stay in Italy
longer than three months are obliged to apply in person

for the residence permit. This is done at the Foreigners' Office (**Ufficio Stranieri**) of police headquarters, 2 Via Genova, near the Quirinal Palace.

You can't be early enough at the Foreigners' Office—there will always be plenty of people before you. Be resigned to standing in line for hours, maybe the entire morning. Take your passport and photocopies of its first three pages as well as three passport photos with you.

Under Emperor Augustus Rome had about 1 million inhabitants, a quarter of whom received free corn from the public granaries. The population shrank to fewer than 30,000 during the Dark Ages, and grew again under the long rule of the popes. When the city became the capital of unified Italy in 1870 it was inhabited by 220,000 people. Since then Rome has grown by leaps and bounds; its residents numbered 1.6 million at the end of World War II and close to 3 million in 1991.

Descendants of families that for generations have lived in the city—they proudly call themselves *romani de Roma* (Romans of Rome)—are a fraction of the inhabitants. Today's Romans are the children of immigrants or have themselves moved to the capital from other parts of Italy, mostly from the Abruzzi Mountains of the interior and from the southern part of the peninsula. Northern Italians, who frequently are critical of the nonchalant Romans, may be heard to assert that their nation's capital has since about 1950 become increasingly "southernized," an appraisal implying ethnic disparagement.

Rome's resident population has been augmented since the end of the 1970s by many thousands of persons from North Africa, other African countries, Asia, and Latin America. The poor immigrants from the Third World, many of whom arrived clandestinely, took over jobs that most Italians spurned—as household workers, kitchen help in restaurants, and manual laborers—or tried to earn a living as street vendors. They form a new, highly visible, and often exploited underclass.

Newcomers to Rome also include the tribes of gypsies that drifted in from the Balkan countries, mostly by way of Yugoslavia. Begging gypsy women and children have become a common sight in the city center, although virtually all of the gypsies live in trailer camps and slums on the far outskirts.

Refugees from Poland, Albania, and other countries that until recently were under Communist rule added to the foreign population of Rome. The influx of tens of thousands of destitute non-Italians has strained Rome's housing market and school system and caused other social tensions. Nevertheless, the Romans as a whole are taking the current ethnic and social transformation of their city in stride. The general atmosphere remains relaxed.

Plenty of people still sit in the wine shops for hours, nursing their carafe of blond Frascati and discussing the soccer championship with fellow patrons in the broad local vernacular. Romans still buy bread and bologna at the neighborhood outdoor market or a slice of pizza at a nearby shop for a snack on the steps of some church that may overlook a charming piazza where others with plenty of time on their hands spoon their gelato at the tables of a café. Office workers still knock off every now and then to sip another espresso in a neighborhood bar, exchange banter with colleagues or the counterman, or flirt with the pretty cashier. Children apparently can't do wrong, and when they are cranky they are met with soothing noises and general forbearance. Even the youngsters in leather jackets who ride thundering motorcycles stop if a woman with a baby carriage is about to cross the street.

Visitors should try to blend in to the local scene as

well as they can. Romans are used to strangers and their
outlandish ways; yet the guests shouldn't advertise their
foreignness by wearing cowboy hats or visiting a church
in a California-style halter, by talking loudly in their language in the streets or in buses, by dressing up in long
gowns and white dinner jackets for an evening in a popular
trattoria, or by mimicking the traffic policeman in the
Piazza Venezia whose balletlike movements and gesticulat-
ing may strike them as funny.

Some notions of history and the arts will be useful for
full enjoyment of one's sojourn in Rome. Visitors who
have never before heard of, say, the Etruscans or the Renaissance popes who were the employers of Michelangelo
and Raphael will be baffled or bored listening to the explanations by museum guides and tour directors. On the other
hand, the cultural treasures of the city may spur its guests
to read up on the civilizations and creative individuals who
produced them.

The seeming ubiquity of Latin is apt to perplex the
sightseer. As if the epigraphs on ancient Roman monuments and the inscriptions on church facades weren't
enough, quite a few modern buildings carry Latin mottoes
on their walls. Not all of them are as simple as, for instance,
Domi manere convenit felicibus ("It behooves happy people
to stay at home"); even if you have taken Latin in school
you may have a hard time puzzling out the meaning of
some of the texts you encounter in Rome.

Manhole covers and announcements from City Hall
are marked with the letters *SPQR*, standing for *Senatus
Populusque Romanus* (the Senate and People of Rome),
which was already the formula for public authority more
than two thousand years ago. If you ask for police headquarters you'd better use its official name, *questura*, which
is derived from the title of an ancient Roman magistrate,

the *quaestor*. And if you look for the Bureau of Vital Statistics to report a birth, marriage, or death, you must know that it is called by an ancient Greek name, *anagrafe*.

Thus a stay in Rome provides guests with elements of a classical education.

2.

Accommodations

EVEN IN ANTIQUITY Rome had to put up swarms of visitors from Greece and Syria, Spain and Gaul, as well as from other provinces of its far-flung empire. They journeyed to the city of the Caesars on business, to try their fortune, or just to breathe the heady air of their world's power center, marvel at its sights, and bask in its opulence. During the dark centuries of the early Middle Ages pilgrims from as far as Ireland trekked to the despoiled settlement on the Tiber to worship at its Christian shrines; they found shelter in austere hospices.

Dante mentions the multitudes of people from abroad he saw crossing the Tiber on a bridge near St. Peter's during Christianity's first Holy Year, A.D. 1300. And from the Renaissance period onward famous and obscure travelers have flocked to Rome in an unending stream. Still being pointed out are the Augustinian convent where Martin Luther stayed for a few weeks; the Inn at the Sign of the Bear, which counted Rabelais, Montaigne, and Goethe among its guests; and the Palazzo where Stendhal lived.

In the era of jet travel Italy can draw on two millennia

of unbroken tradition in accommodating foreigners. Tourism is still a major Roman industry. The city at present has nearly eight hundred hotels and pensions (distinctions between the two categories are vague). Quite a number of Roman Catholic convents take in paying guests—single and married people and couples with children—and don't necessarily expect them to be of their faith or practice it. The few youth hostels and the camping sites on the city's outskirts are often crowded.

It is advisable to make hotel reservations as early as possible, especially for Rome's main tourist season from the week before Easter to the beginning of November. When rates are quoted, find out whether breakfast is included and whether guests are obliged to take at least one main meal on the premises (in some pensions they are). Also make sure there are no supplements—some hotels charge extra for heating or air-conditioning.

Railroad travelers arriving in Rome without a reservation find an electronic signboard indicating vacant hotel space at the Stazione Termini near the ticket windows in the front hall. Information counters in the arrivals lounge of Fiumicino Airport also assist travelers in need of accommodation.

Hotels that don't include breakfast in their room rates often add substantial extra charges to the bill for morning coffee or tea, a roll or croissant, some butter and jam, and maybe a small glass of orange juice—all described as "continental breakfast." Do as many Italian travelers do: walk a few steps to some coffee bar near your hotel (there invariably is one opposite or at the next street corner), and order a cappuccino or tea, toast or croissants, and orange juice. You will save money, and the coffee will in all likelihood be better than at the hotel. Most Romans have just a cup of espresso or cappuccino, maybe with a *cornetto* (croissant), for breakfast, and around 11 A.M. take a coffee break, thereby building up a robust appetite for their filling lunch.

Hotel rates in Italy are high in comparison with other Mediterranean countries because of the nation's elevated labor costs. The best deals will be found in houses that have recently been refurbished but employ small staffs. In some little hotels, especially during off-season months, the desk clerk may be the only employee in the house after the maid or maids have done the rooms and gone home. Guests arriving late will have to carry their bags up to their rooms themselves. All hotels insist on seeing the passports of guests who are checking in, and annoyingly may keep them for a while; don't hesitate to claim your passport after a reasonable interval for registration.

In high-class hotels with doormen, concierges, assistant managers, cashiers, secretaries, switchboard operators, bellmen, and twenty-four-hour room service, the rates will be stiff. Local taxes and service charges are regularly included in the per diem rates, which should be posted in each guest room.

Italian travelers are often generous tippers, but Roman hotel staff and restaurant waiters have long learned that most foreigners aren't. So don't overtip. A gratuity of, say, the equivalent of $10 to $20 is in order for the concierge who gets opera tickets for you or provides other special assistance. Longer-staying guests should give their room maid $15 or so in lire per week in a medium-priced place. Extra tips are also expected by the room-service waiter, the bellman who takes care of your luggage, and the doorman who calls a cab.

First-time visitors to Rome to whom a place has been favorably mentioned are advised to look up its location on a map of the city, or seek expert opinion. Note that in

Rome's historic center the numeration of buildings often runs up on one side of the street and continues in the opposite direction on the other side. Thus No. 3 may be opposite No. 184. Caution is necessary especially if the address of the prospective hotel or pension is on a major thoroughfare, because of the inevitable traffic noises and polluted air, or close to the railroad terminal (Stazione Termini), a neighborhood that is generally considered undesirable although a few satisfactory hotels have managed to survive in it.

Several hotels and large motels in outlying districts offer gardens, swimming pools, tennis courts, and relative quiet, but would-be guests should keep in mind that each trip to the city center will entail a long ride through Rome's heavy traffic in a cab, hotel coach, or public transport. If you are unfamiliar with the local traffic patterns and the scanty parking facilities, you'd better forget about trying to reach the heart of the city by car from a hotel on the outskirts.

Reception desks and doormen will advise arriving motorists where to park their cars—in the hotel garage at an additional fee, at a nearby commercial garage, or in some area where curbside space can normally be found.

HOTELS

Following are recommended hotels, grouped according to price brackets. No specific room rates are quoted, because of frequent changes due to inflation and other factors. The selection of places named in this guidebook was prompted by their location, comfort, quality of service, amenities, and special atmosphere.

All hotels in Rome are enumerated in the three-volume

Annuario degli Alberghi d'Italia (Yearbook of Hotels in Italy), published periodically by Compagnia Editrice Italiana, which many travel agents keep handy for consultation. The Italian word for hotel is *albergo*; in the Rome telephone directory and Yellow Pages look for the heading *Alberghi*.

Top Hotels

These are around $400 and up per night for a double room with private bath, without breakfast; service and taxes are included.

Hassler-Villa Medici, 6 Piazza Trinità dei Monti (telephone: 6782651, fax: 6799278). A major asset is its central location on a spur of the Pincio Hill, to the right of two Roman landmarks, the Villa Medici and the Church of Trinità dei Monti. The Hassler, opened in 1885 and thoroughly renovated recently, faces the top of the Spanish Stairs and commands a famous view of the obelisk in the foreground, the roofscape of Rome's center, and the dome of St. Peter's on the horizon. The panorama is particularly impressive from the upper-floor suites and the elegant, expensive Roof Restaurant. Swiss owned and managed, the hotel does not accept travel groups and prides itself on the privacy and personalized service it guarantees. Presidents Truman, Eisenhower, and Kennedy, royalty, heads of state, government chiefs, and sundry prominent personages have stayed in its suites and ninety rooms. International financiers and business leaders are regular guests.

Le Grand Hotel, 3 Via Vittorio Emanuele Orlando (telephone: 4709, fax: 474307). When King Umberto I found that the capital of newly unified Italy lacked a world-class hotel, he asked the legendary César Ritz to fill the gap. "Le

Grand Hôtel & de Rome," as it first was called, opened in 1894 near the Quirinal Palace, the official royal residence. Ever since then Italian governments have put up their official guests in the palatial establishment, although the nearby Piazza della Repubblica (formerly Piazza dell'Esedra) has lately deteriorated and is now being used as a terminal area for long-distance buses. King Alfonso XIII of Spain as an exile lived and died at the Grand; diplomats like it. The sumptuous halls are often the setting for opulent wedding receptions and other society affairs. While the ground floor has retained its Victorian splendor, most of the 168 rooms have been redecorated in tune with modern tastes.

Excelsior, 125 Via Vittorio Veneto (telephone: 4708, fax: 4756205). In Fellini's *La Dolce Vita* paparazzi ambush movie stars and other denizens of his pleasure-loving Rome in front of the Excelsior. In fact, Tyrone Power, Elizabeth Taylor, Roberto Rossellini, Ingrid Bergman, the Shah of Iran, and countless members of the international jet set have stayed here. The Via Veneto has meanwhile lost much of its former glamor, but the location on the once-celebrated boulevard, next to the U.S. Embassy, still helps to fill the Excelsior's 320 rooms.

Lord Byron, 5 Via de Notaris (telephone: 3224541, fax: 3220405), with 55 rooms, is a white Riviera-style building in a garden on the highest point of a quiet one-way street near the Villa Borghese gardens in the upper-middle-class Parioli district, a ten-minute cab ride from downtown. It has luxurious rooms and suites. The hotel's intimate restaurant, Relais Le Jardin, is rated among Rome's best. Business executives are conspicuous among the clientele.

Cavalieri Hilton, 101 Via Cadlolo (telephone: 31511,

fax: 31512241), is located in a vast, terraced garden on top of the Monte Mario in the city's north, a fifteen-minute cab ride from the center, with a large outdoor swimming pool, tennis courts, and 380 rooms. It provides grand vistas of Rome. Business conferences, wedding receptions, and other meetings and parties provide frequent bustle, which some guests seem to like. Service and cuisine are good, especially in the rooftop restaurant, La Pergola.

First-class Houses

Doubles with bath cost $250 to $350, without breakfast.

Eden, 49 Via Ludovisi (telephone: 4743551, fax: 4742401), near Via Veneto and Villa Borghese gardens; panoramic roof-garden restaurant. Temporarily closed for repairs and refurbishing in 1992.

De La Ville-InterContinental, 67–71 Via Sistina (telephone: 6733, fax: 6784213), near the top of the Spanish Stairs, next to the Hassler. Attractive suites on the top floor.

D'Inghilterra, 14 Via Bocca di Leone (telephone: 672161, fax: 6840828), on a small square off the fashionable Via Condotti, facing the seventeenth-century Torlonia Palace. Henry James stayed here. The rooms of the old building have recently been redecorated. The bar is a convenient downtown meeting place.

Plaza, 126 Via del Corso (telephone: 672101, fax: 6411575). Central. An old establishment in which the composer Pietro Mascagni lived and died. Of its large rooms and suites, those looking out on the courtyard are quiet. Italian politicians favor the Plaza. An evening restaurant and piano bar, the Mascagni, is in the same building at 95

Via delle Carrozze (telephone: 6791958), around the corner from the main entrance.

Nazionale, 131 Piazza Montecitorio (telephone: 6786677, fax: 6789251). On a well-policed square, close to the Chamber of Deputies; quiet at night. Nice junior suites.

Colonna Palace, 12 Piazza Montecitorio (telephone: 6786594, fax: 6794496). Same location as the Nazionale. Members of Parliament stay here during the week. No restaurant.

Crowne Plaza Holiday Inn, 69 Piazza della Minerva (telephone: 6841888, fax: 6794165), is a reconstructed eighteenth-century palazzo near the Pantheon. Two plaques recall that Stendhal lived here, 1834–36, and that the Latin American revolutionary leader José de San Martín sojourned in what was then the Minerva Hotel in 1846. The old Minerva was favored by visiting Roman Catholic prelates because the offices of the pope's vicar for Rome were nearby (they have long since moved to the Lateran). Though there is now nothing clerical about the refurbished house, shops selling ecclesiastical garb and religious articles are still in the neighborhood.

Cardinal, 62 Via Giulia (telephone: 6542719, fax: 6786376), on a distinguished street near the Tiber, hides an interior of modern comfort behind the noble facade of an old building.

Atlante Star, 34 Via Vitelleschi (telephone: 6879558, fax: 6872300), on a busy street near the Vatican. The roof-garden restaurant Les Etoiles looks out on the dome of St. Peter's.

Cicerone, 55 Via Cicerone (telephone: 3575, fax:

6799584), on a much-traveled street in the modern Prati section, close to the center. Good restaurant.

Jolly Vittorio Veneto, 1 Corso d'Italia (telephone: 8495, fax: 8841104), a concrete-and-glass building near the upper end of the Via Veneto on the edge of the Villa Borghese gardens, with a view of the Aurelian Walls.

Regina Baglioni, 72 Via Vittorio Veneto (telephone: 476851, fax: 485483), diagonally opposite the U. S. Embassy. Good service.

Aldovrandi Palace, 15 Via Ulisse Aldovrandi (telephone: 3223993, fax: 3221435), on the northwestern side of the Villa Borghese gardens, with a swimming pool in a garden. Quiet.

Forum, 28–31 Via Tor de' Conti (telephone: 6792446, fax: 6786479), on a small street in a medieval section near the Roman Forum and the Colosseum. Fine view from the roof-garden restaurant, especially at night when the ancient ruins are floodlighted.

Medium-priced and Comfortable

Doubles with bath or shower average around $150, without breakfast.

Victoria, 41 Via Campania (telephone: 473931, fax: 4941330), facing the Aurelian Walls near the Via Veneto. Swiss owned.

Pensione Scalinata di Spagna, 17 Piazza Trinità dei Monti (telephone: 6793006, fax: 6840598). Only fourteen simply furnished rooms on two floors of a graceful neoclassical building on top of the Spanish Stairs, with a large terrace commanding a panorama of old Rome. Reserve early; habitués send deposits for room reservations months ahead.

Internazionale, 79 Via Sistina (telephone: 6784686, fax: 6784794), on a busy street near the Spanish Stairs. No restaurant.

Gregoriana, 18 Via Gregoriana (telephone: 6794269, fax: 6784258), on a charming sloping street near the Spanish Stairs. Small, no restaurant.

Sole al Pantheon, 63 Piazza della Rotonda (telephone: 6780441, fax: 6840689), near the Pantheon, one of Rome's oldest hostelries, recently thoroughly and somewhat garishly restored. The sixteenth-century poet Ludovico Ariosto stayed here when the place was known as the Albergo del Montone (Inn at the Sign of the Ram).

Valadier, 15 Via della Fontanella (telephone: 3610592, fax: 3201558). Once a house of ill repute, the building on a narrow street close to the Piazza del Popolo has been transformed into an elegant fifty-room establishment. The clientele includes show and media people.

Portoghesi, 1 Via dei Portoghesi (telephone: 6864231, fax: 6876976), near the Tiber and the Piazza Navona, and close to a Portuguese church and college. Twenty-seven rooms; quiet. No restaurant. Reserve early.

Bolivar, 6 Via della Cordonata (telephone: 6791614, fax: 6791025). Central, on a quiet street on the southern slope of the Quirinal Hill.

Cesári, 89A Via di Pietra (telephone: 6792386, fax: 6790882), central, on a narrow street off the Via del Corso. Quiet.

Sant'Anselmo, 2 Piazza Sant'Anselmo, and **Aventino &**

Villa S. Pio (both: telephone: 5743547, fax: 5783604), in three buildings with a garden in one of Rome's quietest neighborhoods, the Aventine Hill, close to the Colosseum and the Palatine. A ten-minute cab ride from the center. Officials of the United Nations Food and Agriculture Organization, which has headquarters nearby, are frequent guests.

Sant'Anna, 134 Borgo Pio (telephone: 6541602, fax: 6548717), very close to the Vatican, on a narrow street in the bustling Borghi section. Eighteen rooms, small garden, no restaurant.

Raphael, 2 Largo Febo (telephone: 6838881, fax: 6878993), on a lovely small, triangular square with tall trees and ivy-covered house walls, near the Piazza Navona. Favored by Italian politicians.

Clodio, 10 Via Santa Lucia (telephone: 317541, fax: 3250754). A modern 115-room house near studios of the State Television (RAI) and law courts. TV personalities and lawyers are among the guests. Ten minutes by cab to the center; good bus connections.

Relatively Inexpensive

These cost $120 and less for a double with or without private bath or shower; no breakfast.

Alba, 12 Via Leonina (telephone: 4884840), near the Colosseum.

Centro, 12 Via Firenze (telephone: 4828002, fax: 4741652), close to Rome's Opera House.

Concordia, 14 Via Capo le Case (telephone: 6791953), central.

Homs, 71–72 Via della Vite (telephone: 6792976), near the Spanish Square; plain.

Margutta, 34 Via Laurina (telephone: 3223674), near Piazza del Popolo.

Prati, 87 Via Crescenzio (telephone: 6897133), on a broad, tree-lined street near the Vatican; plain.

Senato, 73 Piazza della Rotonda (telephone: 6784343, fax: 6840297), facing the Pantheon.

On the Outskirts

Good accommodations at around $200 for a double room with bath; breakfast extra.

Holiday Inn–EUR–Parco dei Medici, 65 Viale Castello della Magliana (telephone: 65581, fax: 6557005), on the motorway to Fiumicino Airport; 330 rooms. Garden, swimming pool, and tennis courts; golf club nearby.

Jolly Hotel Midas, 800 Via Aurelia (telephone: 66396, fax: 6808457), on the highway to Pisa and Genoa, 5 miles (8 kilometers) from the center. Many business and political conventions are held here. It has 360 rooms, a garden, swimming pool, and tennis court.

MotelAgip, Via Aurelia, km 8 (telephone: 6379001, fax: 6379001), a 220-room establishment next to Jolly Hotel Midas. Swimming pool.

CONVENT ACCOMMODATIONS

Quite a few of the hundreds of Roman Catholic communities that have headquarters or branches in Rome take in paying guests. Some offer rooms with private baths or showers, while in others the bathroom is down the hall. Many church-affiliated guest houses prefer groups of pilgrims or travelers but welcome individual visitors if there is enough space. The rates are half or less of what comparable accommodations would cost in a local hotel. Some of the religious houses expect their guests to take at least one main meal on the premises; others serve only breakfast.

Most of the ecclesiastical houses impose a 10 P.M. or 11 P.M. curfew, but some give their guests latchkeys. There is generally no obligation to attend religious services.

Following are some religious houses where English is spoken:

Franciscan Sisters of the Atonement, 105 Via Monte del Gallo (telephone: 630782), on a curving, sloping street, a ten-minute walk south of St. Peter's Square; No. 34 bus from Piazza Cavour, behind the old Palace of Justice. A well-appointed establishment of an American-based order; large pine trees in the garden.

Casa Tra Noi, 113 Via Monte del Gallo (telephone: 630089), higher up the hill than the aforementioned. A cluster of modern guest houses; many rooms have balconies. No curfew.

Suore Teatine, 27 Salita Monte del Gallo (telephone: 6374653), in a modern building near the aforementioned. Garden.

Casa Mater Immacolata, 38 Via Monte del Gallo (telephone: 630863), with a small garden, in the same neighborhood as the three places named above, but closer to St. Peter's.

Pensione Suore Francescane, 35 Via Nicolò V (tele-

phone: 632288), on the south side of the Vatican walls
near their highest point. The roof terrace looks out on the
nearby dome of St. Peter's and into the Vatican gardens.
Bus No. 46 from Corso Vittorio Emanuele II.

Suore Dorotee, 4A Via del Gianicolo (telephone:
6543349), halfway up the Janiculum Hill, a ten-minute
walk from St. Peter's Square. Tall pines in a garden and a
panorama of Rome.

Fraterna Domus, 62 Via di Monte Brianzo (telephone:
6542727), north of the Piazza Navona, near the Tiber.

Santa Brigida, 96 Piazza Farnese (telephone: 6865263), in
the historic center, near the Palazzo Farnese. Saint Birgitta
of Sweden died here in 1373.

**Sisters of the Immaculate Conception (Suore di
Lourdes)**, 113 Via Sistina (telephone: 4745324), near the
Spanish Stairs.

Spanish is spoken in the pilgrims' pension run by the **Suore
Mercedarie della Carità**, 8 Via Iberia (telephone:
7596645), near the Lateran; and **Suore Concezioniste,** 75
Via Bixio (telephone: 4464737), near Stazione Termini.

It is advisable to make reservations by mail or telephone
well in advance, because space in religious houses is limited. Demand is strong most of the year, especially before
Easter. If no vacancy can be found in any of the places
listed above, the sisters usually know of another convent
that might have space, though little or no English may be
spoken there. Parish and pilgrims' groups seeking accommodation at moderate rates in Rome should contact Pere-
grinatio Romana, 10 Via della Conciliazione, 00193 Roma
(telephone: 6865090), an official Vatican office close to

St. Peter's Square that also offers advice to individual pilgrims.

YOUTH HOSTELS AND CAMPING SITES

Members of the International Youth Hostels Federation are entitled to stay at the **Youth Hostel Foro Italico**, 61 Viale delle Olimpiadi (telephone: 3336593), close to the sports complex on the Tiber near the Olympic Stadium. The hostel can accommodate 350 persons. **YWCA Home for Women Students**, 4 Via Cesare Balbo (telephone: 4880460), near the railroad terminal, is available during academic vacations, and **Salvation Army (Esercito della Salvezza)**, 39–41 Via degli Apuli (telephone: 490558, fax: 4456306), near the Campo Verano cemetery in Rome's east (see page 151), has dormitories for men and women.

Camping Sites

These are listed in the Rome Yellow Pages under *Campeggi*. Following are a few in convenient locations:

Country Club Castel Fusano, 1 Piazza Castelfusano (telephone: 5662710), on the seaside near Via Cristoforo Colombo, 15 miles (24 kilometers) from the city center; other camping sites nearby on the waterfront Via Litoranea.

Fabulous, Via Cristoforo Colombo, km 18 (telephone: 5259354).

Flaminio, Via Flaminia (National Highway No. 3), km 8.2 (telephone: 3332604).

Camping Roma, 831 Via Aurelia (National Highway No. 1), about 5 miles (8 kilometers) from the center (telephone: 6623018).

Camping Seven Hills, 1216 Via Cassia (National Highway No. 2), about 6 miles (9.5 kilometers) from the center (telephone: 3710214).

APARTMENTS AND ROOMS

For visitors who intend to stay for at least a week, renting a studio with a kitchenette or a suite in an apartment hotel may be advisable. The Italians call this type of accommodation *residence* or *casa albergo*; full hotel services may be available on demand. Most of these establishments are in outlying districts.

Fairly central and high-class: **Palazzo al Velabro**, 16 Via del Velabro (telephone: 6793450, fax: 6793790), near the Capitoline and Palatine hills; and **Residenza di Ripetta**, 231 Via Ripetta (telephone: 672141, fax: 3203959), near the Piazza del Popolo and the Tiber. For other options, see Rome telephone directory (White Pages) under *Residence*, or Yellow Pages under *Case Albergo*.

Inspect the offered accommodation, make sure its kitchen or kitchenette is fully equipped, and find out whether there are any extra charges for utilities, heating, air-conditioning, telephone, television, maid service, or use of parking lot or garage.

Bed-and-breakfast places are almost completely lacking in Rome. One reason is that the custom of taking a substantial breakfast was until recently alien to local families. The very few households offering a room with a breakfast that is more than just a cup of cappuccino and a roll are almost exclusively those of resident foreigners, and their guests are people they know or who have been recommended by friends and other guests.

Rooms and apartments to let—and apartments, villas, houses, and other real estate for sale—are advertised in the classified sections of the Rome dailies *Il Messaggero* and *Il Tempo*, especially on Sundays, also in the *Trova Roma* supplement of the newspaper *La Repubblica* on Thursdays, and in the all-advertisement periodical *Porta Portese*. Porta Portese is also the popular name of Rome's weekly flea market (see page 227).

The city's many real estate agencies have listings of available properties and may take prospective clients to them by car for inspection. Look for such agencies in the Rome Yellow Pages under *Agenzie Immobiliari;* at any rate, also seek advice from some knowledgeable and trustworthy resident. A real estate exchange organized by the Rome Chamber of Commerce at 10A Via dei Cessati Spiriti, on the southeastern outskirts, is in operation from 10 A.M. to 5:30 P.M. every Wednesday. It has computerized lists of available buildings and apartments as well as of licensed real estate agents who will handle transactions at terms guaranteed by the Chamber of Commerce. Telephone inquiries can be made daily at 7946441.

Rooms, possibly with use of the apartment's kitchen, are usually rented for at least a month. The landlord or—much more often—the landlady needs a police license. If half a dozen or more rooms are being let to different renters, the rooming house will call itself a *pensione*, whether it provides meals or not. There are hundreds of these in all parts of the city, most—but not all—of them listed under *Pensioni* in the White and Yellow Pages of the Rome telephone directory. Some *pensioni* operate like hotels, although they may occupy just a floor or two in some residential building; others are run by householders who take in lodgers.

Many *pensioni* specialize in students or recent immigrants from the Third World who share rooms. Before moving into a *pensione* do some investigating (possibly by speaking to a resident guest), and have the terms clearly explained to you.

For rooms to be let by English-speaking people, scan the bulletin board in the **Lion Bookshop**, 181 Via del Babuino/3 Via della Fontanella (two entrances to the same store), near the Piazza del Popolo (telephone: 3225837). The English-language bookshop is open from 9:30 A.M. to 1:30 P.M. and 3:30 to 7:30 P.M. Tuesday to Saturday, 3:30 to 7:30 P.M. Monday.

To rent or buy a condominium apartment or villa in or near Rome, you may not need a lawyer right away, but a *commercialista* (business and fiscal consultant) is indispensable. The local real estate and tax laws and regulations are a daunting thicket that no foreigner (and almost no Italian for that matter) can hope to overcome without expert advice and assistance. Plenty of such specialists are listed in the Rome Yellow Pages under *Ragionieri* (Accountants). To be sure that the *commercialista* is on your side, choose one who has successfully done work for a resident friend or acquaintance.

If you purchase an apartment or some other real estate, a notary public (*notaio*) will draw up a letter of intent (*compromesso*); when this is coupled with a down payment, he or she will complete the contract. A notary public in Italy is a quasipublic official who must have a law degree and is entitled to substantial fees.

Roman landlords like to let apartments to foreigners in the hope of receiving a higher rent than Italians would normally pay under rent-control laws. It is far easier to evict a noncitizen than a native tenant, who would in all likelihood put up a legal fight. A deposit of three months' rent in addition to the payment for the first month is customary. The deposit is refundable at the end of the contract period, but some landlords will try to retain it on the grounds of real or imaginary damages to the property caused by the tenant. Many Italians simply don't pay the last three months' rent.

It is a good idea to have one's apartment or villa insured against damages and especially against theft; burglaries are rampant in Rome. Insurance companies will insist that entrance doors be fitted with special locks and lined with steel plates, and that windows that are easily reachable from the ground, roof, or terrace be secured by grillwork.

Some residential buildings in the city still have doormen and residential superintendents (*portieri*), but more and more condominium buildings (the prevailing form of home ownership in Rome) are now locked all the time because the apartment owners have decided to do without a *portiere*. Anyone without a latchkey must contact a resident by phone or intercom (*citofono*) to gain access.

3.

Eat as the Romans Eat

EATING OUT IS as essential to Roman life as are espresso breaks, the siesta, *amore*, and soccer. To understand what the Eternal City is all about, visitors who by necessity will have all or most of their meals at restaurants should seek out places with a primarily Italian clientele. Though the badges of major credit cards won't be displayed on entrance doors and the menus won't be in English, the cuisine there will often be better than in the establishments recommended by international food critics, guidebooks, and airlines.

Rome, like other capitals, has its power lunches (and dinners). Business executives from Milan and Turin meet with bankers and high bureaucrats over *spaghetti all'amatriciana* to discuss contracts, licenses, and loans; diplomats and journalists entertain their sources; film directors woo financiers; Vatican prelates are taken out by visiting archbishops from wealthy dioceses; and—above all—many of the nearly one thousand senators and deputies of the national Parliament are forever to be seen plotting the maneuvers of Italy's volatile multiparty politics or being wined and dined by lobbyists.

To countless other Romans a restaurant meal does not mean just feeding but is the preferred way of socializing. The city almost completely lacks clubs, cozy coffeehouses, or literary salons, and only foreign diplomats and a few rich residents entertain at their homes. People meet and chat above all in Rome's several thousand eating places. A typical Roman restaurant lunch may last from 1:30 to 3:30 or 4 P.M., a dinner from 8:30 to 11 P.M., possibly followed by a nightcap or a gelato in a nearby piazza.

Visitors accustomed to other mealtimes will find they aren't served lunch before 12:30 P.M. and dinner before 7:30 P.M. in almost any Roman sit-down eating place. Local people often turn up for lunch as late as 2:30 P.M. Romans, who as a rule eat skimpy breakfasts, will have developed a formidable appetite in time for their midday meal.

The typical lunch consists of three substantial courses: a *primo piatto* (first plate) or *primo*, which may be pasta, soup, or antipasto (hors d'oeuvres); a *secondo piatto* (second plate) or *secondo*—meat or fish with salad or other vegetables; and cheese or a dessert, often fresh fruit. Dinner usually follows the same sequence. Serious eaters will take their antipasto before the ritual pasta, to be followed by the *secondo*, and may insert a little cheese before dessert. Such a lavish meal for lunch, especially if it is washed down by plenty of wine, requires a generous siesta. However, the number of people who can no longer indulge in a postprandial snooze is growing, and as many Romans have become weight watchers, restaurant meals—especially at lunchtime—have lately become streamlined.

Foreigners don't have to fear the manifest displeasure of their waiter if they order just a pasta course and a salad for lunch. If they don't want an alcoholic beverage, a soft drink or a bottle of mineral water will do.

Mineral water, which Romans drink in astonishing quantities, comes in one-liter or half-liter bottles, corresponding to about a quart or half a quart. *Acqua minerale* is offered with a variety of labels, each painstakingly listing the presumably healthy minerals and other trace elements it contains and claiming beneficial consequences for various body organs. Ferrarelle is a frequent brand, also Fiuggi; San Pellegrino is rarer. If you want just a small bottle, ask for *una mezza bottiglia*. Also tell the waiter if you want the kind with bubbles (*frizzante*) or without (*senza gas*). Tap water is *acqua naturale*, and it's quite safe, but the waiter may raise his eyebrows if the patron insists on it. (The masculine form is used in the preceding sentence because waitresses are still rare in Rome restaurants.)

The check will include the item *pane e coperto* (bread and cover charge), the equivalent of $1 to $3 per person; it is due regardless of whether the rolls, slices of fresh bread, or breadsticks put on the table have been eaten or not. Other fixed items on the check are *IVA*, which stands for value-added tax (a sales tax), and usually a service charge. The bottom line on the check will be up to 20 percent higher than the sum of the figures for the items ordered, as listed on the menu. If the menu puts a mysterious code like *s.q.* or *s.g.* (standing for "according to quantity" and "according to size") instead of a figure next to a dish like lobster or prime steak, expect a whopper on the check: it's the management's way of saying, "This is expensive food."

Some run-of-the-mill eating places near the Vatican and in other areas frequented by sightseers offer fixed-price, all-inclusive "tourist meals" (*menù turistico*)—for instance, a pasta course, chicken, and fruit. It will be relatively inexpensive, but don't expect a memorable culinary experience.

When paying the check, Romans today leave no more than a 5 percent tip on the plate, often less. Foreigners who may be used to handing out 15 to 20 percent tips at home should keep in mind that a service charge is already a part of Italian restaurant checks.

Patrons ought to keep the check for a little while, because they may be asked to produce it by officers in plain clothes outside the restaurant. The officers, who are under orders to show identification cards, belong to the *Guardia di Finanza*, or Finance Guard, a fiscal police force. They are in the streets during mealtime to spot-check whether restaurants comply with the tax laws. If a waiter or the maître d' just scrawls a few figures on a scrap of paper, something is wrong; request a formal check (*ricevuta fiscale*) and keep it at least for a couple of blocks when walking out of the establishment. If you have no "fiscal receipt" you may be ordered to pay a fine that may cost more than the meal; penalties for restaurant managements that do not issue such receipts are much stiffer.

Quite a few restaurants balk whenever patrons want to pay with a credit card, even though its logo may adorn their entrance door. It won't happen in first-class places; in other establishments either pay cash and send a protest to the headquarters of the credit-card system in question, or start an argument that you are bound to win although the unpleasantness will spoil the fun of the meal.

ROMAN EATING PLACES have various labels, but the distinctions between them have long eroded and, in any case, have little to do with the quality of food and service.

Ristorante is a term suggesting distinction and refine-

ment—white tablecloths, written or printed menus, cour-
teous waiters. A *trattoria* is supposed to be a less formal
place, possibly still run by the owner, assisted by family
members, with a clientele mainly from the neighborhood.
A few authentic trattorie fitting this description still survive
in outlying districts. In the center of the city and in the
Trastevere section most trattorie are *ristoranti* in disguise—
dressed up in folksy ways with old copper pans on the
walls and strings of dry onions or bulbous garlic hanging
from the ceiling, straw-covered wine flasks on a shelf,
autographed photos of celebrities on the walls, and genial
waiters.

An *osteria* as a rule is a popular establishment, often just
one room and the kitchen, offering robust fare and wines
from the nearby hillside in the characteristic Roman carafe
(*fojetta*) with a leaden seal, guaranteeing exact measure, on
its flaring lip. The host or (often) hostess slams a dish of
pasta in front of the guest, who most of the time is a
regular, and there is much loud talk, banter, and laughter
from table to table. Paper substitutes nowadays for the
cloth napkins that even simple trattorie provide for their
patrons.

The business sign *hostaria*, an archaic form of the word
osteria (comparable to "Ye Olde Tea Shoppe"), often betrays pretension. The food may be all right, but waiters in
folklore costumes may serve it amid faux-rustic decor with
plenty of wood paneling. *Bottiglieria*, which means "bottle
shop," is the dying-out type of one-room business where
working-class Romans relax over a glass or a half-liter
fojetta of Frascati wine with a sandwich or some other snack
that they may have brought with them or bought on the
premises.

Pizza is, of course, the standby of any *pizzeria*; Rome
boasts nearly a thousand of them, and many also offer other

snacks and dishes. A *ristorante-pizzeria* has full restaurant service, with pizza available probably only from late afternoon to closing time. Many hole-in-the-wall businesses sell *pizza a taglio* (pizza by the cut) all day—slices from long strips of bland pizzalike dough, topped with mozzarella cheese and probably reheated on an electric stove. Romans like this for a snack. *Pizza bianca* (white pizza) comes without tomato garnishing.

A *rosticceria* (roasting shop) or *tavola calda* (hot table) is a place where roast chicken and other snacks with side orders of french fries or vegetables can be had, to be eaten on the spot—maybe with a glass of wine—or taken out.

Since the early 1980s fast-food outlets have also appeared in Rome, many of them franchises of American and British chains. In addition to hamburgers—the Romans pronounce the word "am-BOORG-ah"—most such places also serve small reheated pizzas and other home-grown snacks.

For the three thousand or so Roman restaurants, whether they are called *ristorante* or otherwise, the rule of thumb is that the quality of their cuisine is in inverse proportion to the attractiveness of their location. The food served on a terrace with a famous panorama of the city or at the open-air tables in some charming piazza will often be humdrum and probably overpriced; some of the city's best eating places are in narrow, hard-to-find streets.

Most restaurants are closed one day, or one day and a half, each week. A sign outside will read, for instance, *"Lunedì Riposo"* (Monday rest). In the city center, most establishments are shuttered Sunday, or Saturday night and Sunday, whereas in the suburban districts the weekends mean big business for trattorie. Between Christmas and New Year's quite a few restaurants stay closed, and the summer visitor to Rome will have a tough time between

August 10 and the end of the month finding an open eating
place that isn't ultra-touristy (see pages 67–79).

It is advisable to make reservations for all but the popular eating places, although managers will usually try to
accommodate walk-ins. Sightseers who are getting hungry
at mealtime will at any rate have little difficulty spying a
vacant table on the terrace or in the dining room of some
ristorante or trattoria, and may claim it unless there is a
Riservato sign on it. Of course, a single person or a couple
should not expect to be given a large table that can accommodate four or six patrons when business is at its height.
Visitors, however, will find Roman waiters and maîtres d'
far more accommodating and less haughty than some of
their colleagues in the United States or France.

ROMAN CUISINE

Local experts point out that restaurant food in the Italian
capital has lately undergone changes in divergent directions. On the one hand the cuisine has become refined in
a dozen or so deluxe places that can hold their own in
comparison with the culinary shrines of Milan, France, and
elsewhere on the Continent. In contrast to this trend, many
other ristoranti and trattorie that once used to serve honest-
to-goodness dishes of traditional Roman cooking have introduced new decor along with fancy innovations that have
inflated prices and worsened quality. They garnish spaghetti with vodka or gorgonzola cheese, douse all sorts
of pasta in cream, sprinkle risotto with champagne, and
overcook inferior fish.

One reason for the decline in standards at many trattorie is mass tourism. First-time visitors who don't speak
the language are often timid in a mock-folksy restaurant

looking out on a fountain or ancient ruin when a smiling waiter presses the house specialty on them, which may turn out to be a pasta composition drowned in questionable vegetable oil, or a piece of tough meat with a slice of ham and some herbs attached to it by a toothpick. In addition to the "*s.q.*" or "*s.g.*" mentioned previously, beware also of the check-boosting device of listing steak or some other dish on the menu with a cryptic "*p. etto,*" which means "according to weight in hectograms" (3.527 oz.); you won't have a pharmacist's scale with you.

Occasionally, unsatisfactory food in Rome's eating places may also be due to the scarcity of accomplished cooks and other kitchen personnel. Outstanding chefs are relatively rare, command high pay, are often temperamental, and are courted by would-be employers. If readers of this guidebook are disappointed by some restaurant mentioned in the following pages, it may be because its former chef has been hired away by a rival establishment or has opened his own place. Many kitchen workers are recent immigrants from eastern Europe, Africa, or Asia who toil hard enough but still have to sharpen their gastronomic skills.

Genuine Roman cuisine—as distinct from what is usually served in hotel dining rooms, by luxury restaurants, and at diplomatic affairs—is avowedly plebeian. Its pasta, lamb, veal, pork, sausages, and poultry have been cooked and eaten by the farmers of the Sabine and Abruzzi mountains of the nearby interior in the same way for centuries; its vegetables and wines are all being grown in the city's vicinity; its fish were caught in the offshore waters before those got thoroughly polluted; its olive oil was, and in part still is, pressed in the hills of Latium and Umbria (although few eating places today still use good olive oil, substituting other vegetable oils for it).

Romans have for many generations liked hefty and uncomplicated fare; they want their meat and vegetables served in natural juices and flavors rather than disguised in sophisticated sauces. Mincing, ornamental nouvelle cuisine was never much of a success in the Italian capital. To underline the inelegant but sincere tradition of local cooking, quite a few restaurants write their menus in *romanesco*, the earthy, even vulgar, local dialect (see page 201). Foreigners, even those who know Italian, will have to ask what it all means.

Pasta

Most Romans have pasta almost every day (some eat it for lunch *and* dinner) and are likely to order the national staple as their *primo* whenever they go to a restaurant. The filling dish, especially when it comes without such exotic trimmings as chunks of salmon or a sprinkling of whiskey, is always the safest bet in any eating establishment throughout the city. No trattoria or osteria could stay in business for long if its spaghetti were consistently overcooked instead of al dente (slightly firm), or its tomato sauce rancid.

The varieties of Italian pasta are endless. A number of them are most common in Rome. *Spaghetti*, thin strings of pasta, is served with tomato sauce (*al sugo*) or ragout, or with butter or olive oil (*in bianco*). More fanciful preparations are: *All'amatriciana* (often misspelled *alla matriciana*), in the style of Amatrice, a town and culinary beacon in the hillside northeast of Rome, with lard and pepper. *Alla puttanesca* (literally: whore's style), with black olives. *Primavera* (springtime), with fresh green peas. *Alla carbonara* (charcoal burner's style), with beaten eggs, small chunks of bacon, and olive oil. *Alla pescatora* (fisherman's style), with seafood, parsley, and garlic. *Aglio-olio*, a very popular form of enjoying one's pasta with olive oil, garlic, and hot red peppers.

Fettuccine and *tagliatelle* are pasta ribbons of varying breadth. Some brands are bright yellow, a color produced by fresh eggs or, more likely, by artificial coloring in the dough. Garnishings are similar to those of spaghetti.

Local purists eat the pasta strands and ribbons by deftly winding them around their fork—not too many at a time—without the aid of a spoon. The unpracticed visitor may safely use a spoon; quite a few Italians do likewise. Never, never cut spaghetti or any other kind of pasta with a knife if you don't want to draw stares and hear snickers from the neighboring tables.

Penne (feathers) are short pieces of macaroni; long macaroni, hollow tubes of pasta, are rare in Rome. *Penne all' arrabbiata* (angry style) come with tomato sauce, garlic, and plenty of red peppers. *Rigatoni*, very popular, are short, broad, ribbed pasta tubes. *Pappardelle* are broad bands of dough, usually with a venison sauce. *Cappelletti* (little hats) are small, round pieces of pasta with a meat filling that come in consommé or with the usual pasta garnishings. *Ravioli* are larger, usually square pasta envelopes containing ground meat, cheese, or spinach. *Agnolotti* too are packages of dough with various fillings.

Lasagne, a Bolognese specialty familiar also to Romans, are layers of pasta with ground meat, cheese, and maybe tomatoes in between, baked in the oven and often dripping with oil. A good-sized helping of lasagne will blunt the appetite for any following dish. *Cannelloni*, Sicilian-style, are pasta rolls with various fillings. *Gnocchi* are small balls or dumplings of semolina or potatoes, therefore not strictly pasta but served with pasta garnishings. Roman trattorie have offered gnocchi every Thursday since time immemorial. Saturday is the day for tripe, *trippa*.

Many eating places promote their own house specialties of pasta, often touted under the owner's or chef's first name (*"spaghetti alla Mario"*). They add cream, diced bacon, or chunks of eggplant, if not more expensive ingredients like sliced truffles or inferior caviar, to regular pasta to jazz it up. In the more pretentious restaurants some insistence will be necessary to obtain the basic plate of spaghetti with nothing more than a sauce of fresh tomatoes.

Risotto and *polenta* (cornmeal mush) are northern Italian specialties, often offered by some restaurants in Rome.

Soups

The choice of soups is much narrower than that of pasta. Clear meat soup (*brodo*), all too often made from bouillon cubes, is usually enriched with tiny pieces of pasta or with rice (*pastina in brodo* or *riso in brodo*). *Minestra di verdura* is a soup that may contain beans and potatoes in addition to green vegetables. *Minestrone* is a thick soup, a chewy mix of green vegetables, beans, chick-peas, potatoes, and pasta. Related are *pasta e fagioli* (short pasta and beans) and *pasta e ceci* (pasta and chick-peas).

Appetizers

Antipasti, if they are ordered at all, may precede pasta or replace it. An old, rustic standby that has lately become fashionable is *bruschetta*—a few slices of peasant bread, slightly rubbed with garlic, spread with olive oil and toasted.

The truck farms around Rome furnish delicious vegetables from early spring to late autumn. Asparagus, from March to June, comes almost exclusively in the slender green (wild) variety. Plump, tender artichokes from plan-

tations near the capital (*carciofi romaneschi*) are eaten as hors
d'oeuvres in spring, and artichokes from Sardinia, Sicily,
and other areas around the Mediterranean are available
most of the year. Zucchini, eggplant, mushrooms, beans,
and other vegetables in many different combinations and
preparations as well as cold cuts adorn the sideboards on
which many Roman restaurants display their antipasti.

Waiters will often suggest ham with melon or, in season, with peeled fresh figs as an appetizer. The *settembrini*
figs, coming to Roman tables from the surrounding coun-
tryside during September, are justly praised. The priciest
ham is supplied by San Daniele and Parma, both in northern Italy, but the pork products from areas closer to Rome
are also satisfactory.

A recent favorite as an appetizer or light main course
is *insalata caprese* (Capri salad): slices of fresh tomatoes and
mozzarella cheese with basil on a plate or, alternately, arranged on a skewer.

Meats, Poultry, and Game

After the glories of antipasti and pasta, the meat courses of
the Roman cuisine may seem something of a letdown,
because the first courses will have taken the edge off one's
appetite. Veal (*vitello*) dominates.

Veal comes in grilled, roasted, or breaded slices (*fettine*);
as *spezzatino* in small chunks in a stew that may also contain
fresh peas; and in several other guises. *Saltimbocca* (literally,
"jump into the mouth"), a Roman specialty, is a strip of
veal with a slice of ham on top, fried in oil or butter with
a shot of sweet wine, and spiced with sage.

A T-bone steak is known as *bistecca alla fiorentina* (beef-
steak, Florentine style); in some restaurants it's grilled over
charcoal before the patrons' eyes and it is expensive. The

juiciest steaks come from beef raised in the coastal low-
lands, the Maremma, of southern Tuscany. Choice cuts of
veal or beef filet are also served raw in thin strips, with
seasoning, as *carpaccio*, a relative novelty imported from
Venice.

Ossobuco, a cut of veal or beef around the marrow bone,
regularly served with rice or mashed potatoes, is a Milanese
dish that has become popular in Rome as well. Better
restaurants offer cuts of various meats from the steam table
or steam cart.

Lamb is a Roman favorite, often eaten on festive occasions. Baby lamb is *agnello*; meat from an older animal is
called *abbacchio*. Roast lamb, *abbacchio al forno*, is considered
a peak of the Roman cuisine.

Chicken is roasted or prepared in other ways: *alla dia-
vola* (devil's style) with hot peppers, or *alla cacciatora*
(hunter's style) with tomatoes, mushrooms, and herbs.
Chicken breast *alla parmigiana* (Parma style) comes with a
slice of soft cheese.

Among larger poultry, pheasant (*fagiano*) and guinea
hen (*faraona*) are preferred. Romans with an upset stomach
order chicken soup and maybe a bit of the boiled hen
(*gallina bollita*) that yielded it.

Down-to-earth treats best sampled in the trattorie in
the Testaccio section and near the wholesale food market
are *coda alla vaccinara* (oxtail, cowherd's style) and *pajata*, a
cooked length of a calf's intestine, still filled with curdled
milk. Working-class eateries display a whole suckling pig,
roasted on the spit and filled with herbs (*porchetta*), from
which slices are cut off on demand.

Breaded and fried meat is *alla milanese* (Milan style).
Fritto misto is mixed grill, which may also include fried
artichokes and zucchini. Artichokes cooked in oil with

garlic and herbs and then deep-fried are a local treat called *carciofi alla giudía* (artichokes, Jewish style).

The legal hunting seasons in the nation's various regions, from September to spring, are the time for ordering *selvaggina* or *caccia* (game): rabbit (*lepre*), boar (*cinghiale*), and various fowl.

Seafood

Fresh fish and other seafood have lately become expensive in Rome because the nearby Tyrrhenian Sea is overfished and, in large stretches, fouled by organic and industrial wastes. Some of the day's catches of fishing boats off Sicily and Sardinia and in the Adriatic Sea are rushed to Rome by air or in refrigerator trucks, but freshness is relative. Lobster is, by local standards, very expensive. Scampi, shellfish, and other seafood should be thoroughly cooked. Shun oysters and raw mussels in Rome.

Most of the seafood eaten in Italy comes deep frozen from far away. Under the law all public eating places must advise patrons whether the fish they serve is fresh or frozen, but menus often identify the latter by a discreet "(*refr.*)."

Dried codfish from the Atlantic has long played a prominent role in the Roman diet and is prepared in various ways. Cod or any other fish *alla livornese* (Leghorn style) comes with tomatoes and garlic; *alla pescatora* (fisherman's style) with garlic, olive oil, and a dash of white wine; and *alla siciliana* (Sicilian style) with olives. Cod in Italian is *baccalà*.

The best fresh sole (*sogliola*) is supposed to come from Ancona on the Adriatic Sea, but most of the sole served in restaurants has been deep frozen.

Cheese (*Formaggio*)

Mozzarella is the favored cheese in Rome. Newcomers may at first be less than thrilled by its rubbery texture and its blandness, but they soon come to like it: mozzarella is an acquired taste. Ideally the soft, satiny cheese should be made with the milk of the water buffalo, which are bred in the Naples area; great quantities of mozzarella, however, are now being turned out industrially in various parts of the country with cow's milk as the basis.

Harder than mozzarella but still semisoft, *caciotta* is a family of cheeses produced in Tuscany, Umbria, Latium, and other regions, and is usually marketed in loaves. *Provolone* is somewhat harder. *Gorgonzola* is a soft, spicy import from northern Italy, as is the high-calorie, creamy *mascherpone*. Italy's food industry supplies a wide range of cheese spreads, like the mild *Belpaese* and more pungent types, generally available in restaurants. The hardest Italian cheeses are Parmesan (*parmigiano*) from the Parma area, and *pecorino*, made of sheep's milk. Most pasta dishes are eaten with a generous sprinkling of Parmesan.

Desserts

Lately *tiramisù* (literally, "pick-me-up"), a creamy confection of cocoa powder, chocolate, and sweetened *mascherpone* cheese (see above), has lately all but supplanted the classic *zuppa inglese* ("English soup"). *Zuppa inglese* is neither English nor a soup; it is a very soft and rich sponge cake—soaked in sweet liquor and topped with custard and whipped cream—that few Roman restaurants still offer. *Tiramisù* is much easier to make.

Many restaurants also display chocolate cakes and other sweets on sideboards or carts. A growing number of Romans who patronize such eating places appear to be calorie-conscious today; they order fresh or stewed fruit or fruit salad (*macedonia*) for dessert, or skip dessert altogether, topping their main course with just a cup of espresso.

DRINKS

Waiters in places frequented by foreigners will ask whether the guest would like an *aperitivo* before the meal. The aperitif may be a Campari or some other concoction of the nation's thriving liquor industry. Don't ask for a martini—you will in all likeliness get a vermouth. Most Romans will ask for wine right away, or just for mineral water.

Time was when the waiter in the average trattoria, a napkin under his left arm, would routinely ask a guest, *"Bianco o rosso?"* (white or red?)—meaning, which one of the two house wines in carafe were preferred—even before the new arrival had had a chance to study the menu or ask what dishes were available. By now many eating places are more sophisticated with regard to wine, but not very much. Relatively few restaurants in Rome have a wine list; the waiter may instead point at a shelf where various bottles are arrayed, leaving it to the guest to examine their labels and make a selection. As for carafe wines in Rome, the whites are usually better than the reds.

Open wines come most often from the hillside southeast of the city, the Castelli Romani. The whites are generally called Frascati, regardless of whether they have been grown in vineyards near that town on a slope overlooking Rome, or near such other towns as Grottaferrata, Marino, Albano, or Velletri. Colorless or in shades from light yellow to amber, these wines are refreshing in taste and seem light but can be treacherous. Be on your guard if you detect a sulfurous taste—it indicates wine tampering. The reds from the Castelli Romani and other wine-growing areas around the capital tend to be dense and at times sweetish.

Bottled wines available in almost any trattoria include the pleasant light whites from Orvieto and Montefiascone, and red Chianti from Tuscany, which is dry and has remarkable body (white Chiantis are much harder to find in Roman restaurants).

Better places may also offer aromatic red Valpolicella and white Soave from Venetia; strong red Barolo and other wines from Piedmont; effervescent, violet-flavored red Lambrusco from the Emilia region; heady Corvo from Sicily; and sparkling wine (*spumante*) from Asti.

Italy, which rivals France as the world's leading wine producer, grows hundreds of distinctive vintages, but few Roman restaurants offer much choice. Wine connoisseurs should turn to an *enoteca* (wine shop or wine bar; see page 74).

Bottles displaying a special seal by a vintners' association guaranteeing authenticity contain what is called DOC wines; the acronym stands for "controlled denomination of origin." European Community rules reserve the commercial use of the terms *champagne* and *cognac* for French products; their Italian counterparts are labeled *spumante* and *brandy*.

Italian beers are light. The dominant brand in Rome is Peroni, from a brewery on the city's eastern outskirts. Czech, Danish, Dutch, and German imports are widely available.

Quite a few Romans like to conclude a substantial meal, before or after espresso, with a small glass of a cordial, known as *digestivo*. It is supposed to have been distilled from herbs to aid the digestion, is bitter (*amaro*) or syrupy, and always has a high alcohol content. Some restaurants offer their brand of *digestivo* on the house, and courtesy dictates that the guest take at least a sip.

EATING PLACES

The following lists are far from complete. They include establishments that—at the time when this guide was compiled—were found to deliver outstanding or at least satisfactory value for their price bracket. Cuisine, decor, and service were considered. Visitors to Rome who want to go by themselves on culinary exploration will doubtless discover other restaurants and trattorie that would deserve mention.

If some establishment is missing here though it is prominently named by other travel literature and is advertising widely, the reason is not necessarily that its performance is poor. It might just be, or have lately become, touristy. Many restaurants—not only in Rome or elsewhere in Italy—that once were excellent and deservedly recommended by experts have meanwhile been overrun and have found it hard to maintain their original high standards.

Expensive Restaurants

Several fine restaurants in hotels have been mentioned in chapter 2: they are **Relais Le Jardin**, 5 Via de Notaris (telephone: 3220404) in the Lord Byron Hotel, with French-inspired cuisine; **La Pergola**, 101 Via Cadlolo (telephone: 31511), on the top floor of the Cavalieri Hilton Hotel; and **Les Etoiles**, 34 Via Vitelleschi (telephone: 6879558), the roof-garden restaurant of the Atlante Star

Hotel. The clientele of all three places includes persons who are not hotel guests. Calculate $75 to $100 per person for a full dinner with wine. Other highly rated and equally expensive restaurants:

El Toulà, 29B Via della Lupa (telephone: 6871115), central, near the imposing Borghese Palace (see page 200). Venetian cuisine. Fancied by business executives from northern Italy.

Ranieri, 26 Via Mario de' Fiori (telephone: 6791592), near the Spanish Square. Small, with Old World grace. Diplomats favor it.

Alberto Ciarla, 40 Piazza San Cosimato (telephone: 5818668), in Trastevere. On a piazza that during the day is filled with the bustle of an outdoor market. Evenings only; outdoor tables when the weather permits. The focus is on seafood.

Cul de Sac 2, 21 Vicolo dell'Atleta (telephone: 5813324), in Trastevere; dinner only. Understated decor, very extensive wine list.

La Rosetta, 9 Via della Rosetta (telephone: 6861002), near the Pantheon. Specializes in seafood.

Al Fogher, 13B Via Tevere (telephone: 8417032), in the north of Rome. Venetian-Friuli cuisine and wines. Polenta, risottos.

Coriolano, 14 Via Ancona (telephone: 8551122), near the Porta Pia; modern decor.

Piperno, 9 Monte de' Cenci (telephone: 6540629), on a small piazza in the former Jewish ghetto. Outdoor tables. Artichokes *alla giudía* and other Roman specialties, good wines.

Vecchia Roma, 18 Piazza Campitelli (telephone: 6864604), on a small piazza near the Capitoline Hill, with outdoor tables. Traditional Roman cuisine. Open Sunday.

La Maiella, 45–46 Piazza Sant'Apollinare (telephone: 6864174), near Piazza Navona. Abruzzi specialties, game in season, seafood. Italian politicians like it.

Taverna Giulia, 23 Vicolo dell'Oro (telephone: 6869768), off the Corso Vittorio Emanuele II near the Tiber. Pasta garnished with *pesto* (a greenish sauce containing olive oil, basil, garlic, pine nuts, and Parmesan cheese) and other Genoese specialties; seafood. Ligurian wines.

Casina Valadier, Via Valadier (telephone: 6794189), on the Pincio, has a famous panorama but indifferent cuisine. However, it's worthwhile for just coffee, tea, drinks, or gelato, which are served from morning to late at night.

Augustea, 6 Via della Frezza (telephone: 3226089), off the Via del Corso, is for people watching. Politicians and other celebrities frequent this bustling place for late suppers; also, business lunches.

Medium Price Range

These average $30 to $60 per person for dinner and are good quality:

Il Buco, 8 Via di Sant'Ignazio (telephone: 6793298), central. Tuscan cuisine and wines, truffles and game in season. Biscuits and *digestivo* on the house. Open Sunday.

Al Moro, 13 Vicolo delle Bollette (telephone: 6783495), near Trevi Fountain. Traditionally Roman. The owner's father, Mario Romagnoli, had a part in Fellini's film *Satyricon*, set in ancient Rome.

Fortunato, 55 Via del Pantheon (telephone: 6792788). Traditional, relaxed.

L'Angoletto, 51 Piazza Rondanini (telephone: 6868019), near the Pantheon, with outdoor tables.

La Campana, 18 Vicolo della Campana (telephone: 6875273), central, near the Tiber. Claims to be Rome's oldest trattoria.

Mario alla Vite, 55 Via della Vite (telephone: 6783818), near the Spanish Square. Lavish hors d'oeuvres; Tuscan wines.

Colline Emiliane, 22 Via degli Avignonesi (telephone: 4817538), on a narrow street near the Piazza Barberini. Renowned for its fettuccine. Open on Sunday.

Cesarina, 109 Via Piemonte (telephone: 4880828), near Via Veneto. Lasagne and other Bologna specialties.

Checco er Carettiere, 10 Via Benedetta (telephone: 5817018), in Trastevere, with outdoor tables. Pseudo-rustic; reliable food.

Dal Bolognese, 1–2 Piazza del Popolo (telephone: 3611426), with a terrace looking out on a famous square. Open Sunday.

La Carbonara, 23 Piazza Campo de' Fiori (telephone: 6864783). Lunch starts as the stands on the square close for the day (see page 89). Outdoor tables, open Sunday.

Da Pancrazio, 92–94 Piazza del Biscione (telephone: 6861246), near Campo de' Fiori. Open Sunday.

L'Antiquario, 27 Piazzetta San Simeone (telephone: 6879694), on a small square near Raphael's house (see page 87). Outdoor tables, open evenings only.

Taverna Flavia, 9/1 Via Flavia (telephone: 4745214), near Porta Pia. VIPs like it.

Da Cesare, 13 Via Crescenzio (telephone: 6861227), near the old Palace of Justice; affluent trattoria-pizzeria.

Giggetto, 21A Via del Portico d'Ottavia (telephone: 6861105), in the former Jewish ghetto. Roman-Jewish cuisine: artichokes *alla giudía*, fried mozzarella; wines from the Roman hillside.

Kosher cuisine: **Uno al Portico d'Ottavia,** 1E Via del Portico d'Ottavia (telephone: 654934), in the former Jewish ghetto.

On the outskirts in pleasant surroundings: **L'Archeologia**, 139 Via Appia Antica (telephone: 7880494), and **Cecilia Metella**, 125–127 Via Appia Antica (telephone: 5136743), both on the Ancient Appian Way, both open on Sunday. **Nino**, 64 Via della Camilluccia (telephone: 3420829), on the Monte Mario. Plain, but in a large garden with a grand panorama. Open on Sunday.

Relatively Inexpensive

These are less than $30 a person for dinner, with beverage; also for snacks:

Bottiglieria Gino, 4 Vicolo Rosini (telephone: 6873434), near the Chamber of Deputies. One of the very few remaining family-run places in the center.

Armando, 31 Salita dei Crescenzi (telephone: 6543034), near the Pantheon.

Galleria Sciarra, 75 Piazza Oratorio (telephone: 6790766), near the Trevi Fountain, with terrace.

Polese, 40 Piazza Sforza Cesarini (telephone: 6861709), off the Corso Vittorio Emanuele II, with outdoor tables.

La Pollarola, 24–25 Piazza Pollarola (telephone: 6541654), near Campo de' Fiori, with outdoor tables.

International Cuisine

The commonplace opinion is that the Romans are so fond of their own way of cooking and eating that they don't care for the food of other countries and civilizations. However, there has been a recent proliferation of Chinese restaurants, while the number of other foreign-oriented eating places has remained limited. What seems true of the far more than a hundred Chinese establishments that have opened lately in all city neighborhoods is that they are comparatively inexpensive, although the quality of their cuisine often does not meet their exotic decor.

If you can't do without chopsticks in Rome, try **Taverna di Bambù**, 2 Via di Santa Dorotea (telephone: 5806065) in the Trastevere section. It practices good Shanghai-style cooking, and unlike other Chinese places it has a respectable wine list. Reservations recommended.

JAPANESE

Mitsukoshi, 34 Via Torino (telephone: 4873920), near the Rome Opera House. On the main floor, guests can watch the kitchen proceedings; the lower level includes a sushi bar and tatami rooms.

FRENCH

Charly's Saucière, 270 Via San Giovanni in Laterano (telephone: 736666), near the Lateran. Open evenings only. Also French-Swiss specialties, like fondue.

L'Eau Vive, 85A Via Monterone (telephone: 6541095), in a sixteenth-century palazzo near the Pantheon, is unusual in several respects. It is operated by a Roman Catholic missionary society, the Travailleuses Missionnaires, with young members from Third World countries in their national costumes serving at the tables. Churchmen visiting Rome and Vatican prelates are often among the patrons, but lay guests need not expect attempts at proselytizing. French-style à la carte dishes are served in the frescoed second-floor halls; an inexpensive "tourist menu" is on the ground floor. The kitchen is competent and the wine list satisfactory.

AUSTRIAN AND GERMAN

Wiener Bierhaus, 21 Via della Croce (telephone: 6795569), and **Birreria Bavarese**, 44–47 Via Vittoria (telephone: 6790383), both near the Spanish Square. Sausages and other Teutonic treats, and imported beer.

NORTH AFRICAN

Taverna Negma, 92 Borgo Vittorio (telephone: 6865143), near the Vatican. Couscous and other Arab specialties.

VIETNAMESE

Mekong, 333 Corso Vittorio Emanuele II (telephone: 6861684), near the Tiber.

Pizza Places

Picchioni, 16 Via del Boschetto (telephone: 4885261), near the Colosseum. It guarantees that its mozzarella is made with buffalo milk.

La Capricciosa, 7 Largo dei Lombardi (telephone: 6878636), off the Via del Corso, with a terrace.

Panattoni, 53 Viale Trastevere (telephone: 5800919), on the right bank of the Tiber.

Snack Bars

Rosticcerie and the like; here are a few of many:

Al Picchio, 40 Via del Lavatore (telephone: 6781602), near the Trevi Fountain.

Franchi, 204 Via Cola di Rienzo (telephone: 6874651), in the Prati section.

Liberti, 27A Borgo Pio (telephone: 6540355), near the Vatican.

Wine Bars

Trimani, 37 Via Cernaia (telephone: 4958343), near the Stazione Termini.

Enoteca al Corso, 293–295 Corso Vittorio Emanuele II (telephone: 6541594), near the Tiber.

Enoteca al Parlamento, 15 Via dei Prefetti (telephone: 6873446), near the Chamber of Deputies.

Bar Gli Angeli, 3 Galleria Margherita/Via Agostino Depretis (telephone: 4821304), near the Rome Opera House. Part of a "megastore" with books, records, games, and an espresso bar.

Cul de Sac, 73 Piazza Pasquino (telephone: 6541094), near the Piazza Navona.

ESPRESSO, CAFÉS, AND GELATO

Rome boasts nearly six thousand espresso bars, and many of them also offer sandwiches, pastry, gelato, fruit juices, soft drinks, and milk shakes, as well as beer and other alcoholic drinks.

Most patrons drop in for coffee and maybe a quick snack or for a drink taken at the counter. Many espresso bars have a few tables inside and put others outside if the weather permits.

Customers pay the cashier first, then place the sales slip on the counter and tell the man or woman behind it, the *barista*, what they want. Many people still put a coin, the equivalent of 5 to 10 percent of the price of their coffee, on the pay slip or in a little bowl on the counter, but the habit of tipping the *barista* seems to be slowly on its way out. Coffee, gelato, drinks, or snacks served at the table of an espresso shop are more expensive than at the counter, and a tip for the waiter is in order.

Romans don't usually order an espresso or cappuccino without adding specifications: *lungo* (diluted), *ristretto* (short and dense), *macchiato* ("spotted" with a drop of cold or hot milk), *senza schiuma* (without the customary ring or top of foam), *al vetro* (in a glass instead of in the standard ceramic cup), *amaro* (without sugar), *freddo* (iced, especially in the hot months), or *corretto* (with a shot of grappa—brandy—which costs a little more). Decaffeinated coffee is ordered by a brand name, *caffè Hag* (pronounced "AHG"). *Latte macchiato* is a large glass of hot milk with a shot of espresso.

Fierce competition among the many espresso places—there are often several on the same block—results in a satisfying brew in almost all of them. Roman connoisseurs will nevertheless go out of their way to get the invigorating cup at some bar that is particularly famous for its potent coffee. Among them are:

Tazza d'Oro, 86 Via Orfani (telephone: 6798212) and **Caffè Sant'Eustachio**, 82 Piazza Sant'Eustachio (telephone: 6861309), both close to the Pantheon. The neighborhood is still being supplied with water from an aqueduct, the Aqua Virgo or Acqua Vergine, that Agrippa had built for his temple-and-baths complex (see page 83).

Torrefazione F. Boso, 23 Via dei Serpenti (telephone: 4882319), off the Via Nazionale. A sign over the large coffee-bean roaster in the shop reads "The Pope's Coffee." When Karol Wojtyla, later Pope John Paul II, was a theology student at the nearby Angelicum College, he used to take his cappuccino at Boso's.

Castroni, 30 Via Flaminia (telephone: 3611029), near Piazza del Popolo.

Bernasconi, 1 Largo di Torre Argentina (telephone: 6548141), adjoining the Teatro Argentina; also renowned for its pastry.

Coffeehouses where patrons may spend hours over little more than cappuccino while they are chatting, dis-

cussing ponderous issues, reading newspapers, or even do-
ing some work, have almost completely died out in the
Italian capital. An illustrious survivor that is more than
two hundred years old is **Caffè Greco**, 86 Via Condotti
(telephone: 6782554), near the Spanish Square. Writers like
Stendhal and the visiting Mark Twain, artists from the
Romantic Age to Giorgio de Chirico (who lived nearby),
and uncounted intellectuals have sat in its stuccoed rooms.
The self-exiled Gogol wrote much of his *Dead Souls* at
its marble-topped tables. Ceremonious waiters still wear
frock coats and black ties, but salesladies from the nearby
boutiques and cabdrivers also drop in for a quick espresso
at the front bar. The Caffè Greco has been designated as a
historic landmark.

The Roman intelligentsia used to meet also at **Rosati**,
4–5A Piazza del Popolo (telephone: 3225859), with outdoor tables. Whenever Jean-Paul Sartre and Simone de
Beauvoir visited Rome, they used to discuss literature and
exchange gossip with Alberto Moravia and his writer wife
Elsa Morante there. More recently Rosati has become essentially a gelato haven.

Opposite is **Canova**, 16 Piazza del Popolo (telephone:
3612231), an espresso and snack bar frequented by artists.
The cafés lining the upper part of the Via Veneto (see page
104) do most of their business on Riviera-style sidewalk
terraces where Italians from the provinces and foreign tourists take position for people watching—"people" being
mostly other provincials and foreigners.

The atmosphere is very English at **Sala da Thè Babington**, the city's only genuine tearoom, 23 Piazza di
Spagna (telephone: 6786027). Opened in 1892, it is still
a meeting place for Britons and other English-speaking
residents and visitors who care for tea and scones. Snacks
and light lunches are also served; prices are high.

Sunday brunch is a novelty for Rome, introduced by resident foreigners but also adopted by a few cosmopolitan-minded Romans; there is still no Italian word for it. Brunch is served at hotels like **Le Grand Hotel** and the **De La Ville-InterContinental**; **Babington**'s tearoom; and at a few trendy restaurants like **Caffè degli Specchi**, 5 Via degli Specchi (telephone: 6861566).

Gelato is a local delight in which Romans and tourists indulge copiously, not only in summer. Ice cream can be had in most espresso bars and in many other places; if a shop advertises that its gelato is *produzione propria* (our own production) or *artigianale* (product of craftsmanship), this means it isn't the industrial kind but made according to original recipes, possibly on the premises. Outstanding gelato places:

Giolitti, 40 Via degli Uffici del Vicario (telephone: 6794206), near the Chamber of Deputies; an old creamery that counts many lawgivers among its gelato customers.

Tre Scalini, 28 Piazza Navona (telephone: 6541996); specialty: iced chocolate "truffle."

Fassi, 123–127 Via Nomentana (telephone: 8552363); in the city's northeast.

Tazza d'Oro, 86 Via Orfani (telephone: 6798212), near the Pantheon; only *granita di caffè*, a soft, grainy coffee ice that comes with or without whipped cream.

PICNICS

Many Romans who cannot go home for lunch (as many thousands of office workers and store personnel still do) and don't want to depend on a restaurant or snack bar enjoy their midday meal in the open. In the warm months they look for a place in the shade, and on one of the occasional sunny days in winter they sit down on the steps of some church or the base of a monument in the nearest piazza. There they eat, picniclike, what they have brought with them from home or bought in a store or outdoor market.

Foreigners can do likewise—nobody cares if you munch a sandwich in St. Peter's Square or on the Spanish Steps: there is no law against loitering. If the weather is right, a picnic in some spot along the Ancient Appian Way or in Ostia Antica or elsewhere on the outskirts may be more fun than a restaurant meal.

Sandwiches may be bought and taken out from many espresso bars, but they have usually been prepared early in the day and may have wilted by lunchtime; especially in summer caution is advisable if they contain mayonnaise, as they often do.

Much better, go to one of the many grocery stores (*salumeria, pizzicheria,* or *alimentari*) and ask the sales attendant to build you a sandwich to your taste. You will have a choice of rolls and breads, tempting hams, salami, bologna, and cheeses, maybe with olives or sliced tomatoes for garnishing. Don't be shy about pointing at whatever you want.

Grocery stores dot residential neighborhoods in a city where supermarkets still aren't numerous. In the center, where fewer and fewer people live, look for **Fratelli Fabbi**, 26–27 Via della Croce, near the Spanish Square, or **Salsamenteria**, 31 Via della Scrofa, near the Tiber.

You will save money on edibles, and fruits will be fresh, if you shop at an outdoor market. In the historical core, go to the stands in the Via del Lavatore, near the Trevi Fountain, or browse at the Campo de' Fiori market.

4.

What to See:
The City Core

IT WAS NOT built in a day, nor can Rome be fully explored in a day, a week, or even a month. Foreigners who have been living in the city for years still keep learning fascinating things that they didn't suspect, and many native Romans who have stayed in place for most of their lives know less about the city than do some of their guests.

The metropolis that has shaped or endured history for 2,500 years is like a parchment on which many scribes have been writing again and again. Traces of erased earlier texts can still be read here and there: churches are found to have been built into the ruins of pagan temples; the lone marble column of an ancient edifice stands out of the white-washed wall of a trattoria; recent immigrants from Africa seek shelter for the night under a vault that belonged to Nero's Golden House (see page 123); haughty fashion models parade in the stuccoed hall of a palazzo where cardinals once ruled.

Visitors whose time is limited will first want to get an overview of the city, and then maybe focus on some special aspect—archeology, religion, monuments, gardens, fountains, picturesque views, the arts, shopping, food, or just the theater unrolling in the streets and piazzas all day until late at night.

The bus tours conducted by travel organizations provide a chance for glimpsing the principal sights in a few hours or half a day. However, passengers will find their coach repeatedly stuck in traffic. They will have to climb out from time to time and walk for lengthy stretches before boarding the coach again, because the bulky vehicle is not allowed to park and must drive around the neighborhood while its passengers fling their coins into the Trevi Fountain or listen to the tour guide in St. Peter's Square.

Sightseers who hate getting in and out of buses all the time may as well reconnoiter Rome's historic center on foot and reach outlying points of interest by public transport or cab. The stroller will always find an espresso bar, or a fountain base or pillar to rest upon for a while and to take in the kaleidoscope of Roman street life.

If you plan to visit one of Rome's many museums and other public or private collections, make sure your destination is accessible. Official opening times are noted in the following pages, but a sightseer may nevertheless find closed doors because of a sudden strike, staff shortage, or absenteeism. Many institutions shut down in August, particularly around the middle of the month, the Ferragosto period.

The language barrier should not prevent a would-be visitor from finding out in advance whether a museum or gallery is *aperto* (open) or *chiuso* (closed). Telephone numbers are listed.

This guidebook does not quote admission fees. Because of inflation and budgetary reasons the price of admission to many excavation areas, collections, and other sights has repeatedly been increased lately. In 1992 prices ranged

from the equivalent of $1.40 for the Museum of the High
Middle Ages (see page 136) to $7.50 for the Roman Forum
or the Palatine (see pages 117, 119). Where admission is
free, it is noted.

Churches usually don't charge entrance fees, but they
may be closed during parts of the day, particularly between
1 and 5 P.M. Visitors to churches should refrain from loud
talk or laughter, especially during services. Women should
not wear short shorts or very revealing or sleeveless
dresses, and men should enter a church bareheaded.

MANY CHURCHES AND monuments dominate their
neighborhood; others have to be discovered in a hidden
piazza or in a maze of crooked lanes. Sloping streets exist
all over Rome. The City of the Seven Hills has in fact more
elevations than this name implies. The historic seven are
the Capitoline, Palatine, Aventine, Quirinal, Viminal, Esquiline, and Caelius—all east of the Tiber. Other hills are
the Pincio, parts of the modern and affluent Parioli district,
and the Monte Sacro, all on the east bank; the Janiculum,
Vatican, and Monte Mario rise on the opposite side of the
river.

The Tiber (*Tevere* in Italian) meanders across the city,
spanned by twenty-four bridges. The Tiber Island, near
the Capitoline Hill, lies in a bend where the river runs
shallow—the only ford between Rome and the sea and for
many miles upstream. This strategic wading passage was
a reason why traffic and commerce concentrated at this
point, and why temples and fortifications rose nearby at
the dawn of history. The early settlement of farmers, fish-
ermen, traders, and warriors was to reach predominance
throughout the region by the fourth century B.C. and eventually would become the capital of the ancient world.

BETWEEN PANTHEON AND TIBER

A good place to start or end a stroll around the heart of Rome is the Pantheon. It marks the geographical center of the old town, and it is the best-preserved building from antiquity in all of Rome. Present-day life swirls around it. The Piazza della Rotonda in front of the ancient edifice is closed in part to motor vehicles, and during the day one sees many tourists sitting at the outdoor tables of its cafés or on the steps of the sixteenth-century fountain in the middle, which is crowned with an ancient Egyptian obelisk. At night a Roman crowd takes over the square.

To Americans and Britons who see it for the first time, the Pantheon will seem somehow familiar. No wonder. Its symmetry and its majestic portico deeply impressed the sixteenth-century architect from Vicenza in northeastern Italy who became known by his nickname Palladio; the Palladian style in turn influenced the neoclassical buildings by Inigo Jones and Sir Christopher Wren in England, echoed by Thomas Jefferson's mansion Monticello and thousands of courthouses, post offices, and banks all over the United States.

The name *Pantheon* is variously interpreted as "temple of all gods" or "most sacred." The building is believed to have been dedicated originally to the gods of the seven planets then known, including Jupiter and Saturn. The large inscription on the architrave (the section supported by the columns of the portico) reads, in translation: "M. Agrippa, Consul for the Third Time." Marcus Vipsanius Agrippa, general, admiral, and son-in-law of Emperor Augustus, had the temple erected in 27 B.C. as part of a complex that also included public baths and gardens, with an artificial lake and fountains. To feed the waterworks, Agrippa had an aqueduct built, the Aqua Virgo, which is

functioning to this day. Its soft water, from a source at an
elevation of 1,800 feet (about 550 meters), 10 miles (16
kilometers) east of Rome, flows out of fountains and fau-
cets in the Pantheon area and in some other central neighborhoods, and is reputed to be excellent for cooking pasta
and brewing espresso. City officials say, however, that the
output of the Aqua Virgo is today being mixed with waters
from Rome's various other aqueducts.

Each of the sixteen columns of the Pantheon's portico
was cut by masons from a single huge chunk of Egyptian
granite. The edifice, through the ages despoiled of its marble and bronze adornments, has served as a Christian
church since the seventh century.

Its grandiose circular interior contains the tombs of
Raphael (to the left), of various other artists, and of the
first kings of unified Italy: Victor Emanuel II (died 1878)
and Umberto I (assassinated in 1900). A central opening
30 feet (9.15 meters) in diameter at the top of the hemi-
spherical dome lights the vast inner space.

The Pantheon is open 9 A.M. to 1 P.M. and 2 to 5 P.M.,
Tuesday through Saturday; 9 A.M. to 1 P.M. Sunday. Free
admission.

At the rear of the Pantheon some remains of Agrippa's
extended thermae, or baths, can be seen. A few steps to
the east is the Piazza della Minerva, with a church that in
the early Middle Ages was erected on the ruins of a temple
of Minerva, the goddess of wisdom. The interior of the
church of Santa Maria sopra Minerva (St. Mary above
Minerva) is noteworthy because it is about the only genuine example of the Gothic style in Rome.

The chapel on the right, close to the high altar, was
frescoed by the Renaissance painter and sometime Carmel-
ite friar Filippo Lippi. Michelangelo's statue, *Risen Christ
with the Cross* (it was completed by the artist's disciples)

stands to the right of the high altar. The bronze loincloth is a later addition, as is the bronze shoe protecting the right foot from the kisses of worshippers.

Outside the church, at the center of the square, is a marble elephant carrying a small Egyptian obelisk, one of the many works around Rome by Giovanni Lorenzo Bernini.

Walking westward from the Pantheon one passes the **Palazzo Madama**, the seat of the Italian Senate, or upper house of Parliament. The imposing baroque building, commissioned by the Medici of Florence, is named after Madama Margherita of Austria, the illegitimate daughter of Emperor Charles V and child bride of the infamous Duke Alessandro de' Medici; he was assassinated six months after their wedding. (His widow later married Ottavio Farnese of Parma.) Catherine de' Medici, who was later to be queen of France, also lived for some time in the palace.

To the north of the Senate building, the **Church of St. Louis of the French**, the French national church in Rome, rates a visit. It contains famous paintings by Caravaggio representing scenes from the life of Saint Matthew (in the fifth side chapel on the left); frescoes of episodes from the life of Saint Cecilia by Domenichino are in the second chapel on the right.

From the straight Corso del Rinascimento, opposite the main entrance to the Senate building with its military sentries, two narrow passages—the Corsia Agonale and the Via dei Canestrari (Basketmakers' Street)—lead to the celebrated **Piazza Navona**. The vast, elongated square, now closed to motor vehicles, provides breathing space for the *popolino* (little people) still living in the cramped, twisting alleys and lanes of the old quarter and serves as a playground for their children. At the same time, Romans consider it the peak of sophistication nowadays to inhabit one of the penthouses with which high-fee architects have topped the old buildings bordering the piazza.

Foreign tourists and visitors from the Italian provinces who have heard that Piazza Navona is where the action is crowd the outdoor tables of the restaurants and cafés around the square in the warm months.

From before Christmas to Epiphany (January 6) vendors offering toys, candy, comic books, sportswear, and souvenirs, as well as novelty stands and shooting galleries, invade the piazza, attracting jostling crowds. It is the way the city pays tribute to the *Befana*, a benign witch who, riding on a broomstick, brings gifts to good children and a bagful of coal to bad ones. (The word *Befana* is a corruption of *Epiphany*.) Piazza Navona also witnesses noisy carnival frolic in the days just before Ash Wednesday. If you want to watch the fun, dress down. Young Roman revelers delight in squirting passersby with shaving cream or other foam from aerosol cans. Fur coats are favorite targets.

The shape of the Piazza Navona, particularly its rounded northern side, betrays that in antiquity it was a racecourse, a stadium built during the reign of Emperor Domitian (A.D. 81–96). Over the centuries Domitian's "circus" was used for athletic games, festivals, and pageants and was occasionally flooded to create an artificial lake for mock naval battles (whence the name *Navona*).

The baroque church of Sant'Agnese, between two palazzi, dominates the square's west side. It is believed to rise on the spot where Saint Agnes was martyred in A.D. 304. Inside, paintings and marble sculptures represent the virgin saint's ordeal.

Three elaborate fountains adorn the piazza. The largest is Bernini's central *Fountain of the Rivers*, with statues by his disciples symbolizing the Danube, Ganges, Nile, and Rio de la Plata. The personification of the Nile hides his face behind a veil, a sculptural allusion to the supposed mystery of the river's headwaters (then still unexplored). The malicious Romans joked that Bernini had meant to suggest that the Nile was covering his eyes so as to be spared the sight of the concave facade of Sant'Agnese, designed by Bernini's archrival Francesco Borromini. An obelisk, originally put up in honor of Domitian, surmounts the four river statues.

Bernini's river fountain is flanked, lengthwise, at the northern side by a nineteenth-century fountain showing Neptune fighting a sea monster, surrounded by Nereids and seahorses; and to the south by another Bernini fountain, representing an Ethiopian (*The Moor*) and Tritons struggling with a dolphin.

Excavated ruins of Domitian's stadium can be seen under a vault of a modern building at 13 Piazza di Tor Sanguigna, at the end of the Via Zanardelli on the outer side of the curved north end of the Piazza Navona. From there turn west into the narrow **Via dei Coronari** (Rosary Sellers' Street). Once a road where pilgrims on their way to St. Peter's would buy devotional objects, the lively street is now lined with antique shops and artsy boutiques. Don't think you can pick up bargains there!

In the Via dei Coronari and in the side alleys, as indeed throughout the old section between the Pantheon and the Tiber, the *popolino* who have been living in humble dwellings amid stately palaces for generations are being squeezed out by entrepreneurs and big-money newcomers who have had the neighborhood's cold-water flats and artisans' shops restructured and modernly equipped. The narrow six-story house at 124 Via dei Coronari was owned by Raphael and mentioned in his will; there is no plaque.

A good part of medieval and Renaissance Rome, of which Via dei Coronari is typical, is wedged into a sharp loop of the Tiber and bisected by the broad, busy **Corso Vittorio Emanuele II**. At the south side of that thoroughfare, which was opened after 1870, is the massive, five-hundred-year-old Palace of the Apostolic Chancery (entrance at 1 Piazza della Cancelleria). Built at the end of the fifteenth century with travertine blocks taken from the Colosseum, it incorporates the ancient Church of San Lorenzo, and is graced by a courtyard with arcades in two stories attributed to Bramante. One of the outstanding Renaissance edifices in the city, the Apostolic Chancery is the seat of Roman Catholic Church tribunals.

Nearby, at 168 Corso Vittorio Emanuele II (telephone: 6540848), is the **Museo Barracco**, a gallery of ancient sculptures in a graceful Renaissance palace that Antonio da Sangallo the Younger erected for a French prelate in 1523. The architectural jewel is also known as the Little Farnesina.

Among the collection's nearly four hundred treasures are Sumerian, Egyptian, Etruscan, Cypriot, Greek, and Roman works. The sculptures were assembled by the wealthy collector Baron Giovanni Barracco (1829–1914) and donated by him to the Italian state. Open 9 A.M. to 1 P.M. Thursday to Sunday, also 5 to 7 P.M. Tuesday and Thursday.

Diagonally opposite, on a small square opening from the Corso Vittorio Emanuele II, stands the large Palazzo Braschi, a late-eighteenth-century building.

The Palazzo Braschi, 10 Piazza San Pantaleo, houses the **Museum of Rome** (telephone: 6875880). On view are paintings, drawings, prints, plans, and other items illustrating the life of the city from the Middle Ages to the present. The collection includes frescoes and other art salvaged from condemned buildings. The Palazzo Braschi is also used for special exhibitions, often of modern art, which are usually announced by streamers strung across the Corso Vittorio Emanuele II. Open 9 A.M. to 2 P.M. Tuesday to Saturday, also 5 to 8 P.M. Tuesday and Thursday, and 9 A.M. to 1 P.M. Sunday.

In the maze of small streets southwest of the Corso Vittorio Emanuele II, walk past the entrance to the Palace of the Apostolic Chancery, to the **Campo de' Fiori** (Flower Field). During the week the large rectangular square is the principal outdoor market in Rome's center. In the early afternoon sanitation workers clean up the piazza, and it becomes a meeting place for motley people, some of them drug addicts. Radicals occasionally hold rallies in front of the monument to Giordano Bruno, erected in 1887 at the approximate spot where the Dominican philosopher was burned at the stake as a heretic in 1600. Campo de' Fiori was also the scene of other executions at various times.

From the Campo de' Fiori it is a short walk to the much quieter Piazza Farnese, where two Renaissance fountains pour water into antique basins of Egyptian granite. The square is named after the magnificent building on its southwestern side, the **Palazzo Farnese**, since 1874 the seat of the French Embassy to the Italian state.

Some of the most famous architects of the Renaissance era worked on the edifice—Antonio Sangallo the Younger, Michelangelo, and Giacomo della Porta. Sightseers are admitted to parts of the building and the garden between 11 A.M. and noon on Sundays (67 Piazza Farnese; telephone: 686011).

Walk around the large palace to its river side with della Porta's loggia, which looks out on the noblest street of old Rome, the **Via Giulia**. It owes its name to Pope Julius II,

the patron of Michelangelo and Raphael, who had it laid
out as a straight major road. It is lined with dignified
buildings; at No. 85 is one of the houses of Raphael (no
plaque). Today Via Giulia is again a most desirable address
for a townhouse, apartment, boutique, or art gallery.

Return to Campo de' Fiori and turn eastward. In the
small Piazza Capo di Ferro stands the sixteenth-century
Palazzo Spada; with statues on its facade, it houses a charming art gallery and is the seat of the Council of State, a high
administrative body of the Italian Republic.

The **Galleria Spada**, 13 Piazza Capo di Ferro (telephone: 6861158), contains a collection started in the seventeenth century by members of the wealthy Spada family,
which occupies four rooms and includes paintings mostly
from the sixteenth and seventeenth centuries. There are
works by Titian, Rubens, Domenichino, and Guido Reni,
as well as a few ancient Roman sculptures. Open 9 A.M. to
2 P.M. Monday to Saturday, 9 A.M. to 1 P.M. Sunday.

The little Piazza del Biscione nearby is the probable site
where Julius Caesar was slain on March 15, 44 B.C. On
that day, the Senate held a meeting in a hall, the curia, of
Pompey's Theater. The plotters, led by Brutus and Cas-
sius, assailed the ruler of the empire with their daggers.
That the remains of the curia can be seen in the *ristorante*
Da Pancrazio is a characteristic Roman connection and a
historical selling point.

A few minutes' walk through Piazza del Paradiso and
Via del Paradiso leads to the large **Church of Sant'Andrea
della Valle**, facing the Corso Vittorio Emanuele II and the
Corso Rinascimento. The baroque church is crowned with
the inner city's most imposing dome next to that of St.
Peter's. (Only the cupola of the modern Church of Saints
Peter and Paul in the EUR district is larger than that of
Sant'Andrea della Valle.) Opera fans will be thrilled to see

the interior of the church in which Puccini set the first act of *Tosca*.

Proceed eastward on the Corso Vittorio Emanuele II to the **Largo di Torre Argentina**. This is a vast square and traffic hub with an important bus stop, a taxi stand, an old stage for legitimate drama—the Teatro Argentina—and ancient ruins.

In the rectangular excavation area in front of the Teatro Argentina, the remains of four temples of the third century B.C. are visible. The ruins, much older than those of the Roman Forum, were dug up during 1926 to 1930, when a cluster of decrepit houses was being torn down. Get an overview from the street level, or take the stairs down to see the foundation walls and damaged columns of rectangular and circular sanctuaries from ancient Rome's Republican era. Scholars are unable to say to which gods the temples were dedicated. Open 9 A.M. to 2 P.M. Tuesday to Saturday, 9 A.M. to 1 P.M. Sunday. Free admission.

The ruins of the Largo di Torre Argentina are inhabited by a tribe of stray cats. Animal-loving Romans, most of them elderly women known as *gattare* (cat fans), bring them tripe, fish heads, and other feline treats. Colonies of stray cats, occasionally cared for by some *gattara*, can also be seen in odd corners of other city neighborhoods, especially among ruins. Domesticated cats were first brought to ancient Rome by traders from Egypt, where they were considered sacred. The animals seem to have been cherished by the Roman populace since their initial appearance in the city, long before the Christian era. During the Middle Ages, however, cats were victims of persecution as embodiments of Satan, especially those that had the misfortune of being black. Stray cats, at any rate, were always conspicuous in Rome, and have done little to thwart the rat population from thriving as well.

From the Largo di Torre Argentina it is a five-minute walk back to the Pantheon.

AROUND THE SPANISH SQUARE

The irregularly shaped Spanish Square (Piazza di Spagna) was the center of Rome's foreigners' district from the seventeenth century to the early twentieth. It is at present still a magnet for tourists. (American Express has its offices at 38 Piazza di Spagna; telephone: 6764.) The famous square owes its name to the Spanish Embassy to the Holy See, located since the seventeenth century at No. 57, and is dramatically enhanced by the Spanish Stairs.

The south side of the piazza, to the left of the Spanish Embassy, is occupied by the narrow facade of the elongated palace of the Propaganda Fide, the Vatican's missionary department. (In Latin the Vatican body is called *Sacra Congregatio de Propaganda Fide*, or Sacred Commission in Charge of Propagation of the Faith; whence the term *propaganda* in modern languages.) Bernini and Borromini, the rival colleagues, designed parts of the palazzo, which incorporates a church.

The ancient column in front of the palace of the Propaganda Fide, topped by a nineteenth-century statue of the Madonna, was erected in 1854 to commemorate the proclamation of the dogma of the Immaculate Conception of the Virgin Mary by Pope Pius IX. On December 8, the Roman Catholic feast of the Immaculate Conception, the pope usually leaves the Vatican to pray below the statue of Our Lady. He always finds the column surrounded by flower offerings that devotees and city authorities have placed there since the morning of that day.

The pink building at 26 Piazza di Spagna is the **Keats-**

Shelley Memorial House. It contains a library and a small museum with memorabilia of the English poets John Keats and Percy Bysshe Shelley. Keats died in the house in 1821; Shelley was drowned off Viareggio on Italy's west coast in 1822. Both poets are buried in Rome's Cemetery of Non-Catholics. The Keats-Shelley Memorial House (telephone: 6784235) is open 9 A.M. to 12:30 P.M. and 2:30 to 5 P.M. (summer months: 3:30 to 6 P.M.), Monday to Friday.

At the center of the Spanish Square is the fountain known as *Barcaccia* (Rotten Boat), designed in 1627 by Pietro Bernini, the father of the more famous Giovanni Lorenzo. It represents a flooded boat leaking water from various cracks. In the warm season Romans and visitors sit around the oval basin. The short street to the left of the Spanish Stairs, Via del Bottino, gives access to the Spagna station of the subway's Line A. Graceful tall palms rise in the northeastern corner of the piazza.

What makes the square a permanent outdoor theater is the celebrated rococo stairway that leads from opposite the Barcaccia to the Church of Trinità dei Monti. Built 1721–25 with French money, the **Spanish Stairs** sweep up scenically in 137 steps that on the first landing divide into two branches and, after a second level, reach a stone balustrade commanding a fine view of the piazza below and the old city.

Even in cold weather some tourists and young people camp on the stairs and landings, while itinerant artists design portraits of paying customers, musicians perform, and souvenir peddlers spread out their wares. In the warm months the Spanish Stairs are crowded until late at night; sanitation workers in the morning have quite a job cleaning up. Around yuletide the city erects a life-size crèche, a representation of the Nativity scene, at the middle of the stairway. In spring the municipal park department covers a part of the steps with hundreds of blooming white and purple azaleas.

As a prime tourist sight and a frequent setting for happenings, the Spanish Stairs attract thieves, drug pushers, and other shady people. Although the police are vigilant and visible in the Spanish Square most of the time, caution is necessary.

The church at the top of the Spanish Stairs, **Trinità dei Monti** (Trinity on the Hills), has a stone facade in warm yellows and browns and two short bell towers. One of several French churches in Rome, it was started on orders from King Charles VIII of France in 1495 during his invasion of Italy, which took him and his army as far south as Naples. The obelisk in front of the church is an ancient Roman copy of the authentic Egyptian obelisk in the Piazza del Popolo.

Walk a few hundred yards to the left to another twin-towered edifice, the **Villa Medici**. Built originally for a cardinal in the middle of the sixteenth century, the mansion was subsequently purchased by the Medici family of Florence and eventually became French property. Napoleon made it the seat of the prestigious French Academy in Rome in 1803, which it still houses.

The French Academy often organizes art shows and other cultural events. A part of the building and its walled Renaissance gardens with their statuary can be visited on Sunday mornings during certain periods of the year. Inquiries: telephone 6761270.

Proceeding to the left of the Villa Medici, the stroller enters the **Pincio Gardens**, a vast park on a hill named after an ancient Roman clan, the Pincii, who dwelled on it. The gardens were designed by Giuseppe Valadier, a Roman architect and champion of the neoclassical style, and were completed by the middle of the nineteenth century.

After the unification of Italy many busts of notable Italians (some of whom are all but forgotten today) were put up along the Pincio paths. The City of Rome employs a team of stonemasons to replace the noses of the busts on the Pincio and on the Janiculum, which vandals knock off consistently. The terrace of the Pincio, projecting westward, is noted for its grand panorama, as is the charming little edifice, the Casina Valadier, on the highest point of the hill.

A bridge spanning the low-lying Viale del Muro Torto (Street of the Bent Wall) joins the Pincio with the **Villa Borghese**, a vast public park, 3.75 miles (6 kilometers) in circumference, created in the seventeenth century by Cardinal Scipione Borghese. The oval Piazza di Siena at the center, surrounded by pines and other evergreen trees, is the setting for the Rome International Horse Show, held every spring. (Old Romans say the fashionable riding contests are regularly marred by downpours, and that fine weather starts directly after the society event.)

Rome's Zoological Garden, **Giardino Zoologico** (telephone: 322103), is in the north of the Villa Borghese gardens. Local people have somewhat neglected it lately; the city does not seem to care much about it; and animal rights advocates are lobbying to have the zoo closed altogether.

The **Borghese Gallery**, the finest of Rome's collections of old master paintings and famous sculptures outside the Vatican, is on the northeastern edge of the Villa Borghese gardens. The collection is housed in the Casina Borghese, 5 Piazza Scipione Borghese (telephone: 8548577), built in 1615 by the Dutch architect Jan van Santen (Italianized into Giovanni Vansanzio). Much of the building has been closed to visitors since 1984, and work has since been underway to save the structure from termites, other decay, and collapse.

The ground floor contains ancient mosaics, reliefs, and statuary as well as sculptures of the baroque era and the eighteenth and nineteenth centuries. Outstanding among these are *David* and *The Rape of Proserpine* by Bernini; the famous reclining figure of Pauline Bonaparte, Napoleon's favorite sister and the wife of Prince Camillo Borghese, pictured as Venus, was sculpted by the classical revivalist Antonio Canova in 1807.

A limited number of visitors (twenty-five persons at a time) are admitted to the ground floor of the Borghese Gallery every morning, Tuesday to Sunday. The picture gallery on the upper floor, which features Titian's *Sacred and Profane Love*, Raphael's *Deposition,* and important works by Sodoma, Correggio, Caravaggio, and others, was still inaccessible in 1992. Some of the paintings were temporarily shown in the Museum of the Palazzo Venezia.

Another stroll from the Spanish Square may lead through the straight **Via del Babuino** (Street of the Baboon), starting at the northwest corner of the square, to the Piazza del Popolo. The "baboon" of the street's name is the sixteenth-century fountain statue of a satyr that the populace derided as a monkey. What remains of the pock-marked sculpture sits now in front of a low building at No. 150A. The Via del Babuino is lined with art and antique stores.

The short Vicolo Alibert on the street's right side connects it with the relatively quiet Via Margutta, parallel to Via del Babuino. As late as the 1960s many artists had their studios here; now Via Margutta is a coveted address of the affluent. Painters and sculptors nevertheless gravitate to the Via del Babuino and Via Margutta to patronize art supply shops and insiders' espresso bars.

Opposite the Vicolo Alibert, at the left side of the Via del Babuino, is the Via Vittoria with the Academy of Santa Cecilia (at No. 6; telephone: 3234775). Rome's foremost musical institution, it was founded in 1566 and is housed in a former convent. Proceeding along the Via del Babuino, you pass on the left the Greek-Catholic Church of St. Athanasius (No. 150B) and the Anglican Church of All Saints (No. 153C) to reach the vast oval **Piazza del Popolo**.

Before the aviation and railroad ages, this square was what uncounted pilgrims and travelers to Rome from the north saw first of the city proper on passing the **Porta del Popolo**. The monumental gate was built, probably from a design by Michelangelo, in 1561–65 on the spot where the Flaminian Gate of the ancient Aurelian Walls once rose.

In the northeast of the square stands the 700-year-old Church of Santa Maria del Popolo, which was rebuilt in the fifteenth century. Next to it are remains of the Augustinian convent where Luther stayed during his Rome visit, 1510–11, seven years before his break with the papacy.

In the church's baroque interior two dramatic paintings by Caravaggio, *The Conversion of Saint Paul* and *The Crucifixion of Saint Peter*, can be seen in the chapel on the left, closest to the choir. Paintings by Pinturicchio adorn chapels on the right side. Pinturicchio also frescoed the ceiling of the choir with a coronation of the Virgin and scenes of the evangelists and fathers of the Church.

In the 1950s the clergy of Santa Maria del Popolo, acknowledging the character of the nearby Via del Babuino–Via Margutta neighborhood, opened a modern-art gallery adjacent to their church.

Facing Santa Maria del Popolo from the opposite side

of the Porta del Popolo is a barracks of the Carabinieri that looks more like an art school than a military building. Mussolini was taken there after King Victor Emanuel III had him arrested on July 25, 1943. The deposed dictator was held in the barracks briefly before being flown as a prisoner first to the Island of Ponza, south of Anzio, and then to the Island of Maddalena off Sardinia.

An Egyptian obelisk, 79 feet (24 meters) in height, stands at the center of the Piazza del Popolo, carrying hieroglyphics in praise of the pharaohs Ramses II and his son Merneptah (thirteenth century B.C.). It is one of a dozen obelisks placed at crossroads and in public spaces all around the city, like huge exclamation marks commenting on the sweep of history.

The emperors of ancient Rome, fascinated by the giant stone needles their generals and surveyors had found in conquered Egypt, had many of them shipped across the Mediterranean and up the Tiber to adorn their temples, circuses, and mausoleums in Rome. When the Roman Empire crumbled and fell, the obelisks tumbled too. They were dug up again more than a thousand years later, together with plenty of ancient statuaries, and put up as landmarks in papal Rome.

The obelisk in the Piazza del Popolo was erected on orders from Pope Sixtus V, a Franciscan friar who as Felice Peretti had been a zealous official of the Inquisition, and who as pontiff during the brief five years of his reign (1585–90) tackled a Roman building program of near-pharaonic ambition. The restless pope, one of history's foremost obelisk fanciers, redeveloped entire neighborhoods and adorned them with rediscovered Egyptian trophies.

Brought to Rome from Heliopolis under Emperor Augustus, the obelisk rising now in the Piazza del Popolo was found in the ruins of the Circus Maximus. More than two-hundred years after Sixtus V placed it in the square, the obelisk was surrounded with fountains and stone lions during Valadier's transformation of the entire area.

The entrance to the heart of the city, the **Via del Corso**, is impressively flanked on the south side of the scenic piazza by two domed churches, both built in the second half of the seventeenth century, and both—like the church across the square—dedicated to the Virgin Mary. While a segment of the Piazza del Popolo is today a parking lot, motor traffic in much of the square is restricted, making way for recreation areas with benches.

The straight Via del Corso (to Romans, simply "the Corso"), nearly a mile (about 1.5 kilometers) long, cuts across the inner city as did an ancient Roman street underneath that led from the Capitol to the Via Flaminia.

Corso means racecourse: horses were run along the street periodically through the centuries, particularly at carnival time. Today only city buses, cabs, ambulances, and other authorized vehicles may pass the Corso, although at night it is invaded by other traffic.

Bordered by baroque palaces, the Corso in the eighteenth and nineteenth centuries was Rome's most elegant street. Since then banks have moved into formerly aristocratic buildings. Lately casual-wear emporiums (which Italians call *jeanserie*) and shoe stores have crowded out the established and more distinguished businesses and cafés.

At the right side of the Corso is the white baroque facade of the recently restored Church of San Carlo al Corso, dedicated to Saint Charles Borromeo (1538–84), the champion of the Counter-Reformation and bishop of Milan whose heart is contained in a reliquiary behind the altar.

Proceeding along the Corso, note on the right side, at

No. 418A, the massive **Palazzo Ruspoli** (formerly Palazzo Caetani), designed by the famous Florentine architect Bartolomeo Ammanati in 1556. It now houses a private gallery in which periodic art shows are held. Information: 6832179.

At the south side of the Palazzo Ruspoli opens the Piazza di San Lorenzo in Lucina, named after a porticoed basilica that is one of the city's oldest churches, founded in the fifth century and repeatedly rebuilt. A *Crucifixion* above the high altar is by Guido Reni.

If, from the Piazza del Popolo, you walk into the Via di Ripetta rather than the Via del Corso, you enter a neighborhood that has only recently become fashionable. Fancy bars and restaurants have sprung up along the straight Via di Ripetta as well as in the side streets. Leading to the Tiber near the Cavour Bridge, the Via di Ripetta passes the Piazza di Augusto Imperatore, which holds the remains of the circular **Mausoleum of Emperor Augustus**.

Facing the emperor's tomb on the river side is a modern cage of travertine and glass enclosing a famous ancient monument. Augustus's Ara Pacis (Peace Altar) was recomposed in 1936 from slabs and fragments dug up in the nearby Campo Marzio, in the vicinity of the Chamber of Deputies, during various periods. Through the windows of the enclosure reliefs showing the triumphant Augustus and allegorical scenes can be seen. On the wall of the modern base below the Ara Pacis a long Latin text is engraved; it is the record of Augustus's military campaigns and conquests as he himself had written it.

From this monument of Augustean majesty turn left to the Corso. The buildings on the east side of the Piazza di Augusto Imperatore are a good example of the so-called Mussolini Modern style, architecture characterized by straight lines, severe columns, and frequent pomposity.

The **Via dei Condotti** (Street of Water Pipes) from the Corso to the Spanish Square is Rome's smartest shopping area. Stores and boutiques with internationally renowned names line it: Bulgari, Cartier, Ferragamo, Gucci, Valentino, Van Cleef & Arpels, and others. Fashionable stores also take up the ground floor of the building at No. 68, though it is largely extraterritorial—the Italian state has no jurisdiction there.

The eighteenth-century edifice is in fact the headquarters of the Sovereign Military Order of Malta, a transnational entity that Italy and a few other nations recognize as an independent state. The Knights of Malta, whose nucleus is a small Roman Catholic religious order, own other choice property in Rome and operate medical and relief services in Italy and around the world.

COINS IN THE FOUNTAIN

The **Trevi Fountain**, made famous by pop songs and movies such as Fellini's *La Dolce Vita*, is hard to find. Located amid a maze of narrow streets, it can be reached through the curving Via della Stamperia or the straight and short Via Poli, both branching off the Via del Tritone, a thoroughfare perpendicular to the Corso that most of the time is filled with traffic, noise, and exhaust fumes.

The largest of Rome's many water marvels, the Trevi Fountain was built between 1732 and 1762 at a spot where three streets met, whence its name—*tre vie* (three roads)—soon became Trevi. A big statue of Neptune, flanked by sculptures in niches representing Health (right) and Fertility (left) look down on a wide stone basin. Allegorical reliefs tell the legend of the Aqua Virgo or Virgin Water, the aqueduct that feeds the fountain as it does the Pantheon area: a rustic girl led thirsty Roman legionnaires to a spring that Agrippa would later harness. Other baroque statuary is underneath.

From midmorning to late at night Romans and tourists sit on the iron rails around the basin and the steps leading down to it, or take pictures of someone tossing a coin into the water. The rite, which is supposed to make sure that the visitor will one day return to Rome (*"Arrivederci, Roma!"*) is old; to conform to tradition, one must fling the coin into the basin over one's shoulder. Police who keep patrolling the small, often crowded Trevi Square blow their whistles whenever some overenthusiastic tourist tries to wade into the water the way Anita Ekberg does in Fellini's picture. It is likewise prohibited to fish out the small change that often covers the basin's floor; City Hall claims the money as its property.

Turn your back on the Neptune and walk away from the Piazza di Trevi. On your left you will soon see the sloping Via della Dataria climbing up the Quirinal, one of Rome's seven historic hills. It is topped by the vast **Quirinal Palace**, now the official residence of the President of the Italian Republic. Military sentries guard the main entrance on the Piazza del Quirinale and the entrance on the side wing that is known as the "long sleeve" of the building. The presidential palace cannot ordinarily be visited, but a stroller may get a glimpse of its lush gardens through the doorway of the "long sleeve" (don't linger, though!).

The Quirinal Palace was built at the end of the sixteenth century to provide the popes with a summer residence that was cooler and healthier than the Vatican. It was the seat of Italy's royal court from 1870, when the troops of King Victor Emanuel II conquered Rome and thereby completed the unification of Italy, until the 1946 plebiscite that established the Italian Republic and sent the nation's last sovereign, King Umberto II, into exile.

The Piazza del Quirinale in front of the palace's main facade is like a huge terrace commanding a panoramic view of Rome with the dome of St. Peter's as a backdrop. The scene is particularly impressive at sunset. The Egyptian obelisk at the center of the square is 50 feet (15.2 meters) high, and once adorned the Mausoleum of Augustus. It is flanked by two larger-than-life statues of horse tamers, usually identified as the twin brothers Castor and Pollux, the Dioscuri, who in Greek myth were sons of Zeus and formidable hunters and warriors. The statues are copies, made in Roman imperial times, of long-lost Greek originals. A fountain with an ancient Roman granite basin completes the monumental composition in the piazza.

Opposite the Quirinal Palace is the eighteenth-century Palace of the Consulta, once an administrative office of the papal government and now seat of Italy's Constitutional High Court. To its right, at 43 Via Ventiquattro Maggio, is the sumptuous Palazzo Rospigliosi with a garden and a private art gallery.

A separate building of the complex, the Casino Rospigliosi, is famous for a ceiling fresco by Guido Reni, the *Aurora*. It can usually be viewed on the first day of each month. (Information: 474019.)

Walking up the Via Quirinale past the "long sleeve" of the palace, note on the right side of the street the elliptical Church of S. Andrea al Quirinale, an elegant building by Bernini (around 1670) in which Roman society weddings are often performed (there is a waiting list). Proceed to the next intersection, known as Quattro Fontane (Four Fountains), with water spurting at its four corners. If the traffic permits, pause a moment to glimpse three obelisks—in the Piazza del Quirinale to the southwest, in front of the Church of Trinità dei Monti to the northwest, and behind the Basilica of Santa Maria Maggiore to the southeast—from the same spot, like huge trigonometrical markers.

Turn left and walk down the Via delle Quattro Fontane toward the Piazza Barberini. The imposing edifice on the right side of the steep street is the **Palazzo Barberini**, built in the first half of the seventeenth century. The palace is the seat of a branch of the National Gallery of Ancient Art, with the entrance at 13 Via Quattro Fontane (telephone: 4814591), on the left side. The other branch of the gallery is in the Palazzo Corsini on the right bank of the Tiber. The treasures in the Palazzo Barberini include paintings by Fra Angelico, Filippo Lippi, Andrea del Sarto, Titian, El Greco, and many other masters. The portrait *La Fornarina,* the dark-eyed baker's daughter who is believed to have been Raphael's mistress and who has lent her features to many female figures in his compositions, always attracts much attention; it was painted either by Raphael himself or by his pupil Giulio Romano. Also noteworthy: a portrait of King Henry VIII of England by Hans Holbein the Younger (circa 1540). The Barberini Gallery is open 9 A.M. to 2 P.M. Monday to Saturday, 9 A.M. to 1 P.M. Sunday.

VIA VENETO GLITZ

In the **Piazza Barberini** traffic wheels around Bernini's *Fountain of the Triton,* a sea god surrounded by four dolphins. Another Bernini fountain in the square's north corner, with a queen bee and two other bees in stone, marks the beginning of the Via Vittorio Veneto, a street named after an Italian World War I victory (1918) and commonly called Via Veneto.

The broad Via Veneto, lined with trees in its lower part, curves upward in an inverted S to the Villa Borghese gardens. To many foreigners and provincial Italians the boulevard, glamorized by Fellini, seems the quintessence of Roman sophistication. Elegant hotels, high-priced cafés, travel bureaus, and stores catering mainly to tourists line it.

At 27 Via Vittorio Veneto is a church of the Capuchin friars with a Franciscan museum that will appeal to morbid tastes. This is an underground cemetery in which the bones of four thousand friars, forming decorations and designs, are displayed on the walls and under the arches. Skeletons and mummies of Franciscans are clothed in the garb of their order. Open 9 A.M. to noon and 3 to 6 P.M. daily (telephone: 4871185).

The **Palazzo Margherita**, housing the U.S. Embassy to the Italian Republic (119A Via Vittorio Veneto; telephone: 46741), stands at the upper bend of the street, close to the Excelsior Hotel. The stately turn-of-the-century building is named after Queen Margherita, who resided there after the assassination of her husband (and cousin) King Umberto I in 1900; she died in 1926. The vast embassy compound, guarded by Italian police around the clock, includes the American Consulate (121 Via Vittorio Veneto; telephone 46741).

Many Romans shun the Via Veneto after dark, when touts for nightclubs and prostitutes abound there. The newsstands along the boulevard carry newspapers and magazines from many countries, are well supplied with English-language paperbacks, and do business until late at night.

The Via Veneto ends at a particularly well-preserved stretch of the **Aurelian Walls**. Emperor Aurelian had this fortified ring, 12 miles (nearly 20 kilometers) in circumference, built around Rome between A.D. 271 and 275 to protect the city from possible raids by barbarian hordes. The battlemented brick walls, initially about 22 feet (6.7 meters) high, linked 381 rectangular towers, incorporating earlier structures at some points and reinforced by outworks at others.

Between A.D. 306 and 312 Emperor Maxentius strengthened the walls and added galleries on top, doubling the height of the bulwarks in many sections. Fortified gates opened to the main roads.

The portion of the Aurelian Walls between what is now the Via Veneto and the Villa Borghese gardens saw furious fighting when Belisarius, the general of Justinian, Emperor of the East, defended Rome from the onslaught of the Goths, A.D. 537–38. (For the Museum of the Walls, see page 136.)

MARCUS AURELIUS IN THE GOVERNMENT QUARTER

The Trevi Fountain may be chosen also as a starting point for another rewarding stroll: facing its Neptune statue, turn left and walk through narrow streets to the Galleria Colonna, an arcade from before World War I in the form of a Y. The galleria attracted homeless people at night until it was recently closed for restructuring. It faces the **Piazza Colonna**, a square owing its name to the Column of Marcus Aurelius at its center.

This monument, 97 feet (31.8 meters) high, has recently been restored. It carries a spiral of reliefs celebrating the Roman emperor's victories over Germanic and Sarmatian tribes on the Danube, A.D. 171–75. A likeness of Marcus Aurelius originally topped the column; it was replaced in 1589 by a statue of Saint Paul.

The large **Palazzo Chigi**, built between 1560 and 1630 for a rich banker's family from Siena, takes up the north side of the Piazza Colonna. It was long the seat of Italy's foreign ministry; now the national government has its headquarters in the palace. Adjacent, linked with the Palazzo Chigi by an overpass, is the extensive complex of the **Chamber of Deputies**. This lower branch of Parliament is housed in the seventeenth-century Palazzo Montecitorio, which has a spacious addition built early in the twentieth century. Piazza Colonna and the nearby Piazza Montecitorio are, not surprisingly, well policed around the clock. At mealtimes the restaurants in the government district, which also includes the Senate building, are populated by lawmakers, their confederates and hangers-on, and favor seekers.

The obelisk in the Piazza Montecitorio, 85 feet (28 meters) high, dates from the seventh century B.C. and was brought from Egypt to Rome under Augustus.

Walking south from the Piazza Colonna along the Corso, note on the right, at No. 304, the rococo facade of the rambling Palazzo Doria, which encloses a well-kept garden. The Palazzo Doria is the home of a remarkable private art collection, the **Galleria Doria Pamphilj** with entrance at 1A Piazza del Collegio Romano (telephone: 6794365) in the rear of the complex. Its best-known asset is the famous portrait of Pope Innocent X (the former Giovanni Battista Pamphilj) by Velazquez. There are also paintings by Filippo Lippi, Titian, and others. Open 10 A.M. to 1 P.M. Tuesday, Friday, Saturday, and Sunday.

One of the largest palaces of the Roman nobility, the

450-room **Palazzo Colonna** faces the rectangular Piazza Santi Apostoli, parallel to the southernmost two blocks of the Corso. Political and labor rallies are held often nowadays in the centrally located square. Unlike many other mansions that were built for aristocratic clans, the Palazzo Colonna is still inhabited by members of the historic family whose name it bears, although much of it is rented out. Four graceful arches spanning the narrow Via della Pilotta behind the palace connect it with its private gardens.

The magnificent private art gallery of the Palazzo Colonna, 230 feet (70 meters) long, contains works by Melozzo da Forlì, Veronese, Tintoretto, Guido Reni, and others. Entrance at 17 Via della Pilotta (telephone: 6794362). Open 9 A.M. to 1 P.M. Saturday.

5.

What to See:
From Capitol to
Colosseum

THE CAPITOL, WHICH since the beginnings of Rome was a citadel and a sanctuary, was once visible from the south end of the Corso. Now the view of the fateful hill is obstructed by the enormous National Monument. Known also as the **Monument to King Victor Emanuel II**, the unifier of Italy, the heap of glaringly white Brescian marble, which by its mineralogical nature will never mellow, was erected between 1885 and 1911. Foreign tourists call it the wedding cake; with its forty-nine tall columns it also looks like a giant typewriter of the old upright kind. It overwhelms the **Piazza Venezia**.

From the large square, a staircase leads up several flights to an Altar of the Fatherland at the foot of a statue of Rome, represented as a goddess with processions of worthies in bronze and marble approaching from either side to pay tribute. Above is a huge equestrian statue of Victor Emanuel II, surrounded by allegorical sculptures and martial symbols.

After the end of World War I Italy's Unknown Soldier was put to rest at the Altar of the Fatherland; servicemen of the nation's armed forces guard his tomb day and night. The Italian president periodically lays a wreath at the **Tomb of the Unknown Soldier**, and visiting foreign personages pay homage there.

On the west side of the piazza is the somber brown **Palazzo Venezia**, from which Mussolini used to rule Italy until King Victor Emanuel III had him arrested by a Carabinieri detail in 1943. From the narrow central balcony the dictator harangued the masses in the square below. The palace, which includes a church, was built in the fifteenth century, one of the first Renaissance edifices in Rome. With its stout, short tower and its battlements it suggests a fortress. It served as a residence for popes, as seat of the embassy of the Republic of Venice to the Holy See and, before World War I, as embassy of Austria-Hungary to the Italian Kingdom.

Part of the Palazzo Venezia is a museum containing paintings, sculptures, ceramics, and tapestries from the Middle Ages to the Renaissance. Special exhibitions are from time to time held in the frescoed state apartments that Mussolini used as his office, including the large Hall of the Globe, where he worked and received visitors. The entrance to the museum is at 1 Via Astalli (telephone: 6798865). It is open 9 A.M. to 2 P.M. Tuesday to Saturday, 9 A.M. to 1 P.M. Sunday.

Two blocks west of the Palazzo Venezia is the Church of the Gesù (Jesus), the main sanctuary of the Jesuit Order, a splendid baroque building completed in 1584. The founder of the Society of Jesus, Saint Ignatius of Loyola, who died in 1556, is buried in the chapel at the left transept. In the right transept is an altar with relics of Saint Francis Xavier, the Basque Jesuit missionary and friend of Saint Ignatius. (Saint Francis Xavier's tomb is in Goa, India.)

GHETTO MEMORIES

To visit the former Jewish ghetto, cross the busy Via delle Botteghe Oscure (Street of Dark Workshops) and penetrate into the maze of alleys and lanes between the **Piazza Mattei** and the Tiber. The quiet Piazza Mattei has in its middle what is often considered the loveliest of Rome's many fountains. It is a seventeenth-century composition of four youths with dolphins and tortoises, by Taddeo Landini.

The Jews of Rome, who were numerous already in the first century B.C., lived for hundreds of years principally in the Trastevere district and later on the opposite bank of the Tiber as well. Pope Paul IV, a stern Neapolitan, ordered the Jews of Rome in 1555 to reside in segregation in an enclave totaling about 7 acres (less than 3 hectares) on the left bank of the Tiber, near the Capitoline Hill. More than three thousand persons were packed into that ghetto, which initially was smaller than a New York city block; later it was slightly expanded. A wall surrounded the area. The gates to the ghetto were closed at 7 P.M. in winter, 8 P.M. in summer, and reopened at sunrise; during the night nobody was allowed in or out of the ghetto.

The ghetto walls were razed when the Romans revolted against Pope Pius IX's government in 1848, but the city's Jews only attained full religious liberty and civil rights after 1870, the year Rome became the capital of unified Italy. From 1907 to 1913 Rome had a mayor of Jewish descent, Ernesto Nathan (who was British-born).

Rome's main synagogue, at 15 Lungotevere Cenci (telephone: 6543168), faces the Tiber at what was the river side of the ghetto. Crowned by a square metal dome, the large building recalls Assyrian-Babylonian architecture; it was completed in 1904. Its **Jewish Museum** (telephone: 6864648), with Jewish art and much material on the ghetto and the long history of the Jews in Rome, is open 10 A.M. to 2 P.M. Sunday to Friday.

Despite complete emancipation after 1870, many Jewish families continued to live in the old ghetto. Many of the neighborhood's dilapidated houses were demolished toward the end of the nineteenth century, but a few old buildings have survived. To this day most stores and eating places in the area are Jewish owned; the distinctive idiom of the neighborhood perpetuates some expressions of the medieval dialect of Rome.

During the Nazi occupation of the Italian capital, 1943–44, SS commandos raided the ghetto section and rounded up about two thousand Jews—men, women, and children—for deportation to the death camps in eastern Europe. Very few ever came back.

The main street of the former ghetto is the Via Portico d'Ottavia, named after the conspicuous remains of a colonnade that Emperor Augustus erected in honor of his sister Octavia. The three hundred columns of the structure enclosed temples of Jupiter and Juno. A few columns remain. In the Middle Ages a church was built into the ruins; it came to stand just outside the walls when the ghetto was established in 1555.

From the synagogue, walk a few steps downstream along the Tiber. The river is divided by the Tiber Island, the site of an old hospital and a church. One of Rome's oldest existing bridges, the **Ponte Fabricio**, built in 62 B.C., links the island with the left riverbank. A few yards farther downstream an arch sticks out of the Tiber; it is what has remained of a much-repaired stone bridge from the first century B.C. that ultimately collapsed during a flood four hundred years ago. The Romans call the relic the Ponte Rotto (Broken Bridge).

One of the most curious structures in a city abounding in bizarre architecture is the **Theater of Marcellus** on the left riverbank, near the Tiber Island: a palace built into the ruins of an ancient amphitheater. The theater, erected toward the end of the first century B.C. and named after a nephew of Augustus (the son of his sister Octavia) who died young, accommodated up to twenty thousand spectators. It was to serve as a model for the much larger Colosseum. Beginning in the fourth century A.D. stone blocks and other material were taken from the already obsolete Theater of Marcellus to be used for construction work elsewhere. In the Middle Ages the ruin of the ancient theater was adapted as a fortress. Aristocratic clans eventually transformed the stronghold into a mansion, which became known, after one of them, as the Palazzo Orsini. It's not open to visitors.

In front of the Theater of Marcellus rise three Corinthian columns that belonged to a temple of Apollo, built in 433 B.C. and restored in 33 B.C. The "archeological area" between the Theater of Marcellus and the Portico of Octavia is used for outdoor concerts in summer; access is from the Via Portico d'Ottavia.

CAPITOLINE GLORY

Ascent to the Capitol is from the Piazza Aracoeli—the Latin words of the square's name mean Altar of Heaven—between the Theater of Marcellus and the Piazza Venezia. Three approaches climb the hill from different directions and angles. The steepest, to the left, is a stairway to the main entrance of the old Church of Santa Maria in Aracoeli, built in the Middle Ages at the site once occupied by a temple of Juno. Many Romans flock to the church at Christmas to worship in front of a crèche with the Infant Jesus represented in a widely venerated image as the Holy Child (the *bambinello* to the Roman populace). Frescoes by Pinturicchio adorn the first chapel on the right.

Vehicles driving to the Capitol take the Via delle Tre Pile that curves up the hill from the Piazza Aracoeli. Between the steps to the church and the driveway a central flight of low steps, designed by Michelangelo, leads to Capitol Square (Piazza del Campidoglio).

Michelangelo also planned the square, with the equestrian statue of Marcus Aurelius at its center. The ancient bronze sculpture of the emperor on his horse, which was once gilded, was transferred to the Capitol from the Lateran in 1538. By the early 1980s the statue was found to be so corroded that it had to be taken off its pedestal for restoration. After several years' treatment in a government laboratory the statue was returned to the Capitol in 1991— but not put back in the piazza. It can now be seen behind glass in the Capitoline Museum (see p. 115). A replica may eventually be placed on the pedestal.

Two ancient milestones, indicating Mile 7 and Mile 1, can be seen on the left and right ends of the front balustrade of the Piazza del Campidoglio; they were transferred there from ancient consular roads. The distances on all these principal highways of ancient Rome were computed with the Capitol as their theoretical starting point.

The smallest of the historic Seven Hills, the Capitol was from the origins of Rome a religious and political center. Since the Middle Ages the hill has been the seat of the city government.

The mayor of Rome has his office in the Palazzo del

Senatore (Palace of the Senator) facing the square, a medieval structure that was rebuilt during the Renaissance, when the bell tower and the fountain in front of the facade were added. The city parliament also meets here. Unless you have official business in the Palazzo del Senatore, you will not be admitted.

To the left and right of the municipal government building are two edifices, both designed by Michelangelo. They are the Capitoline Museum and the Palace of the Conservatori, each a repository of important historic and art collections.

The star of the **Capitoline Museum** (at left) is the sculpture *The Dying Gaul*, the Roman copy of a Hellenistic bronze of the second century B.C. showing a wounded Celtic warrior. (Gauls, the Roman name for Celtic tribes, invaded and sacked Rome in 390 B.C., and the ancient city never forgot the traumatic experience.) Other treasures of the museum: a second-century A.D. statue known as the *Capitoline Venus*, and a gallery of busts of sixty-four Roman emperors.

The pride of the **Palace of the Conservatori**, on the right of the piazza, is the haunting bronze sculpture of the *She-Wolf*, Rome's totem animal, created in the late sixth or early fifth century B.C. by an Etruscan artist who has been identified as Vulca from Veii. The southernmost of the Etruscan cities, Veii or Veio, as it is now known, 9 miles (14.5 kilometers) north of Rome, was then a rival of the struggling settlement on the Tiber. The sculptures of the twins Romulus and Remus, the mythical founders of Rome, suckled by the wolf, were added by Antonio Pollaiuolo in the late fifteenth century. In an adjoining room is the equally famous *Boy Extracting a Thorn from His Foot*, a bronze from the Roman imperial age that is a copy of a Hellenistic work.

The Palace of the Conservatori, with a modern annex, contains a further wealth of ancient statuary, reliefs, and mosaics, as well as a picture gallery with paintings by Titian, Tintoretto, Rubens, and others. Official city ceremonies, civil weddings, and receptions are often held in the front halls of the palace.

The Museums of the Capitol (Capitoline Museum and Palace of the Conservatori; telephone: 67102071) are open 9 A.M. to 2 P.M. Tuesday to Friday; 5 to 8 P.M. Tuesday, Thursday, and Saturday; and 9 A.M. to 1 P.M. Sunday.

The Via del Campidoglio, on the right side of the Palace of the Senator, leads to a terrace with a celebrated view of the Roman Forum with its triumphal arches, upright columns, ruined temples, and foundation walls. The Palatine Hill is on the right and the giant shell of the Colosseum in the background.

The southern height of the Capitoline Hill, with gardens and terraces, also commands fine views of the city below, the Palatine, and the Janiculum. One of the terraces, the Belvedere Tarpeo, overlooks a cliff that is believed to be the ominous Tarpeian Rock. According to tradition, criminals condemned to death were hurled from that precipice; the exact location, however, has remained controversial.

The sixteenth-century **Palazzo Caffarelli** on the southwestern tip of the hill occupies the site where a large temple of Jupiter stood for more than a millennium—from the end of the sixth century B.C. to the sixth century A.D. The colonnaded edifice was long revered as the most sacred shrine in the Roman world. Remains of the temple's foundation can still be seen at various points. The Palazzo Caffarelli, which was the German embassy to the Kingdom of Italy before World War I, now houses municipal collections and offices.

Stairs descending from the left side of the Palace of the Senator take the sightseer to a church, **San Pietro in Carcere** (Saint Peter in Jail). It was built in the sixteenth century over the ruined cells of what was ancient Rome's state prison, the Mamertine Jail. According to legend, the Apostle Saint Peter was held there; historically certain is that the captured Gallic rebel leader Vercingetorix was put to death in the jail after Caesar had brought him to Rome and paraded him in triumph in 46 B.C.

FORUM AND PALATINE

The entrance to the **Roman Forum** is off the straight Via dei Fori Imperiali, which runs from the Piazza Venezia to the Colosseum. Mussolini had the broad avenue laid out after having the old houses that stood in the way of the project bulldozed. Archeologists today would like the Via dei Fori Imperiali to be closed again to permit new excavations, but the broad street has long become an essential traffic artery, and there is little chance that what the dictator did will ever be undone.

The Forum that the visitor sees south of the Via dei Fori Imperiali (on its right-hand side, facing the Colosseum) is only part of the area that in ancient Rome was cramped, crowded, and noisy and was where most of the city's inhabitants and swarms of visitors from the provinces used to spend most of their days. In the Forum the Romans worshipped in magnificent temples that jostled one another, listened to popular orators, cheered generals who were marching under arches that had been expressly built for their triumph, watched trials, struck deals, and—most of the time—gossiped the hours away.

In the early nineteenth century the Forum was a cow

pasture, then known as the Campo Vaccino (Cow Field), with an occasional broken column or decaying arch sticking out from the grass and rubble of the millenia. Systematic excavations started after 1870.

Today the average sightseer may get confused by the jumble of foundation walls, a few upright columns, and other remnants of buildings in a district that, starting around 500 B.C., served for hundreds of years as the center of intense religious, political, judicial, and business life. Classical scholars have identified just about every tufa block and marble fragment that has come to light, although they don't always agree in their attributions.

The nonspecialist might look for traces of the Via Sacra (Sacred Road), a strip that bisected much of the Forum, running from northwest to southeast. Religious processions proceeded on it to one or another of the shrines, and victorious military leaders would march on it in triumph with their soldiers, prominent captives in chains, and glittering spoils.

North of the Via Sacra, close to the Capitol and unmistakable, is the Triumphal Arch of Septimius Severus, 75 feet (nearly 23 meters) in height. The marble monument was erected in A.D. 203 to commemorate a victory over the Parthians by the emperor and his son in what today is Iraq and western Iran.

At a point where the Via Sacra swerves to the left toward the present Via dei Fori Imperiali stood the circular Temple of Vesta, the virgin goddess of house and hearth. Nearby was the large rectangular House of the Vestal Virgins; usually six in number, they were the keepers of the sacred fire.

Also on the left, a little farther along, are three colossal arches that belonged to a huge edifice for legal and commercial business that was started by Emperor Maxentius and completed by his conqueror, Emperor Constantine, after A.D. 312. The enormous ruin, accessible from the Via dei Fori Imperiali, is called Basilica di Massenzio by the Romans. (In ancient Rome any oblong public building with a semicircular apse was called a basilica; the religious significance of the word originated when the early Christians used this architectural form for their cult.)

Mussolini had large stone maps showing the territorial growth of the Roman Empire put on the outside of the ruin, facing the Via dei Fori Imperiali. After the conquest of Ethiopia in 1936 he had another, larger map added, with the African country included in his new "Fascist Empire." The implication was that Il Duce was a modern Caesar. The stone map flaunting the Italian occupation of Ethiopia has long been chiseled away, but the maps recording the development of the Roman Empire from its beginnings to its vastest extension can still be seen on the Via dei Fori Imperiali.

On the southeastern rim of the Forum, close to the Colosseum, is the Triumphal Arch of Titus, which commemorates the defeat of the Jews and the destruction of Jerusalem in A.D. 70. Among the reliefs of the monument are, on the inside, representations of Jewish prisoners and of the seven-branched candelabrum, the menorah.

From the Arch of Titus or from a point near the center of the Forum, climb about 120 feet (36 meters) on winding paths to the top of the **Palatine**. The hill was already inhabited in prehistoric times, as recent excavations have proved. The Palatine, rather than the Capitol, was the heart of early Rome. Later, prominent people went to live there; Cicero had a house, and Augustus was born on the Palatine. The emperors took up their official residence on the hill, building and enlarging their palaces. The word *palace* is, in fact, derived from Palatine, an ancient name that is variously interpreted.

Leave it to the archeologists to determine the exact function of the imposing ruins on the hill. Rather, enjoy the quiet at a happy distance from Rome's traffic noise, the serenity of the gardens in the northeast corner of the Palatine (which were laid out in the sixteenth century), the evergreen trees, and the sweeping panorama. The Palatine is a magic spot.

The Roman Forum (telephone: 6790333) can be visited 9 A.M. to 3:30 P.M. Monday and Wednesday through Saturday, 9 A.M. to 1 P.M. Sunday. The Palatine is accessible also from a separate entrance on the Via San Gregorio, south of the Colosseum, which is open 9 A.M. to 7 P.M. Monday and Wednesday through Saturday, 9 A.M. to 1 P.M. Sunday.

AILING AMPHITHEATER

The gray mass of the **Colosseum**, one of Rome's largest and best known landmarks, has weathered barbarian raids, earthquakes, civil strife, and many other vicissitudes in more than 1,900 years. During the Middle Ages and the Renaissance era contractors used it as a handy quarry for obtaining and carting off marble, stone blocks, and metal that went into the palaces and churches they had to build.

At present the gaunt structure is ailing: exhaust fumes are gnawing at its porous travertine blocks, and the vibrations caused by traffic (including the subway's Line B trains that rumble through a nearby tunnel) impair the monument's stability. Through the ages the stones of the Colosseum were loosened, because the iron clamps that held them together were looted and weeds grew in the cracks. Botanists have classified an astonishing number of species of plant life in the ancient amphitheater. Every now and then a chunk of travertine crashes to the ground, and the authorities close off a section of the walls for urgent repairs.

Visitors may walk into the Colosseum (telephone: 7004261) free of charge from 9 A.M. to sunset, and hundreds do every day. Yet caution is imperative. Pickpockets and robbers, many of them foreigners, prey on tourists, and the few policemen and guardians on duty often seem powerless.

After dark the gates to the interior of the amphitheater are closed, but it is easy to penetrate, and homeless people, petty criminals, and vandals congregate inside every night. Prostitutes of either sex work the Colosseum and its surroundings at night, and the neighborhood appears to attract shady characters. Viewing the giant stone shell of the Colosseum by moonlight seems a romantic experience, but if you want to do it go in a taxi or horse-drawn cab.

Keeping all this in mind, the ancient amphitheater nevertheless merits more than a cursory visit. It inspires awe in view of the achievements of ancient technology and architecture, and at the same time prompts somber thoughts.

The giant structure can best be viewed from the northeast. A section there is fully preserved. Of the amphitheater's four oversize stories, the three lower ones are formed by arcades with half-columns of a different order on each floor: Doric, Ionian, and Corinthian. A fourth tier with windows and blind arcading used to carry masts for awnings that were moved by sailors of the imperial navy to shield spectators from the sun.

The elliptical building, with a circumference of close to a third of a mile (527 meters), could hold up to 50,000

people in seats on the lower three tiers and standing room
on the top gallery. Numbered arcades and staircases were
used to fill and empty the amphitheater like a modern
sports stadium. The upper floors can be reached by stairs
built much later that are not as steep as the ancient ones,
but access is often barred because of restoration work.

Excavations have brought to light what was under the
floor of the arena, which in antiquity was paved with tim-
ber: dressing rooms for actors and gladiators, dens for
animals, elevators operated by hoists, and a system of
drains.

According to ancient reports five thousand wild animals were killed, and many gladiators died, during a hundred days of spectacles that inaugurated the Colosseum
under Emperor Titus in A.D. 80. For hundreds of years
streams of human and animal blood were shed in the arena
to amuse the Roman populace. Whether the Colosseum
also saw the martyrdom of early Christians, as has long
been popularly believed, is a matter of controversy.

Echoing an ancient prophecy attributed to the Venerable Bede, Byron wrote:

> *While stands the Coliseum, Rome shall stand;*
> *When falls the Coliseum, Rome shall fall;*
> *And when Rome falls—the world.*

That the Colosseum, essentially a monument to human
cruelty, should be regarded as a symbol of Rome's grandeur and eternity seems weird.

Southwest of the Colosseum stands the best-preserved
triumphal monument in Rome, the Arch of Constantine.
It was erected, with three passages, after A.D. 312 to celebrate the new emperor's victory over his rival and prede-
cessor Maxentius. To save time and money, and maybe

also because there weren't a great many skilled craftsmen around, the architects stripped existing buildings of decorations and sculptures and slapped them onto the new structure.

The slope northeast of the Colosseum, known as the Oppian Hill (Colle Oppio), is a vast public park with extensive ruins of ancient baths and of the Golden House (Domus Aurea), an extravagant palace that Emperor Nero built himself after the burning of Rome in A.D. 64. The Colle Oppio, like the Colosseum, is at present being taken over by homeless people after dark.

6.

What to See: Rome's East and South

THE PIAZZA VENEZIA is a convenient starting point for a stroll up the Esquiline Hill, with old up-and-down neighborhoods that in City Hall parlance are bunched together as Rione Monti (mountains section). The vast district is bordered on its northwest side by the broad, straight **Via Nazionale**, which was created after 1870. Until recently it was far from chic to live in the Monti section; lately, however, gentrification has started transforming some of its narrow streets and little squares, giving birth to new boutiques and restaurants.

Walking from Piazza Venezia toward the left side of the Via dei Fori Imperiali, one sees the excavations of **Trajan's Forum**, with Trajan's Column rising in the middle. As the population of ancient Rome grew, and more and more power was being wielded and money handled in the city, the old Forum threatened to choke. The emperors ordered wholesale demolition of private houses in adjacent areas to gain more space for public and business affairs. The largest of these new "imperial forums" was a grand complex of colonnades, porticoes, libraries, market halls, and other structures that was completed by Emperor Trajan in A.D. 114.

Trajan's Column, celebrating the emperor's campaigns and victories in Dacia, today's Romania, is the best-preserved example of ancient relief art in Rome. During the 1980s, after the ravages of prolonged air pollution, the monument was painstakingly restored. Built of marble from the Island of Paros in the Aegean Sea, the column, 108 feet (33 meters) high, was originally crowned with a statue of Trajan; some four hundred years ago this was replaced with one of Saint Peter.

A strip of reliefs, 3 feet (about 1 meter) high, spirals up the column. On them some 2,500 figures enact episodes from the Dacian wars—river crossings, sieges, battles, and taking of prisoners, with the emperor conspicuous in most scenes. To the Romanian nation Trajan's Column provides invaluable testimony of its early history.

Trajan's Markets (Mercati Traianei), with a curving facade, is an ancient trading area accessible from Via Quattro Novembre, which links Piazza Venezia with Via Nazionale. Art and handicraft shows are occasionally held in the merchant's center of antiquity. Open 9 A.M. to 1 P.M. Wednesday, Friday, and Sunday, and 9 A.M. to 5 P.M. Tuesday, Thursday, and Saturday.

FINDING MICHELANGELO'S *MOSES*

Near the entrance to Trajan's Markets rises a tall, massive brick tower, leaning slightly toward the east. Local people may tell you in good faith that from its top Emperor Nero watched the burning of Rome while plucking his harp. Don't believe it. The Tower of the Militias, as the structure is called, was erected in the early thirteenth century. It is one of several surviving medieval towers around old Rome that once served as military strongholds in the fierce and incessant fights for control of the entire city or parts of it. A baron owning a fortified tower from which his henchmen might pour forth at any moment had to be reckoned with. He could impose his will on the people living in the neighborhood, as well as on a large chunk of Rome and the papacy.

From Trajan's Forum walk to the broad **Via Cavour**, which ascends the Esquiline from the left side of the Via dei Fori Imperiali at about halfway between Piazza Venezia and the Colosseum. A stairway at the right side of the Via Cavour, after the Via degli Annibaldi, leads to the hard-to-find church with Michelangelo's *Moses*.

The church is known as San Pietro in Vincoli (Saint Peter in Fetters). It was founded in the fifth century to enshrine what were supposed to be the chains in which the Prince of Apostles was held; it was rebuilt during the Renaissance and again later.

Michelangelo's *Moses*, one of his most brilliant sculptures, was to be part of an elaborate mausoleum for his demanding patron, Pope Julius II, in St. Peter's. After that pontiff's death in 1513 the project was scaled down, and a monument of him that didn't contain his body was placed in the church of San Pietro in Vincoli. Julius II was buried in St. Peter's, but his remains vanished during the Sack of Rome in 1527 (see page 185).

The traditional interpretation of Michelangelo's *Moses* is that it represents the prophet on his descent from Mount Sinai, sternly gazing at the idolatrous Jews. "Speak!" Michelangelo is said to have commanded, angrily striking his masterpiece with a hammer. A nick in the marble of the statue's bared right knee is pointed out as evidence of the old anecdote's truth. The statues at the side of Moses are in part by Michelangelo, in part by disciples.

An imitation of Michelangelo's *Moses* can be seen at the center of the showy Fountain of the Acqua Felice, at the corner of Via Venti Settembre and Via Vittorio Emanuele Orlando, to the left of the Grand Hotel. The sculptor Prospero da Brescia copied the masterpiece of San Pietro in Vincoli as his contribution to the fountain by Domenico Fontana in 1587, and is said to have died of heartbreak over widespread criticism of his attempt at emulating Michelangelo.

The Via Cavour leads up to the Piazza dell'Esquilino and the sumptuous Church of Santa Maria Maggiore (St. Mary Major). It is the largest of approximately a hundred churches in Rome that are dedicated to the Madonna, and one of the city's four so-called patriarchal basilicas (the other three are St. Peter's, St. John Lateran, and St. Paul's Outside the Walls). To gain the full spiritual benefits of a pilgrimage to the city of the popes, believers worship in all four basilicas; some pray also in the churches of San Lorenzo, Santa Croce in Gerusalemme, and San Sebastiano (over the catacombs in the Ancient Appian Way) to complete their round of the proverbial Seven Churches of Rome. The number seven recurs in Christian theology and recalls also the seven historic hills of Rome.

The first gold brought from the New World was, according to tradition, used to decorate the magnificent ceiling of the interior when Santa Maria Maggiore was completely rebuilt in the Renaissance. Medieval mosaics in the apse are preserved. An obelisk forty-eight feet (nearly 15 meters) high, found near the Mausoleum of Augustus, stands behind Santa Maria Maggiore.

LATERAN LORE

From the Basilica of Santa Maria Maggiore it is two-thirds of a mile (1 kilometer) along the straight Via Merulana to the Lateran complex. The Lateran can also be reached from the center by the subway's Line A (San Giovanni stop).

The obelisk in the Piazza di San Giovanni in Laterano, 105 feet (32 meters) high, is the tallest and oldest of the Egyptian pillars in Rome. It stood originally in Thebes, erected there by the Pharaoh Thutmose in the fifteenth century B.C., and was in three pieces when it was rediscovered in the Circus Maximus in 1587; the jagged lines where the fragments were again fitted together can be clearly seen.

St. John Lateran (San Giovanni in Laterano) is the Pope's cathedral in his role as bishop of Rome; every pontiff formally takes possession of his local see soon after his election. Until the thirteenth century the Lateran Palace was the official papal residence.

Legally, the Lateran is now considered an appendage to the State of Vatican City, and therefore the Italian authorities have no jurisdiction over it. During World War II prominent Italian anti-Fascists found a refuge in the Lateran.

The **Basilica of St. John Lateran** was founded under Emperor Constantine in the fourth century in an area where the ancient Roman family of the Laterani owned property. The church was repeatedly rebuilt during the following centuries. The present baroque facade is surmounted by fifteen giant statues representing Jesus, Saint John the Baptist, Apostles, and Fathers of the Church. The interior of the basilica is coldly ornate. Beautiful cloisters are accessible from the left of the papal altar (to see them, tip a sacristan).

The **Lateran Palace** at the north side of the basilica, replacing an earlier edifice, was designed by Domenico Fontana, the busy architect of Pope Sixtus V. It houses the offices of the Pope's cardinal-vicar for the city of Rome.

Frescoed staterooms, called the papal apartment, can be visited between 8:45 A.M. and 1:45 P.M. on the first Sunday of every month. To be seen, among other parts of the palace, is the hall in which Mussolini and Pope Pius XI's Cardinal Secretary of State, Pietro Gasparri, signed the Lateran Treaties whereby the State of Vatican City was established on February 11, 1929.

There is also a collection of Vatican curiosities, like the portable throne or gestatorial chair that the popes used until recently, and the uniforms of long-disbanded pontifical armed formations. The collection is officially called the Historical Museum of the Vatican; the entrance is on the right side of the basilica's facade.

Walk around the palace and past the obelisk to see the Lateran's octagonal baptistery near the church's choir. It is the fifth-century prototype of chapels everywhere in which baptisms are performed.

A porticoed edifice diagonally opposite the entrance to the Lateran Palace encloses the Scala Santa (Sacred Stairway). Devotees go up its twenty-eight wood-covered steps on their knees. The marble steps are supposed to have been brought to Rome from Pilate's palace in Jerusalem; Jesus, wearing a crown of thorns, is believed to have been escorted over the stairway by soldiers during his Passion.

Walk six blocks northeast of the Lateran, along a section of the Aurelian Walls, to the Church of Santa Croce in Gerusalemme (Holy Cross in Jerusalem). According to tradition, it was founded by Saint Helena, the mother of Emperor Constantine. Its name is due to relics of the True Cross that Saint Helena is supposed to have recovered in

Jerusalem, and which are treasured, together with other venerated objects, in the Chapel of the Relics on the church's left side. The present dramatic facade of Santa Croce in Gerusalemme dates from the first half of the eighteenth century.

Nearby is the National Museum of Musical Instruments, 9A Piazza di Santa Croce in Gerusalemme (telephone: 7014796). It contains three thousand exhibits, including archeological finds related to music as well as historic and exotic musical instruments. Open 10 A.M. to 1 P.M. Wednesday to Monday.

THE AVENTINE AND ITS SURROUNDINGS

From the Colosseum the broad Via di San Gregorio leads, on the right, to a valley between the Palatine and Aventine hills where the largest racecourse of ancient Rome was located. There, as many as 200,000 people used to cheer or boo racing-chariot drivers, and opposing factions of fans often came to blows. Little has remained of the **Circus Maximus** (Circo Massimo stop of the subway's Line B), but the layout of the elongated racecourse can be guessed. It totaled about three-fifths of a mile (1 kilometer). The last races in the Circus Maximus were held in A.D. 549 when the Ostrogoths under King Totila had occupied Rome.

Adjacent to what was the north curve of the Circus Maximus stands the 1,300-year-old Basilica of Santa Maria in Cosmedin, facing the Tiber; its bell tower is medieval.

On the left side of the church's vestibule is a large, round stone mask of a river god that in antiquity probably capped a steam pipe in a public bath, releasing vapor through the openings representing eyes, nose, and mouth. According to a time-honored local belief, the mask snaps its mouth shut on perjurers who put their right hand into it; hence the name Bocca della Verità (Mouth of Truth). Replicas of the mask that may bite off a liar's hand are a frequent prop in Italian film and television farce.

The Aventine Hill on the southwest side of the Circus Maximus, today a comparatively quiet, and therefore coveted, neighborhood, was the plebeian quarter of ancient Rome.

Don't miss the famous peep through the keyhole of the entrance to the Priory of the Knights of Malta in the attractive little Piazza dei Cavalieri di Malta in the northwest of the hill's plateau: you will see the distant dome of St. Peter's as if it were floating in the air, framed by the greenery of the gardens in the foreground behind the door. The priory is the seat of the Italian branch of the Sovereign Military Order of Malta.

From the Circus Maximus or the Aventine proceed south, along the Viale Aventino and the Via della Piramide, to the Piazza di Porta San Paolo (Piramide stop of the subway's Line B). The stone pyramid in that square, 121 feet (37 meters) high, marks the tomb of Caius Cestius, a Roman official who died in 12 B.C. The ancient Romans occasionally modeled funeral memorials after the Egyptian pyramids. The neighborhood is known as the Ostiense section. The City Air Terminal and the old terminal of the Rome-Ostia railroad are nearby.

The walled Protestant Cemetery, officially called Cemetery of the Non-Catholics (Cimitero degli Acattolici), is behind the pyramid, with its entrance at 6 Via Caio Cestio (telephone: 5741900). If it is closed, try ringing the bell.

Some four thousand British, American, German, Scandinavian, and Russian visitors or residents of the city are buried in the slightly rising grounds in the shade of cypresses. The tomb of Keats, near the pyramid, bears the inscription: "Here lies one whose name was writ in water." Shelley's ashes were interred near the upper wall. The cemetery is a melancholically romantic corner of the Eternal City.

A few steps to the east of what Romans usually call the "foreigners' cemetery," across the Via Nicola Zabaglia and close to the Tiber, is a conical hill, Monte Testaccio, that rises 115 feet (35 meters) above the flat ground. It is named after the Latin word for potsherd, and consists entirely of broken pottery—the remains of large amphorae or jars (the barrels of antiquity) in which wine and olive oil were imported to Rome from the empire's provinces around the Mediterranean. The cargo was unloaded in the nearby river port and stored in vast warehouses, traces of which were dug up in the 1980s.

The **Testaccio** section, a former workers' neighborhood with a still-functioning outdoor market in the Piazza Testaccio, has many taverns and has lately become trendy. New cafés, small theaters, and night spots are springing up (or closing down) in the area all the time. Local boosters talk of "Testaccio Village," an allusion to New York City's Greenwich Village.

Turn back to the Pyramid of Caius Cestius. Behind it is a stretch of the Aurelian Walls, with the Porta San Paolo. This is a gate flanked by two round, battlemented towers that controlled access to Rome from the seaside at Ostia. The broad, straight Via Ostiense runs past the city's wholesale food market (Mercati Generali), to the ancient Basilica of St. Paul Outside the Walls, 1.25 miles (2 kilometers) to the southwest (San Paolo stop of the subway's Line B).

Together with the adjoining monastery, the large church is a dependency of the State of Vatican City, like the Lateran. The basilica was founded in the fourth century and repeatedly rebuilt, the last time after a devastating fire in 1823. It stands at the site where, according to tradition, Saint Paul was buried after his martyrdom.

Inside the church patches of medieval mosaics, a thirteenth-century tabernacle above the high altar, and other parts of the old edifice that survived the 1823 blaze are interspersed with the nineteenth-century reconstruction and some more recent additions. Mosaic medallions with the traditional representations of the Apostle Peter and all his successors, including the modern popes, form a band on the walls.

TO EXPLORE ANOTHER evocative area of the city's southeast, turn from the Circus Maximus into the broad Via delle Terme di Caracalla, which is shaded by old trees.

The obelisk at the street's start rose in the Ethiopian city of Aksum, a center of Coptic Christianity since the fourth century A.D., and was brought to Rome at Mussolini's orders after Italian forces had conquered Ethiopia in 1936. The monument bears no hieroglyphics but has windowlike geometrical ornaments.

Opposite the obelisk is the sprawling modern headquarters of the United Nations Food and Agriculture Organization (FAO). Farther on the right side of the street are the grandiose ruins of the **Baths of Caracalla**.

The magnificent thermae, or public bathing establishment, built in the early third century A.D. by emperors Septimius Severus and Caracalla, could accommodate thousands of people; no fewer than 1,600 were able to use the pools, tubs, and steam chambers at the same time, while many more were lounging or gossiping in halls and porticoes.

On summer nights outdoor opera is produced amid the giant brick walls, which originally were clad in marble. Archeologists have lately urged City Hall to designate another site for the open-air performances, to prevent further decay of the Baths of Caracalla.

WORLD'S FAIR THAT NEVER WAS

The **Piazza Numa Pompilio**, outside the thermae, is a traffic circus: straight ahead is the narrow Via di Porta San Sebastiano, leading to the Ancient Appian Way; the Via delle Terme di Caracalla turns south, passes the Aurelian Walls, and becomes the Via Cristoforo Colombo, a multilane road to the seaside. About 4 miles (more than 6 kilometers) south is the **EUR** section, a modern satellite district (EUR Marconi and EUR Fermi stops on subway Line B).

EUR stands for Esposizione Universale di Roma (Rome World's Fair)—an event that didn't take place. Mussolini had planned to celebrate the twentieth anniversary of his Blackshirts' "March on Rome" in 1922 with an international exhibition, and in the 1930s ordered a favorite architect, Marcello Piacentini, to design the fairgrounds for the projected 1942 event. The site on the city's southern outskirts, close to the Tiber, was chosen to help channel Rome's future growth toward the sea. Piacentini was something like the Fascist regime's Bernini, a champion of the Mussolini Modern style.

World War II intervened, and the world's fair that was supposed to glorify Mussolini's dictatorship was canceled. The half-finished buildings that the new Italian Republic inherited from Fascism were completed by Pier Luigi Nervi and other architects during the 1950s. Among the

EUR's outstanding structures are a white Palace of the Civilization of Labor with six tiers of arcades, nicknamed "the square Colosseum" by the Romans, and the equally glaringly white Church of Sts. Peter and Paul on a ridge overlooking the Tiber, with a dome that in Rome is surpassed in size only by that of St. Peter's.

Government departments, museums, and various public and semipublic agencies moved into Piacentini's buildings, and large corporations built themselves skyscraper headquarters in the area. An amusement park sprang up on the northern edge of EUR. A large circular Sports Palace was built at the district's south side near an artificial lake and is being used not only for athletic contests but also for rock concerts. Condominiums and other residential buildings went up, attracting businesses to serve the new inhabitants of EUR.

To many Romans the EUR district has nevertheless remained the "Italian Brasilia"—a futuristic government enclave in the wilderness. On working days the satellite district looks lively enough, but after dark and on weekends, particularly in winter, some of its straight alleys look eerily abandoned, while its major streets teem with prostitutes and the autos of their clients.

Following is a list of the public collections in the EUR district:

Museum of Roman Civilization, 10 Piazza G. Agnelli (telephone: 5926135), with scale models of ancient buildings and monuments and plaster casts of famous sculptures. Open 9 A.M. to 1:30 P.M. Tuesday through Saturday, also 4 to 7 P.M. Wednesday and Saturday, 9 A.M to 1 P.M. Sunday.

Prehistoric and Ethnographic Museum Luigi Pigorini, 1 Viale Lincoln (telephone: 5910702), named after a nineteenth-century scholar and collector, contains a wealth of objects dug up all over Italy and in other countries as well as artifacts and other materials from all continents. Open 9 A.M. to 2 P.M. Monday to Saturday, 9 A.M. to 1 P.M. Sunday.

Museum of the High Middle Ages, 1 Viale Lincoln (telephone: 5915656). Exhibits of works from the eighth to the tenth centuries A.D. and Byzantine art. Open 9 A.M. to 2 P.M. Monday to Saturday, 9 A.M. to 1 P.M. Sunday.

National Museum of Popular Arts and Traditions, 10 Piazza Marconi (telephone: 5926148). On display are Italian regional costumes, rural and urban furniture, tools, Nativity scenes and other religious objects, photos illustrating folklore, and the like. Open 9 A.M. to 2 P.M. Tuesday to Saturday, 9 A.M. to 1 P.M. Sunday.

TO THE APPIAN WAY

Sightseers who want to visit the Ancient Appian Way instead of the modern EUR district proceed from the Piazza Numa Pompilio straight to the Porta di San Sebastiano (it can be reached also by the No. 118 bus from the Colosseum). Originally known as the Appian Gate, this passage in the Aurelian Walls controlled the principal road to southern Italy. The two round towers flanking it were erected in the Middle Ages.

The **Museum of the Walls** in the recently restored Porta di San Sebastiano (telephone: 7575284) is remarkable above all because it provides a chance to see the walkways inside the fortifications. The exhibits consist of archeological finds and other material connected with the Aurelian Walls. Open 9 A.M. to 1:30 P.M. Tuesday to Saturday, also 4 to 7 P.M. Tuesday and Thursday, 9 A.M. to 1 P.M. Sunday.

The Via Appia, the "Queen of Roads" of the ancients, starts with a slight downgrade from the Porta di San Sebastiano; at the right the first milestone soon comes into view. The street gets interesting after about half a mile (800 meters). On the left is the small church called Domine, Quo Vadis? (Lord, Where Art Thou Going?), a name derived from the legend that Saint Peter, fleeing from persecution, met Jesus at this spot and was shamed into returning to Rome to suffer martyrdom under Nero.

The Via Ardeatina to the ancient town of Ardea, branching off the Appian Way on the right side, leads in about half a mile (less than a kilometer) to a memorial recalling a World War II atrocity. An SS detail shot 335 men, including many Jews, in a tufa cave (the Fosse Ardeatine) here on March 24, 1944, in reprisal for the killing of 32 German soldiers by Italian anti-Nazi urban guerrillas in Rome's central Via Rasella, off the Piazza Barberini, the day before. To go by public transport to the Ardeatine Caves, take the No. 218 bus from the Lateran.

Shortly after the turnoff to the Ardeatine Caves is the entrance to the **Catacombs of Saint Calixtus**, 110 Via Appia Antica. The principal of the early-Christian underground cemeteries on Rome's outskirts, it is named after one of the Apostle St. Peter's successors who is believed to have been martyred in A.D. 222. The subterranean vaults and a maze of mile-long galleries on various levels served the Christians of the first centuries A.D. as burial places and supposedly as refuges in times of persecution. This underground world has not yet been completely explored. All Christian catacombs in Rome, as anywhere

else in Italy, are under the supervision of the Vatican's
Commission for Sacred Archeology, 1 Via Napoleone III
(telephone: 4465610).

Guided tours of a part of the Catacombs of Saint Calixtus are conducted from 8:30 A.M. to noon and from 2:30
to about 5 P.M. daily, except on Wednesday and Roman
Catholic feast days. The crypts and corridors, 21 to 60 feet
(7 to 20 meters) below the surface, are often very crowded
with groups of pilgrims and tourists; there are no special
facilities for disabled persons.

The No. 118 bus turns after the Catacombs of Saint
Calixtus into the Via Appia Pignatelli, to the left. To see
the most noteworthy stretch of the Ancient Appian Way,
proceed on foot or go by car.

At the left side of the road, at 119A Via Appia Antica,
is the entrance to the Jewish catacombs, one of the burial
places of ancient Rome's Jews. Simple tombs decorated with representations of the seven-branched candelabrum, other Jewish symbols, and inscriptions in Hebrew,
Aramaic, Greek, and Latin can be seen. The Jewish Community of Rome, 15 Lungotevere Cenci (telephone:
6875051), organizes guided tours at infrequent intervals.

A little farther, on the right side of the street, is the
Church of St. Sebastian, built over another subterranean
network of early-Christian burial sites on four levels.
Guided tours take place daily, except Thursday, at the same
times as at the Catacombs of Saint Calixtus.

Nearby, on the left side of the road, are the remains of
a circus, a racecourse that Emperor Maxentius founded in
the early fourth century A.D. It measures 530 by 86 yards
(484 by 79 meters) and could accommodate up to fifteen
thousand spectators in ten tiers of seats.

At 1.75 miles (2.8 kilometers) from the Porta di San
Sebastiano the Via Appia Antica reaches, on the left side,

the monumental Tomb of Cecilia Metella, long a favorite with painters, designers, and photographers. Built for the wife of a wealthy official who served as a general under Caesar in Gaul, the well-preserved memorial is a circular tower 65 feet (19.8 meters) in diameter. Like many other large structures from antiquity, the massive tomb served as a fortress during the feuds and wars of the Middle Ages.

A short distance from the majestic memorial the most characteristic section of the Ancient Appian Way begins. Patches of the original pavement with well-worn flagstones become visible and tax the shock absorbers of cars.

The road narrows and is flanked by pine trees, cypresses, and shrubbery. To the left and right are decayed ancient tombs and memorial statues, mutilated by the vandalism they had to endure through the ages. The ancient Romans used to bury prominent people along their highways; the Appian Way above all was lined with illustrious tombs. The arches of ruined ancient aqueducts that for centuries conveyed water from the southern hills to Rome can be seen to the left.

At a few points the visitor may still imagine the romantic mood of the Campagna Romana—the plains around the Eternal City—that its sun-baked loneliness, classical ruins, clumps of umbrella pines, and occasional flocks of sheep evoked in the travelers and artists of the early nineteenth century.

Yet the old, melancholy charm of the venerable road has long faded as new constructions closed in on it. The government decreed in 1965 that the Ancient Appian Way and a broad belt on either side were to become an archeological park. Landowners and contractors, however, found legal loopholes or simply ignored the zoning laws, building more than two hundred villas and other structures in the supposedly restricted area. Gina Lollobrigida and other

movie personalities, tycoons, and rich professional people
went to live in fancy homes, often masked by walls and
shrubs along the choicest stretches of the ancient road.

At about 5 miles (8 kilometers) from the Porta di San
Sebastiano the Ancient Appian Way becomes scrungy,
with garbage piling up left and right, and ends up as a mere
track that joins the Via Appia Nuova at a suburb called
Frattocchie.

This "new" Appian Road starts at the Lateran, and
after merging with the old one continues as the much-
traveled National Highway No. 7 to the Alban Hills and
southern Italy.

7.

What to See: Right Bank and Random Sights

TRASTEVERE AND JANICULUM

IN JULY EVERY year the Trastevere district, facing the core of the city from the west bank of the river, celebrates its *Festa de Noantri*. The dialect phrase means celebration of "us others." The populace of Trastevere (pronounced trahs-TAYH-ve-rayh) has maintained through the centuries that it is distinct from the rest of the Romans—proud to be plebeian, speaking an idiom of its own, and content with its earthy way of life. Fireworks crackle in the summer night, and streams of Frascati wine are poured in Trastevere's many trattorie during the two-week reassertion of the neighborhood's diversity.

Yet there are few genuine *trasteverini* left. Families whose great-grandparents already lived in the district have lately moved elsewhere, allowing architects and interior designers to transform their modest flats in elevatorless, decrepit buildings into elegant high-rent studios and apartments. Trastevere is today the city's favorite section for well-heeled foreigners and Italians from other parts of the

nation who want to live in comfort near the center of
Rome, but in a relaxed, pseudobohemian ambiance.

Trastevere means "beyond the Tiber"; the once folksy
neighborhood is a ten-minute walk across the Garibaldi
Bridge from the Largo di Torre Argentina, fifteen minutes
from the Pantheon. You may take buses Nos. 44, 56,
or 60 from Largo di Torre Argentina to reach the Piazza
Gioacchino Belli, the vestibule of Trastevere at the south
end of the Garibaldi Bridge.

Stroll in Trastevere's narrow and occasionally winding
streets and in its little piazzas or watch the neighborhood's
vibrant outdoor life from the table of some osteria. The
heart of the once proletarian and now fashionable district
is the Piazza di Santa Maria in Trastevere, from which
cars are banned. Junkies and purse-snatchers unfortunately
aren't. The inside of the old church, Santa Maria in Trastevere, in the square is noteworthy for the twelfth-century
mosaics in the apse and on the triumphal arch framing it.

From Trastevere the Via Giuseppe Garibaldi and the
Via Dondolo curve up to the top of the **Janiculum** (Gianicolo), a ridge 3.5 miles (5.7 kilometers) long and, at its
loftiest point, 269 feet (82 meters) high. Much of it is
covered with gardens. Take the No. 41 bus from the end
of Corso Vittorio Emanuele II near the Tiber, or the Nos.
44 or 75 from Piazza Sonnino in Trastevere.

Walking or driving up the Via Giuseppe Garibaldi, one
passes the Church of San Pietro in Montorio adjoining
a convent in whose courtyard stands a graceful circular
building with sixteen columns, the Tempietto (Little Temple) by Bramante. He built the Tempietto at the spot where
according to legend, Saint Peter the Apostle was crucified.

The street continues to rise to a baroque fountain, the
Acqua Paola. It is the showpiece of an aqueduct that the
ancient Romans built and which Pope Paul V had repaired

in 1612. The old aqueduct still brings water from Lake Bracciano, more than 20 miles (about 35 kilometers) to the northwest, to neighborhoods on the right bank of the Tiber.

Farther up, near the summit of the Janiculum, is the Porta San Pancrazio, a nineteenth-century gate at the site where the Aurelian Gate of the ancients stood. The Via Aurelia, National Highway No. 1, starts here.

To the right is the entrance to the Janiculum park and promenade, adorned with busts of prominent nineteenth-century Italians, quite a few of them vandalized. Follow the promenade to a large square with an equestrian statue of Garibaldi, the national hero who on the Janiculum defended the Roman Republic from the attacks of French troops, 1848–49. After an initial defeat the French eventually won, permitting Pope Pius IX to return from the southern seaport of Gaeta to which he had fled when the revolution broke out in Rome in 1848. Garibaldi and his ragtag forces managed to escape to the north.

Step to the parapet in front of the monument to enjoy the vast panorama of the city. A few feet below the terrace is an old field gun that artillery soldiers fire at noon every day. Meant as an exact-time signal, the midday boom is drowned out in most parts of the city by the din of traffic.

From the Garibaldi Monument the promenade continues northward, affording other fine vistas—the dome of St. Peter's, the Castel Sant'Angelo (see page 184), and the Tiber. On the northwest of the Janiculum is the modern complex of the Pontifical North American College, which trains seminarians from the United States for the priesthood. The steep Salita di Sant'Onofrio and the curving Via del Gianicolo descend to the Tiber embankment close to Vatican City.

On the slope of the Janiculum, below the Garibaldi

Monument and close to the Tiber, is Rome's Botanical Garden (Orto Botanico), 24 Largo Cristina di Svezia (telephone: 6832300), with fine palms and six thousand other plants, many of them rare. Open 9 A.M. to 1 P.M. Monday to Friday, 9 to 11:30 A.M. Saturday. Closed all of August.

Nearby is the **Palazzo Corsini**, a baroque edifice at 10 Via della Lungara. Built for Roman nobility, it was the residence of Sweden's former Queen Christina from 1668 until her death in 1689. She had abdicated in 1654, converted to Roman Catholicism, and gone to live in Rome.

More than a century later, relatives of Napoleon, including the emperor's mother Letizia Bonaparte, lived in the palace.

The Palazzo Corsini is at present being shared by two institutions: the Accademia dei Lincei, a nearly four-hundred-year-old learned society; and a branch of the National Gallery of Ancient Art (telephone: 6542323). On view in the gallery are works by artists of the sixteenth and seventeenth centuries, including Caravaggio and his school. Open 9 A.M. to 2 P.M. Tuesday to Saturday, 9 A.M. to 1 P.M. Sunday. (The other branch of the National Gallery of Ancient Art is in the Palazzo Barberini.)

Opposite the Palazzo Corsini, at 230 Via della Lungara, is the elegant **Villa Farnesina** and its garden. The Renaissance building is adorned with frescoes by Raphael and his disciples. Particularly remarkable are a cycle, *The Myth of Psyche*, and the famous *Galatea*, which depicts the beautiful statue of Greek myth coming to life as it is carried across the sea in a shell. The Villa Farnesina houses the National Gallery of Prints (telephone: 6540565). Open 9 A.M. to 1 P.M. Tuesday to Saturday.

Proceeding along the river embankment toward the Castel Sant'Angelo, you pass the grim old Regina Coeli (Queen of Heaven) prison at 29 Via della Lungara. Although Rome has a modern penitentiary complex with a high-security section in the Rebibbia district on the far northeastern outskirts, Regina Coeli is still in use. The fetid jail near the Vatican is in fact often overcrowded with inmates awaiting trial; a women's prison is around the corner in the Via delle Mantellate. Local people say sardonically that in order to be an authentic Roman one must spend time in a Regina Coeli cell.

Next to the Castel Sant'Angelo is the mammoth **Palace of Justice**, built of white travertine stone. At the beginning of the twentieth century this edifice housed most of the city's law courts. Only sixty years later, the building, long acknowledged as an eyesore, threatened to collapse and most of the courts and judiciary offices moved to a new, modern complex at the foot of the Monte Mario known as Judiciary City (Città Giudiziaria). The Court of Cassation, Italy's highest tribunal in civil and criminal cases, continues using a part of the restored Palace of Justice.

The **Prati**, **Mazzini**, and **Trionfale** sections north of the Palace of Justice and the Vatican were mostly developed during the twentieth century. They are predominantly middle-class neighborhoods with broad streets in regular patterns, residential and office buildings, and large army barracks.

ITALIC FORUM

Farther toward the northern outskirts is the Foro Italico (Italic Forum), a sports complex founded by Mussolini. To reach it from the city center, take the No. 1 tram or No. 48 bus from Piazzale Flaminio outside the Porta del Popolo.

Mussolini Dux can still be read on a gold-tipped marble pillar, 56 feet (17 meters) in height, at the beginning of the Viale del Foro Italico. *Dux* is Latin for leader, the root of the Italian appellation "Duce" by which the dictator wanted to be addressed.

The various athletic installations include the **Olympic Stadium** (Stadio Olimpico), swimming pools, and tennis courts. The stadium was enlarged for the 1960 Olympic Games in Rome, and again for the World Cup soccer finals in 1990. It can now accommodate up to 100,000 spectators; during top soccer matches it is filled to capacity.

Close to the Olympic Stadium is Italy's huge white Foreign Affairs Ministry, known as Palazzo della Farnesina, a superpower-size inheritance from Fascism. The Italian government entertains visiting royalty and heads of state or government in its official guesthouse, the Villa Madama, on a nearby slope of Monte Mario. The sixteenth-century building, designed by Raphael, and the surrounding gardens are off limits to sightseers.

Farther northwest, close to the Foro Italico, is the **Milvian Bridge** (Ponte Milvio) across the Tiber. Built toward the end of the second century B.C., it was still used by motor vehicles as recently as the 1960s and continues to be open to pedestrians. Upstream is the broad, Mussolini Modern Ponte Flaminio (Flaminian Bridge), which was opened after World War II. It carries traffic between the center of Rome and two important national highways, Via Cassia and Via Flaminia.

Overlooking the city from the northwest, the **Monte Mario** has an altitude of 456 feet (139 meters), the highest elevation within Rome's boundaries. During the second half of the twentieth century it has become a vast, pleasant residential district with many upper-middle-class condo-

miniums and villas. Public transport: take the No. 991 bus
from Piazza Resorgimento, north of the Vatican, or No.
999 bus from the Ottaviano terminal of the subway's Line
A (Viale Giulio Cesare at Via Ottaviano).

Several points on the Monte Mario command impressive views of the city below, especially the Cavalieri Hilton
Hotel and a promenade at the Caffè Zodiaco, 90 Viale
Parco Mellini (telephone: 3451032), near the Astronomi-
cal-Meteorological Observatory, which can be reached by
car or on foot from the Piazzale Medaglie d'Oro, north of
the Cavalieri Hilton Hotel.

RANDOM SIGHTS

Murmuring Fountains, Talking Statues

Rome has always been a city of waters. The first aqueducts
that channeled water from the nearby hills were built in
the fourth and third centuries B.C. As the city was expanding, the officials and emperors of ancient Rome conveyed more water to it, constructing impressive conduits;
their ruined arches and bridges can still be seen on the
outskirts today. Water pipes supplied the public and private
baths and the homes of the wealthy; other Romans bought
water from public distribution points or took it from the
many public fountains.

The admirable system of aqueducts was damaged by
barbarian invaders and decayed in the Middle Ages, when
the Tiber remained the main water supply. During the
Renaissance the popes had several ancient aqueducts repaired and put into service again. Hundreds of new public
fountains were built. Today cool drinking water still spills

out from the mouths of stone divinities and from bronze naiads and tritons, turtles, lions, sea monsters, and fish all over the center. Water escapes from a leaking marble boat in the Spanish Square and from a huge sandstone tureen in the Corso Vittorio Emanuele II. Water pours from the beaks of eagles or griffins into sidewalk bowls and soars into the air to fall languidly into granite basins that graced the monumental baths of antiquity.

At the center and in outlying neighborhoods you will find some curbside *fontanella* (little fountain) in stone or cast iron dispensing fresh water around the clock. The upper side of the metal spout has a little hole through which, by closing the main opening with your thumb, you can divert the stream for convenient drinking.

A favorite drinking place is the little Fontana del Facchino (Servant's Fountain) on the side of a Renaissance palace in Via Lata, just off the Via del Corso near Piazza Venezia. The water comes out of a little marble casket offered by a stone fellow in the dress of the medieval guild of water carriers; his nose has long been broken off, and his features have been defaced over the centuries by the innumerable hands that touched them.

The faceless water carrier was one of Rome's "talking statues" on which anonymous satirists, working by night, would hang wooden tablets with pasquinades—biting attacks on the high and mighty. The word *pasquinade* is derived from a legendary acerbic hunchback tailor, Master Pasquino. The populace thought they had identified Pasquino's likeness in the fragment of an ancient sculptural group located in the beginning of the sixteenth century in a square near the Piazza Navona now called the Piazza Pasquino. The first pasquinades were affixed to the torso of the ancient statue, and then they appeared often on other Roman monuments as well, including the fountain of the water carrier in the Via Lata and the "baboon" of the Via del Babuino.

Minishrines

On many street corners in the center of Rome, representations of Jesus, the Virgin Mary, or saints in medallions are surrounded by stucco work or enclosed in small shrine-like structures. Often illuminated with candles or electric light, these small street sanctuaries are known as *edícole*, Italianized from the Latin term *aedicola* (little temple or little house). Devotees adorn them with fresh flowers, and a few people will cross themselves as they pass. A typical *edícola* is near the Trevi Fountain at the corner of Piazza di Trevi and Via del Lavatore, opposite the recently restored Church of Saints Vincent and Anastasius: an image of the Madonna is flanked by two angels in soft stone holding up a wreath, all topped by a canopy.

Museums and Other Attractions

National Museum of the Villa Giulia, 9 Piazza di Villa Giulia (telephone: 3201951), on the northern edge of the Villa Borghese gardens. This is one of the world's largest collections of pre-Roman and, especially, Etruscan antiquities. Much of its wealth is in its storerooms, accessible only to scholars. The museum occupies a richly decorated building, erected for Pope Julius III between 1551 and 1553 by leading Renaissance architects with Michelangelo as a consultant. The Nymphaeum (Ninfeo), an airy structure in the courtyard, is occasionally used for literary or social events.

Most of the objects in the showrooms were dug up north of Rome, mainly during the exploration of Etruscan burial sites. Among the most famous exhibits is the *Apollo of Veii*, a life-size statue in painted terracotta, found with other sculptures at what is now Veio, north of Rome. The sculptural group to which the Apollo belonged was executed in an orientalizing style—note the seemingly ambiguous smile of the Apollo—toward the end of the sixth century B.C. by the artist Vulca or his school.

Also remarkable: the often reproduced *Sarcophagus of a Married Couple*, fitted together from many fragments excavated at Cerveteri, northwest of Rome; it shows a husband and wife serenely on a couch.

The Villa Giulia Museum is open 9 A.M. to 7 P.M. Tuesday to Saturday, 9 A.M. to 1 P.M. Sunday.

National Gallery of Modern Art, 131 Viale delle Belle Arti (telephone: 3224151), close to the Villa Giulia. In addition to many works by Italian painters and sculptors of the nineteenth and twentieth centuries, this collection has some non-Italian art too, but none really outstanding.

Special shows of modern art on loan from other institutions or from private collectors are held from time to time. The National Gallery of Modern Art is open 9 A.M. to 2 P.M. Tuesday to Saturday, 9 A.M. to 1 P.M. Sunday.

Baths of Emperor Diocletian. These are the ruins of the largest thermae in ancient Rome, occupying a vast space opposite the front gallery of the Stazione Termini. A part of the baths, which were built after A.D. 300, was transformed by Michelangelo into the Church of Santa Maria degli Angeli (St. Mary of the Angels) between 1563 and 1566. State funerals are usually held in this church, which faces the circular Piazza della Repubblica, near the Grand Hotel. The National Roman Museum, also known as the Thermae Museum (Museo delle Terme), took up many halls and courtyards of the ruined Baths of Diocletian for more than a century, but lately most of its thousands of exhibits have been inaccessible to sightseers.

A large portion of the long-neglected collection is to be transferred into a readapted former Jesuit school, the Palazzo Massimo, on the southeast side of the Piazza dei Cinquecento near the railroad terminal. For information call the museum's secretariat, 4824181.

Servian Walls. An old tradition credits Servius Tullius, the sixth of Rome's seven semilegendary kings (a personage who lived presumably in the sixth century B.C.), with having built fortifications around the nascent city-state. Short sections and fragments of the so-called Servian Walls have survived to this day in a few points. Scholars assume that the ancient walls, nearly 7 miles (11 kilometers) in circumference, actually went up after the invasion by the Gauls in the early fourth century B.C.

The most substantial remainder of the stone walls, up to 40 feet (13 meters) high, stands at the left side of the front gallery of the railroad terminal (Stazione Termini). Other short stretches of the Servian Walls can be seen in the middle of the Largo Magnanapoli at the lower end of the Via Nazionale and in the Piazza Albania on the southern slopes of the Aventine.

San Lorenzo Fuori le Mura (St. Lawrence Outside the Walls), one of Rome's seven pilgrimage churches, at Piazza San Lorenzo, is close to the city's main cemetery, Campo Verano (No. 71 bus from downtown). The edifice was formed by the merger of two basilicas that since the early Middle Ages had been standing on the site, back to back.

In July 1943 the old church was heavily damaged during the first Allied air attack on Rome. Some bombs destined for the nearby railroad yards missed their targets and fell on and near St. Lawrence's. The church was repaired

in the late 1940s. Alcide de Gasperi, eight times Italian
prime minister between 1945 and 1953 and a champion of
European unification, is buried in a crypt in St. Lawrence's.

Porta Pia. This is a gate in the northeastern section of
the Aurelian Walls, built in the second half of the sixteenth
century from designs by Michelangelo. (No. 60 or No.
62 bus from Piazza Barberini.) Facing the gate from the
outside, you will see to its left a marble column and plaque
marking the spot where the soldiers of King Victor Emanuel II breached the walls and penetrated into Rome on
September 20, 1870, meeting no resistance. The "breach
of the Porta Pia" meant the end of papal rule in Rome.

Via Nomentana. This straight, tree-lined street, running from the Porta Pia northeast, passes at its right side
the Villa Torlonia, the nineteenth-century mansion of a
wealthy princely family that was Mussolini's private residence until his arrest in 1943.

The vast gardens of the Villa Torlonia are now a public
park. Its subsoil is pierced by vast, largely decayed Jewish
catacombs. For information, call the Jewish Community,
telephone: 6875051.

About 2 miles (a little more than 3 kilometers) from the
Porta Pia, the Via Nomentana crosses the Rome–Florence
railroad tracks and the Aniene River, a heavily polluted
tributary of the Tiber, and reaches the **Monte Sacro** (Holy
Mountain). This gentle hill, about 100 feet (30 meters)
high, saw the first walkout of the plebeians from Rome,
supposedly in 494 B.C. As the story goes, Menenius
Agrippa, a conciliator who was almost certainly fictional,
told the secessionists on the hill the parable of the stomach
and the limbs, persuading them to strike a deal with the
patricians and return to the city. Today the Monte Sacro
section is an uninspiring lower-middle-class neighborhood.

Exhibition Palace (Palazzo dell'Esposizione), 194 Via Nazionale (telephone: 4817648), below the Quirinal Hill, is a city-sponsored arts center, opened in 1990 in a re-adapted vast edifice erected in the eclectic Beaux Arts style in the early 1880s. Periodic shows are held on three exhibition floors; there is also a bookshop, a cafeteria, and a rooftop restaurant. Open 10 A.M. to 10 P.M. Wednesday to Monday.

Napoleonic Museum, 1 Via Zanardelli (telephone: 6540286), near the Piazza Navona, is a collection of memorabilia of the Bonaparte family, especially of those of its members who lived in Rome: paintings, drawings, portraits, sculptures, autographs, and such curious items as a Turkish sword and a tobacco box owned by the emperor. Open 9 A.M. to 2 P.M. Tuesday to Saturday, also 5 to 8 P.M. Tuesday and Thursday, 9 A.M. to 1 P.M. Sunday.

Albergo dell'Orso (Inn at the Sign of the Bear), 25 Via dei Soldati, between the Piazza Navona and the Tiber, is a dark brown Renaissance building that functioned as a hotel for four hundred years. If you are told that Dante stayed here, smile politely—the Florentine poet visited Rome in A.D. 1300, and the "Bear" was built toward the middle of the fifteenth century. But Rabelais, Montaigne, and—probably—Goethe were guests, as were many other distinguished visitors through the centuries. A graceful arched loggia surmounts the main entrance; the former inn's side facade on the Via dell'Orso shows traces of old frescoes. Formerly known as Hostaria dell'Orso, the building housed a luxury restaurant and nightclub.

8.

Visits to the Vatican

VATICAN CITY, a sovereign enclave on the right bank of the Tiber, is the smallest independent state in the world. At the same time it is an organic part of Rome, connected with it by history, religion, language, culture, currency, economic interests, and uncounted personal relations.

The miniature state's territory is 108.7 acres (44 hectares)—about seven times the area of the New York City headquarters of the United Nations (which lacks sovereignty) or less than a sixth the size of another dwarf country, the Principality of Monaco. Under the Lateran Treaties of 1929, which carved the State of the Vatican City out of the Italian capital, certain buildings in other parts of Rome, such as the Lateran complex and the papal summer residence at Castelgandolfo (see page 242), are considered appendages to the pontifical state. Therefore these structures are outside the jurisdiction of Italian authorities.

Some seven hundred persons—clerics, nuns, and lay people—live in Vatican City and four hundred have Vatican citizenship. The Pope carries Vatican passport No. 1. Vatican citizens and residents ride in cars with SCV (State of Vatican City) license plates and are customers of a Vatican supermarket. About four thousand persons, including cardinals and gardeners, computer programmers and art restorers, who live elsewhere in Rome come to work in the Vatican every weekday.

The heart of the Vatican is the **Basilica of St. Peter**, the largest church in Christendom, built over what Roman Catholics believe is the burial site of the Prince of the Apostles. St. Peter's is adjoined, mainly on the north side, by a cluster of buildings including the Apostolic Palace, in which the pope lives and works.

The Vatican encompasses nearly two thousand halls, chambers, chapels, air-conditioned offices, corridors, galleries, and stairways, with twelve thousand windows. There is also a railroad station, linked by a spur line with the Italian rail network. It serves mainly for importing merchandise to the Vatican; the pope travels by train only on very rare occasions. He does, however, often use the heliport near the highest point of his tiny state.

Except for St. Peter's and the square in front of it, the Vatican is enclosed by high walls that were erected during the Renaissance period, replacing much older fortifications.

Pedestrians who aren't afraid of braving the Roman traffic may walk around the State of Vatican City in forty to forty-five minutes, but they won't see much more than some towers and broadcasting antennas sticking out. By chance they may stroll by just as a helicopter takes off from behind the walls to ferry the pope to one of the Roman airports or to some other nearby destination.

The Vatican is not only one of the world's great religious shrines, it is also the administrative center of a tightly structured organization that spans the globe, and a treasure house of priceless art. Ecclesiastics who have spent most of their adult lives in the papal enclave say that every week they still discover curious things of which they had no previous knowledge. The sightseer with limited time can hope to glimpse only the highlights. Visitors to the Vatican should start early in the morning, because its museums close early in the afternoon except during the peak tourist seasons.

KEYHOLE SQUARE

A ribbon of bright stone slabs set into the pavement separates the cobblestones of the Piazza di Pio XII from the cobblestones of the **Piazza San Pietro** (St. Peter's Square) and marks the border between Italian and Vatican territory. St. Peter's Square, however, is open to any comer. There are no frontier controls. Under a special convention between the Holy See and Italy, Italian policemen patrol the area on foot, watching out for pickpockets and other possible trouble.

One of the earth's great public spaces, St. Peter's Square was designed by Giovanni Lorenzo Bernini, the foremost Roman architect and sculptor of the early baroque era. Taking inspiration from the gospel report according to which Jesus promised Peter that he would be given "the keys of the kingdom of heaven," Bernini shaped the access to the sanctuary as a giant keyhole. The semicircular colonnades on either side seem to embrace the pilgrims and faithful flocking to St. Peter's.

Large crowds often gather in the square. Unless the pope is absent from Rome, he shows himself at noon every Sunday in a window on the top floor of the Apostolic Palace to pray the Angelus—a devotion commemorating the Incarnation—with the people in the piazza below. Usually he gives a short speech on an international topic over the public address system.

The **Apostolic Palace**, rising high on the right (north) side of St. Peter's Square, was built between the middle of the fifteenth century and the middle of the sixteenth. The windows on the last floor, visible from the piazza, are those of the pope's private apartment.

On the lower floors are his staterooms, including his private library where the pontiff receives distinguished visitors; a chapel; and the living and working quarters of the Cardinal Secretary of State, the pope's chief aide.

Galleries with large windows, in part visible from St. Peter's Square, belong to the offices of the Secretariat of State, the Vatican's nerve center. A large medallion bearing an image of the Virgin Mary and the Infant Jesus overlooks St. Peter's Square from a side wing. This *edícola* was erected in the early 1980s by order of Pope John Paul II.

At Christmas and Easter the pope appears on the central loggia of St. Peter's to impart his traditional blessing *urbi et orbi* (to the city of Rome and to the world) to the throng of Romans and foreigners in the square below and to a global television audience. St. Peter's Square is also the setting for occasional open-air masses, other pontifical ceremonies, and papal general audiences.

Media reports at times exaggeratedly speak of half a million people in the piazza; actually it can accommodate up to 100,000 persons, with an overflow of additional thousands crowding the Piazza di Pio XII, the Via della Conciliazione, and other approaches.

St. Peter's Square is an oval, 787 by 623 feet (239 by 190 meters), adjoining a trapezoidal space with flights of steps leading up to the church. The total length from the

Italian-Vatican boundary to the portico of St. Peter's is
1,115 feet (340 meters), nearly one-fifth of a mile, or more
than one-third of a kilometer.

The colonnades have four rows of pillars and Doric
columns each, 43 feet (13.1 meters) in height, their thick-
ness increasing in the outer semicircle. The colonnades
form three covered passageways, the central one originally
meant for carriages (no vehicle is allowed there now).

The rectangular bases of the columns are worn smooth
by generations of tired pilgrims and tourists who have used
them as resting places. The few steps leading from the
piazza to the colonnades are often crowded with people
sunning themselves or feeding the innumerable stubborn
pigeons that are constantly underfoot. The colonnades, the
walls of the connecting buildings between them, and the
church are topped with 162 larger-than-life statues of
saints, most of them also designed by Bernini.

Neighborhood residents regard St. Peter's Square as a
recreational area and safe playground for their children,
especially during the afternoon and on days when the
square isn't host to some special event. Vehicles are banned
from the square, except authorized ones that use the **Archway of the Bells**, to the left of the church facade, a passageway under the bells of St. Peter's. Coaches of pilgrim
groups are permitted to park in the square only for brief
periods of time.

On each side of St. Peter's Square, between the central
obelisk and the two fountains, a round stone slab set into
the pavement indicates the point from which the four columns of each series in the colonnade appear as one.

At the end of the right colonnade is the **Bronze Door**
(Portone di Bronzo), where Swiss Guard sentries (see page
179) in Renaissance uniforms wield halberds. The Bronze
Door is one of the three main entrances to Vatican City;

the others are the Archway of the Bells and the Gate of St. Anne (see page 178).

The obelisk at the center of St. Peter's Square is 82 feet (25 meters) high—135 feet (41 meters) including its large base and the cross on top. The reddish-brown granite stalk bears no hieroglyphics. Emperor Caligula (A.D. 12–41) had it shipped to Rome from Heliopolis to embellish a new circus on the right bank of the Tiber. One of Caligula's successors, Nero, shocked the Romans by competing with professional charioteers in that racecourse, which from then onward was known as Nero's Circus. Saint Peter the Apostle, Roman Catholics believe, suffered martyrdom in it. Pope Sixtus V ordered the enormous tapered stone, found in the ruins of Nero's Circus, to be raised in front of the still uncompleted Basilica of St. Peter.

It took 900 workmen and 140 horses four months in 1586 to do the job. According to a story that may or may not be true, Sixtus V's architect, Domenico Fontana, almost bungled the critical phase of the enterprise. The colossal weight of the obelisk, it seems, strained the ropes of his system of winches and pulleys to a degree that they started smoking. Silence had been imposed on all workers and bystanders on pain of death, but a sailor from San Remo who knew what might happen yelled, "Water on the ropes!" He saved the day and the obelisk.

The trophy from Heliopolis and Nero's Circus is crowned with a brass cross containing a relic from the Holy Land and rests on a stone pedestal. A Latin inscription on the base proclaims that Sixtus V consecrated the Vatican obelisk "to the invincible Cross," having reclaimed it from "impure superstition." This alludes to the Romans' belief at the time that obelisks had something to do with witchcraft.

The base of the obelisk is surrounded, at some distance,

with slabs in the pavement indicating the winds of Rome. The two graceful fountains, 45 feet (13.7 meters) high, between the obelisk and the colonnades look like twins but were actually erected sixty-two years apart during the seventeenth century. (The right one is older, installed in 1613.) The fountains are fed with water from Lake Bracciano via the Acqua Paola aqueduct.

At the right side of St. Peter's Square, close to the north colonnade, stand two trailers. One is a first-aid station, while the other serves as a Vatican post office during the summer months.

Another Vatican post office is behind the left colonnade, near the Archway of the Bells, as well as a Vatican bookshop and an information office for pilgrims and tourists. Public restrooms are behind the left and right colonnades. Souvenir vendors are barred from St. Peter's Square but hang around the approaches to it.

ST. PETER'S

The St. Peter's we see today replaced an ancient church that Emperor Constantine the Great, urged by the bishop of Rome, Pope Sylvester I, had built over the supposed gravesite of the Apostle Saint Peter, near Nero's Circus. Consecrated in A.D. 326, the original Church of St. Peter, also known as the Constantinian Basilica, was often altered and enlarged during the Middle Ages. At Christmas in A.D. 800 Charlemagne was crowned emperor in it by Pope Leo III. The ruler of the Franks and their conquests, Charlemagne was the first of several heads of the Holy Roman Empire to receive the imperial crown in St. Peter's.

By the middle of the fifteenth century the ancient church threatened to collapse, and it was decided to rebuild it completely. To raise the immense funds needed for the undertaking, the popes pressed churchmen and the faithful all over Europe for contributions; the discontent caused by the canvassers from Rome was one of the many factors leading to the Protestant Reformation. After initial work the forceful Pope Julius II (1503–13) commissioned Bramante to furnish designs for a new St. Peter's. These were repeatedly changed as new architects took over after Bramante's death in 1514.

The greatest architects of the Renaissance and the early baroque eras took turns in the construction of the central sanctuary of the Roman Catholic faith and symbol of the papacy, the Basilica of St. Peter. Between the beginning of the sixteenth century and the middle of the seventeenth, Bramante, Raphael, Giuliano da Sangallo, and his nephew Antonio da Sangallo the Younger, Michelangelo, Giacomo da Vignola, Domenico Fontana, and Carlo Maderna either supervised the giant building project or did important work for it. After the building's official consecration in 1626 Bernini also made many decorative additions.

The visitor walking across St. Peter's Square is impressed by the church's facade. It is so high that, as one approaches it, the dome gradually disappears. Eight huge columns, four pilasters, and six half-pilasters in Corinthian style support a broad shelf (the entablature) with open, quadrangular windows. The bells of St. Peter's can be seen through the window on the left.

The entablature carries two large clocks and is crowned with statues, 18 feet (5.5 meters) high, of Jesus, Saint John the Baptist, and the Apostles. A large Latin inscription on the frieze indicates that the facade was erected in honor of the Prince of Apostles in 1612 by Pope Paul V "Borghesius" (a member of the Borghese family).

The central loggia or balcony from which the pope

imparts his blessing on solemn occasions is located below the frieze, over the central entrance. Newly elected pontiffs make their first public appearance on this loggia, before crowds of Romans who gather in St. Peter's Square to greet their new bishop.

Anyone may enter the Basilica of St. Peter from 7 A.M. to 6 P.M. in winter and to 7 P.M. from May to October. In the portico, uniformed and plainclothes lay officers of the Vatican's security service will bar persons who are in their judgment inappropriately dressed. For women, pants are acceptable, as are bare legs. Miniskirts, hot pants, bare midriffs, and very low necklines are not. Men wearing wide open shirts may be asked to button up.

Briefcases and bulky bags must be deposited, free of charge, at a checkroom outside the portico, to the right. Cameras can be used inside the church, even with flashes. A gate on the right side of the portico leads to a courtyard with a souvenir shop and restrooms.

The portico is 233 feet (71 meters) long and paved with mosaics, including a modern one at the center that shows the coat of arms of Pope John XXIII (1958–63). Five doors lead from the portico into the church; the central entrance is closed by bronze doors executed by the Florentine sculptor Antonio Filarete from 1443 to 1445, made with material saved from the Constantinian Basilica. In the manner of the Renaissance, the bronze doors depict Christian and classical pagan scenes. The other doors are modern; the most recent one (1963), to the left of the central entrance, is a work by Giacomo Manzù, who was a friend of Pope John XXIII.

The far-right door is the Porta Santa (Holy Door) by Vico Consorti (1950). It is opened only during a Holy Year. Such a church jubilee is ordinarily celebrated every twenty-five years, when the faithful who fulfill certain conditions (like a pilgrimage to Rome or special devotions at home) earn extraordinary spiritual benefits. Popes may proclaim additional Holy Years to solemnize important events or recurrences, as did John Paul II by designating 1983/84 as a special jubilee to mark the 1900th anniversary of Christ's Passion and Resurrection. The next ordinary Holy Year is in 2000.

The visitor entering St. Peter's is awed by its size and theatrical splendor. The interior is 610 feet (186 meters) long and 90 feet (27.5 meters) wide at the nave, 449 feet (137 meters) wide in the transepts. The nave is 144 feet (44 meters) high. The entire interior surface is 163,000 square feet (15,160 square meters), as compared with 109,000 square feet (10,126 square meters) in the Cathedral of St. John the Divine in New York City.

The length, in meters, of some of the world's great cathedrals is indicated by metal markers on the floor of the nave: Notre-Dame in Paris, St. Paul's in London, and so on. A 331.9-foot (101.19 meters) marker for "Neo Eboracen[sis]" refers to St. Patrick's in New York. (*Eboracum* was the name of the ancient Roman garrison city that today is York in England; *Neo Eboracum* is curial Latin for "New York.")

A round porphyry slab embedded in the pavement near the central entrance shows the spot where, in the Constantinian Basilica, Charlemagne knelt during his imperial coronation.

The chapel on the right, closest to the entrance, guards the moving *Pietà*, a representation of a youthful Virgin Mary with the dead Jesus on her lap, executed by the twenty-five-year-old Michelangelo from 1499 to 1500. The celebrated sculpture, which was on display in the Vatican Pavilion of the 1964/65 New York World's Fair, is protected by plate glass. In 1972 a deranged Hungarian-born Australian attacked it with a hammer, causing serious, though not permanent, damage. Whenever the pope makes a solemn entrance into St. Peter's, he and his large retinue emerge processionally from a door near the Chapel of the *Pietà*.

At the fourth pillar on the right side of the nave is a darkened bronze sculpture of St. Peter, seated on a marble throne under a canopy. The thirteenth-century statue's right foot, which is thrust forward, is worn by the kisses of devotees. On the feast of Saints Peter and Paul, June 29, the statue is clad in pontifical vestments.

The papal altar, at which the pontiff alone may officiate, rises above the presumed grave of Saint Peter. The high altar is surmounted by a dramatic bronze canopy resting on four gilded spiral columns. This architectural extravaganza—praised or condemned by art critics over the centuries—is a creation by Bernini (1633). In front of the high altar is a pit surrounded by a marble balustrade with ever-burning sanctuary lights. Two flights of stairs descend to the so-called Confession, a now-empty space on the level of the grottoes. The space was for many years occupied by a large statue of Pope Pius VI by Canova (1822), which was removed to the grottoes in the 1980s.

Looking up, the visitor sees a Latin inscription in dark blue mosaic letters on gold ground on a frieze, 6.5 feet (2 meters) high, around the circumference of the dome, which measures 630 feet (192 meters). The text is from Matt. 16:18–19: "Thou art Peter, and upon this rock I will build my church . . . I will give thee the keys of the kingdom of heaven." The passage completes other scriptural quotations in Latin and Greek around the nave and apse.

The nave continues beyond the high altar and ends with a sumptuous apse, called the Tribune. It is dominated by an elaborate bronze throne, known as the Cathedra of Saint Peter, enclosing an ancient wooden chair that, according to pious tradition, served the Prince of the Apostles.

Four large statues representing doctors of the church— saints Ambrose, Augustine, Athanasius, and Chrysostom—flank the throne. The triumphant Cathedra composition is by Bernini. The dove in the circular stained-glass window above the throne symbolizes the Holy Spirit.

Confessionals are lined up in the transepts; to the right for faithful who want to do penance in Italian, to the left for confessions in other languages. On rare occasions, usually during the week before Easter, the pope hears confessions in person. His presence in one of the confessionals in the transepts is never announced beforehand.

The faithful may receive communion every day during masses celebrated either by members of the chapter of St. Peter's or by visiting priests. At various times during the day, mass is said at one of several altars, especially in the two large rectangular chapels on either side of the nave, the Chapel of the Choir (left) and the Chapel of the Sacrament (right).

Close to the entrance a visitor may encounter the christening of a newborn Roman baby. A crowd of relatives and guests will gather in the Chapel of the Baptismal Font, the first to the left.

Outside that chapel, under the first arch to the left, is Canova's monument to the last of the Stuarts, the family that once ruled Scotland and England. The white memorial carries busts of the "Old Pretender" (James II, who, according to Jacobite style, is identified as James III) and his sons Charles Edward (the "Young Pretender") and Henry, Duke of York, who died in 1807 as Cardinal of Frascati near Rome.

St. Peter's is filled with other sculptures, monuments of popes, mosaics, stucco work, and paintings. To study them all would require many hours.

The **Sacristy**, a building adjoining the left side of the basilica, is an eighteenth-century addition. Besides the halls in which priests are robed for liturgical functions, the Sacristy houses a collection known as the Historical-Artistic Museum/Treasury. In addition to ecclesiastical vestments, chalices, and other religious objects, the exhibits include a gem-studded cross from the sixth century, a donation by Emperor Justinian.

The Historical-Artistic Museum/Treasury is open 9 A.M. to 5:30 P.M. daily, except during major rites in St. Peter's, and is accessible through an entrance on the left side of the nave.

A narrow stairway near a large statue of Saint Longinus, right of the papal altar, descends to the **Vatican Grottoes**, or crypts. Several popes, including all since Benedict XV (1914–22), are buried in separate chapels and cells. Devotees are often seen praying at the tomb of Pope John XXIII, who is believed to be a candidate for church-proclaimed sainthood.

One of the few women buried under St. Peter's is former Queen Christina of Sweden; her tomb is close to that of John XXIII.

The one-way visitors' circuit, covering only a part of the grottoes, passes a glass door under a Latin inscription translating as "The Sepulcher of the Holy Apostle"; it looks out on the empty floor of the Confession.

The itinerary leads past some stumps of columns and sections of ancient brick-and-stone walls saved from the Constantinian Basilica, to reach an exit outside St. Peter's on the right side of the portico.

The grottoes can be visited from 8 A.M. to 5 P.M. on weekdays, except during major functions in St. Peter's. Admission is free.

For an ascent to Michelangelo's dome, look for the sign *Cupola*—it is either inside the left aisle, near the baptismal chapel, or outside near the exit from the grottoes. Sightseers usually have a choice between climbing stairs or using an elevator that was installed in 1910. Along the winding stairs one sees wall tablets recording past visits by royalty.

A first stop is on the roof of St. Peter's, on which rise two smaller decorative cupolas on either side of the dome. Other structures, not visible from the ground, include huts of the *sampietrini*, the old Roman name for the stonemasons and other maintenance workers of St. Peter's.

A circular gallery inside the dome permits one to look down into the church from 174 feet (53 meters) above its floor—not for people tending to suffer from vertigo. Note huge iron hoops around the dome, put into place in the eighteenth century to reinforce the structure.

Staircases between the dome's outer and inner shells ascend to the loggia of the lantern, 345 feet (108 meters) above the ground. The much-photographed vistas range over Rome and its surroundings, from the Apennine Mountains to the Tyrrhenian Sea. Only the *sampietrini* are permitted to climb higher, on iron ladders, up the lantern and the copper globe, 8 feet (2.5 meters) high, above it to the cross on top of St. Peter's.

Admission to the dome is from 8 A.M. to shortly before sunset daily.

Visitors interested in Christian archeology may ask for admission to one of the guided tours of the excavations below St. Peter's. Apply in person during the morning hours at the Ufficio Scavi (Excavation Office), a few steps behind the Archway of the Bells after explaining what you want to the Swiss Guard sentry.

Tours for a limited number of participants are conducted on most weekdays, lasting about ninety minutes. Expert guides explain the significance of what has been dug up below the level of the Constantinian Basilica since the late 1940s, including a cemetery from the first century A.D. A space there has been identified by Roman Catholic archeologists as the presumable grave of the Apostle; wall scratchings by early pilgrims include invocations to Saint Peter.

VATICAN MUSEUMS AND SISTINE CHAPEL

The Vatican Museums are a cluster of picture and sculpture galleries, frescoed halls and chapels, and collections of antiquities and precious or curious objects. The museums represent one of the world's vastest repositories of historical treasures and timeless art. The wall space within them adds up to a daunting 5 miles (8 kilometers) in length. The Raphael Rooms, Michelangelo's ceiling frescoes and soaring Last Judgment in the Sistine Chapel, ancient sculptures, and famous works by artists from Giotto to Caravaggio are among the major sights.

The Vatican Museums take up parts of the Apostolic Palace on different levels and extensive buildings adjacent to it. The museums are competently administered—better than some Italian state museums and galleries—but at the height of the tourist season seem overwhelmed by floods of visitors: up to twenty thousand on peak days. Tour operators and individual sightseers often set aside just a couple of hours, or even less, for the museums; thus thousands rush every day through their halls, galleries, corridors, and stairways, looking only for the Sistine Chapel and maybe one or two other highlights.

The Vatican Museums are open from 8:45 A.M. to 1:45 P.M. Monday to Saturday, except on Roman Catholic feast days; 8:45 A.M. to 4:45 P.M. Monday to Saturday, July 1–September 30 and during the week before Easter. Ticket sales stop an hour before closing time. On the last Sunday of every month admission is free, 8:45 A.M. to 12:45 P.M.

To cope with the crowds, the museum administrators suggest that visitors select and follow one of four one-way circuits, marked by color-coded signposts. The briefest circuit (A—violet) takes an hour for cursory visits, mainly to the Raphael Rooms and the Sistine Chapel; the longest suggested itinerary (D—yellow) is calculated to take five hours. While tour guides stick to the color-coded itineraries, individual visitors are nevertheless able to take shortcuts, skipping sections of little interest to them or going back to parts of the museums they have already passed. There is, at any rate, a lot of walking to be done.

Disabled persons may obtain a wheelchair, may bypass the crowds at the entrance, and will be shown to elevators. Call 6983333 during operating hours at least a day before the projected visit.

The use of cameras is permitted in most showrooms, but flash photography needs special authorization. No pictures may be taken in the Sistine Chapel.

The complex of the Vatican Museums includes a checkroom, first-aid stations, a coffee shop, a post office, a currency exchange and several sales desks for guidebooks and other literature. Portable sound guides with taped explanations in various languages regarding the Raphael Rooms and the Sistine Chapel may be rented. There is an adequate number of restrooms.

The entrance to the Vatican Museums is at Viale Vaticano on the northwest side of the papal state, a ten- to fifteen-minute walk from St. Peter's Square across the right-hand colonnade and following the Vatican walls. A Vatican bus takes visitors from St. Peter's Square, near the Archway of the Bells, to the museum entrance at hourly intervals from 8:45 A.M. to 12:45 P.M. The ride, lasting only a few minutes, isn't cheap: in 1992 it cost two and a half times the price of a ticket for Rome's municipal bus and streetcar network. However, passengers get glimpses of the Vatican Gardens.

The entrance hall of the Vatican Museums is noteworthy for its double-helix staircase (built in 1932), with one spiral for access to the ticket offices and showrooms, the other for the descent of exiting visitors. There is also an elevator. Not all parts of the museums are accessible every visiting day: a signboard near the entrance indicates which exhibits are open. Following is a brief description of the various units of the Vatican Museums, which are visited by an average of two million persons every year.

The **Pio-Clementine Museum**, named after popes Clement XIV (1769–74) and his successor Pius VI (1775–99), who were both avid collectors of antiquities, contains Greek and Roman sculptures. Its most famous exhibits are in two corner alcoves of its Octagonal Courtyard: the *Laocoön*, depicting the priest Laocoön and his two sons smothered by snakes because they offended the god Apollo; and the *Apollo Belvedere*. The *Laocoön* is a Greek original from the first century B.C., the *Apollo* an ancient copy of a fourth-century B.C. Greek original.

Adjoining the Pio-Clementine Museum is the **Egyp-**

tian Museum (Museo Egizio), with ancient Egyptian statuary, mummies and mummy cases, papyruses and reproductions of papyruses.

Outside the Egyptian Museum lies the vast **Courtyard of the Pinecone** (Cortile della Pigna), named after a huge bronze pinecone on its north wall. The pinecone probably adorned a fountain in antiquity; what it meant is something of a puzzle. A well-kept lawn takes up most of the courtyard with, at its center, a modern globe of yellow metal.

Chiaramonti Museum, named after Pope Pius VII (Barnaba Chiaramonti, 1800–23), in a long corridor, is a collection of Greek and Roman sculptures. Among them are what is believed to be the best existing likeness of Emperor Augustus, with his right arm raised, and an ancient copy of a statue of the orator Demosthenes.

The **Etruscan Museum** (Museo Etrusco), a floor above the Pio-Clementine Museum, is a display of many notable finds, mostly from tombs north of Rome, including Greek vases that the Etruscans imported into Italy.

Long galleries link the buildings near the entrance to the museum complex with the Apostolic Palace. Their windows look out on courtyards and on the Vatican Gardens. Antiquities, tapestries, ancient geographical maps, and various paintings are arrayed in the richly decorated galleries.

The second-floor galleries lead to the **Stanze of Raphael** (Raphael Rooms), four staterooms that Raphael decorated on orders from Pope Julius II from 1508 to 1520. His murals and ceiling paintings are generally acknowledged as one of the peaks of Renaissance art.

The Stanza dell'Incendio (Room of the Fire) is named after the painting of a conflagration in the old Borgo section near the Vatican in the ninth century, which was, according to legend, miraculously stopped by Pope Leo IV. Note also a mural showing the coronation of Charlemagne, designed by Raphael and executed by disciples.

The Stanza della Segnatura is so called because popes used to sign pardons and other documents in it. The frescoes deal with theology, poetry, philosophy, and justice; they include a celebrated composition, the *School of Athens*, with representations of Plato (believed to be a portrait of Leonardo da Vinci) and of a melancholy Greek scholar resembling Michelangelo.

The Stanza d'Eliodoro derives its name from a fresco showing the unsuccessful attempt of the Syrian raider Heliodorus to despoil the Temple of Jerusalem (2 Macc. 3). The room also contains a mural representing Attila the Hun being repulsed from the walls of Rome by the intervention of Pope Leo I, aided by apparitions of the Apostles Saint Peter and Saint Paul.

The Hall of Constantine, the fourth and farthest of the rooms, is devoted to the Roman emperor who favored Christianity. The paintings were completed by Raphael's pupils after his death.

The **Logge of Raphael**, a long corridor near the rooms, holds paintings by Raphael and his disciples that illustrate biblical themes. This collection was lately closed to the general public, and scholars who wish to see it must submit a special request while restoration work is proceeding.

The **Borgia Rooms** (Appartamento Borgia) in the Apostolic Palace below Raphael's *stanze* are named after Alexander VI (Rodrigo de Borja, or Borgia, 1492–1503), the infamous Spanish pope who lived in them, at times with his son Cesare or his daughter Lucrezia. The walls were frescoed by Pinturicchio, Alexander VI's favorite painter.

Pope Paul VI (1963–78) had the Borgia Rooms and various nearby chambers and halls subdivided and adapted—in part by covering frescoed walls with burlap—to house a new **Gallery of Modern Religious Art**. Paul VI, a collector of modern works who personally knew many contemporary artists, acquired (mostly through donations) paintings and sculptures by Chagall, Dalí, Gauguin, Kandinsky, Klee, Kokoschka, Matisse, Henry Moore, Picasso, Rodin, Graham Sutherland, and others. Roman experts declared in published criticism that most of the works in this vast collection were minor if not disappointing.

The **Sistine Chapel** is reached from the Borgia Rooms or by following signs through the long galleries, which lead to a small door at the right of the altar. Erected between 1473 and 1481 under Pope Sixtus IV, after whom it is named, the rectangular chapel is the place where the cardinals, in secret conclave, have elected all popes since Leo XIII (1878–1903). Other solemn functions are held in the chapel from time to time.

Michelangelo's frescoes, executed between 1508 and 1541, are sublime testimonials to his towering genius. A mirror will help you inspect the paintings on the vaulted ceiling if your neck becomes sore from looking upward. (Michelangelo's neck was so strained after a day's work on the ceiling of the Sistine Chapel that in order to read a message he had to hold it up and tip his head backward.) There are long benches on either side of the chapel, usually crowded with visitors.

The ceiling frescoes were cleaned and restored between 1980 and 1990. Michelangelo's brilliant original colors reappeared as layers of paint and glue from earlier restoration efforts and soot from candle smoke and incense were removed. Almost inevitably, the transformation of the Sistine ceiling sparked international controversy among Michelangelo scholars and art experts. During the restoration work, financed to a large extent by Nippon Television Network Corporation, the Sistine Chapel remained open to visitors of the Vatican Museums.

After completion of the ceiling project in 1990, the art restorers started work on the Last Judgment above the altar. A scale copy of the famous fresco was—for the benefit of sightseers—placed on a screen shielding the original while it was being treated by the restorers.

Michelangelo's ceiling paintings depict an intricate biblical cycle from the Creation to the Fall of Man: the Expulsion of Adam and Eve from Paradise, the Sacrifice of Noah, the Flood, and the Drunkenness of Noah. Flanking these scripture scenes are prophets and pagan sibyls (prophetesses), which portray humankind's hope for redemption; other biblical episodes; and, in the twelve lunettes (window vaults), the ancestors of Jesus. Michelangelo's incomparable design, composed of 343 figures, reflects his belief in the accord between classical (Platonic) philosophy and Christian thought. Most famous are the scenes of the Creator touching Adam with his forefinger to transmit life to him, and the Fall of Man and Expulsion from Paradise. Michelangelo's renowned nudes (*ignudi*), decorative figures on the edges of the main panels, are proof of his mastery in depicting the human body.

The Last Judgment on the altar wall, which is being freed from the grime of centuries, represents Jesus as judge with the Virgin Mary, Saint Peter, saints and angels, the elect ascending to heaven, the damned precipitating into hell.

The other walls of the Sistine Chapel carry frescoes by outstanding painters from Tuscany and Umbria, including Perugino, Pinturicchio, Botticelli, and Domenico Ghirlandaio.

The showrooms of the **Apostolic Library** on the first floor of the long galleries include a Museum of Pagan Antiquities, frescoes, paintings, a rotating exhibition of precious manuscripts and books, and a coin collection.

Scholars and students who want to work in the Apostolic Library, with its more than a million bound volumes and tens of thousands of manuscripts, must apply in person to the secretariat (telephone: 6982, ext. 4037). The library's offices and reading rooms are accessible from the Gate of St. Anne on the Via di Porta Angelica, outside the right-hand colonnade of St. Peter's Square.

The **Vatican Picture Gallery** (Pinacoteca) is in a modern building erected in the early 1930s near the entrance to the museums. The central room (No. 8) contains some of the best-known works by Raphael: the *Coronation of the Virgin*; the *Madonna of Foligno* with the Umbrian town of that name in the background; the *Transfiguration of Mount Tabor* (his last major painting); and various tapestries.

Other treasures of the picture gallery are a tryptych by Giotto; *Madonna with Angels* by Fra Angelico; works by Melozzo da Forlì and Perugino; Leonardo da Vinci's unfinished *Saint Jerome*; and paintings by Titian, Guido Reni, Rubens, Caravaggio, and other sixteenth- and seventeenth-century masters.

Another, even newer, building near the entrance to the Vatican Museums houses collections that before 1970 had been in the Lateran Palace. The **Gregorian Museum of Pagan Antiquities** (Museo Gregoriano Profano), named after Pope Gregory XVI (1831–46), contains antique sculptures, mosaics, and other materials. The **Christian Museum** (Museo Pio Cristiano), founded by Pope Pius IX (1846–78), displays early Christian sarcophagi, reliefs, inscriptions, and other objects found in the catacombs and in other ancient places of worship. Both museums are open on most visiting days. The **Ethnological Missionary Museum** (open only Wednesday and Saturday) acknowledges non-Christian religions with images of divinities, models of temples, and other objects, and illustrates the work of Roman Catholic missionaries on various continents.

VATICAN GARDENS AND ADMINISTRATIVE DISTRICT

About a third of the pontifical state is taken up by buildings from various epochs, another third by large and small squares and courtyards, and the last third by a vast park on the gentle slopes of the Vatican Hill.

The Vatican Gardens can be visited in guided tours on weekdays, except Wednesday. A coach leaves from the Archway of the Bells at 10 A.M. with a polyglot guide; the tour takes about two hours. Make reservations in person and buy tickets at least a day ahead at the information office at the left side of St. Peter's Square, open 8:30 A.M. to 6 P.M. Monday to Saturday. Visitors who decide to join the tour at the last minute are accommodated if there is space on the bus.

After passing the Archway of the Bells tour participants are shown, to their left, the Camposanto Teutonico (Teutonic Cemetery), said to have been founded by Charlemagne; German and Dutch clerics and lay people are buried here. The bus passes the Sacristy of St. Peter's and the Convent of St. Martha, today a guesthouse for visitors to the Vatican with a cafeteria for ecclesiastical staff that is said to be a dignified Vatican gossip center.

The spot where the obelisk that now rises in St. Peter's

Square was found is pointed out to visitors. Nearby is a huge stone trough, once used for slaking the thirst of the horses that raced in Nero's Circus.

A few hundred yards farther is the Vatican railroad station, where workmen may be seen unloading containers with United States, French, or German markings or handling merchandise for the Vatican supermarket (Annona), where only Vatican personnel may shop.

The rail station, the Palace of the Governor (which houses administrative offices), and other modern structures in this part of the papal domains were built in the 1930s with funds that the Vatican had received from the Italian state following the Lateran Treaties of 1929. The money was an indemnity for papal properties that Italian authorities had seized in the process of the nation's unification during the second half of the nineteenth century.

Visitors are shown the new papal heliport, wedged into a salient of the old walls. Nearby is a lush park section with cedars from Lebanon, roses from Texas, shrubbery from Japan, and other exotic flora brought to Rome by missionaries or donated by bishops. There is also a patch of vegetation that the papal gardeners leave alone—a miniature Vatican national park and bird sanctuary. A few Vatican cats prowl among the trees.

The tour guide will point out a fenced-in plot with lemon trees, eggplant, artichokes, and other vegetables: the pope's kitchen garden.

Near the highest point of the gardens is the ancient Tower of St. John, a former observatory that Pope John XXIII had adapted as an aerie for himself and as a guest-house for distinguished visitors. Josef Cardinal Mindszenty of Hungary was a guest here for a short time after his liberation.

Nearby is a reproduction of the grotto at Lourdes,

France, where the Virgin Mary is believed to have appeared to Saint Bernadette, a gift of French devotees to Pope Leo XIII (1878–1903). Not far from the Lourdes Grotto is a basketball court where the Swiss Guards compete with the Vatican firefighters and security men.

A building belonging to the Vatican broadcasting services (which operate extensive installations with towering antennas near Lake Bracciano, north of Rome) was once used by Guglielmo Marconi, the inventor who developed wireless telegraphy.

There are also several fountains and pavilions in the manner of the Italian gardens of the Renaissance. An elegant villa, the Casina (Little House) of Pope Pius IV (1559–65), near the buildings of the Vatican Museums (and visible from some of their windows) is now the seat of the Pontifical Academy of Sciences. Nobel Prize winners and other scientists on whom the pope has bestowed membership in the learned body—they need not be Roman Catholics—meet in the frescoed rooms of the Casina from time to time to discuss their findings and theories.

The Vatican's administrative sections and the papal quarters in the Apostolic Palace are off limits to ordinary tourists. Anyone, however, may walk through the Gate of St. Anne to visit the little Church of St. Anne at the right side immediately behind it, which is the parish church of Vatican residents. Couples who don't live in the papal state occasionally choose to be married in St. Anne's.

Sightseers may penetrate farther into the administrative district of Vatican City if they explain to the Swiss Guards and Vatican security officers at the Gate of St. Anne that they want to send a package from the Vatican's central post office or to go to the Apostolic Library or the Pontifical Pharmacy. The pharmacy carries medicines that may not be available in Italy; it helps to be able to show a doctor's prescription.

The Gate of St. Anne is also used by visitors to the offices of the Vatican newspaper *L'Osservatore Romano*, to a printing plant that turns out texts in many languages and alphabets, to an electric power plant, and to other services that are inaccessible to outsiders, such as a bank called the Institute for the Works of Religion.

The Swiss Guards at the Gate of St. Anne wear dark blue fatigues, Renaissance style. At the other two main entrances, the Bronze Door and the Archway of the Bells, the Swiss guardsmen do service in their gala uniforms with yellow, blue, and red stripes. The pattern is said to have been designed by either Michelangelo or Raphael.

The Swiss Guard consists of about eighty volunteers from the Roman Catholic cantons of Switzerland. The mercenary force, bodyguards of the popes for nearly five hundred years, is still armed with halberds and swords. Its men are today all veterans of the Swiss Army, and while in Rome they continue rifle and karate practice. The guardsmen, who speak German or French as their first language, won't object to being photographed, and they may even pose with tourists for group pictures.

The officers of the Vatian Security Service, in blue uniforms or plain clothes, are less likely to have their pictures taken. They are mostly former Italian policemen or carabinieri (see page 218).

The Swiss Guard and Vatican police could not prevent an attempt on the life of Pope John Paul II. On May 13, 1981, a Turk fired shots at the pontiff during a general audience in St. Peter's Square, severely wounding him. Since then the Vatican has stepped up its security measures. During general audiences and ceremonies in St. Peter's or in the square, officers of the Vatican Security Service dressed in plain clothes unobtrusively watch the crowd.

SEEING THE POPE

The easiest way to get a glimpse of the head of the Roman Catholic Church is at noon on any Sunday (unless the pope is absent from the Vatican). The pontiff will show himself in a window on the top floor of the Apostolic Palace to say the Angelus and address the crowd in St. Peter's Square.

On Christmas Day, at Easter, and possibly on a few other occasions during the year, the pope imparts a blessing and delivers a homily from the central loggia of St. Peter's. He makes ceremonial appearances in St. Peter's or in the square outside during canonizations or beatifications, whereby dead persons are proclaimed saints or—a preparatory step on the road to sainthood in the Roman Catholic Church—"blessed." Anyone may join the throng of the faithful during such ceremonies, although special invitations are required for the enclosures near the papal altar.

When the pope is in Rome he holds a general audience every Wednesday, usually beginning at 11 A.M. in the cool months or in the late afternoon during summer. General audiences take place either in St. Peter's Square or in the modern **Audience Hall**. This is a concrete building with bright travertine facings south (left) of St. Peter's, erected in 1971 by the architect Pier Luigi Nervi. Access is through a gate behind the left-hand colonnade of St. Peter's Square, which is opened for the occasion and watched by Swiss Guards.

Tickets are needed for attendance at a general audience, although the security men sometimes allow people without tickets to slip into sections farthest from the dais on which the pope is to appear.

All audience tickets are free of charge. They carry letters corresponding to different enclosures in the Audience Hall, which seats eight thousand persons, or in St. Peter's Square, sectioned up by wooden barriers for the occasion. Special consideration is given to disabled persons, who are assigned space near the pontiff.

Visitors who want to participate in a general audience may apply for tickets in person at the Prefecture of the Pontifical Household, an office beyond the Bronze Door that is open 9 A.M. to 1 P.M. on weekdays (on Wednesday from 9 A.M. until shortly before the audience).

Americans may also write, or apply in person, to the Bishops' Office for United States Visitors to the Vatican, 30 Via dell'Umiltà, 00817 Rome (telephone: 6789184). The office, located near the Trevi Fountain in downtown Rome, is open 9 A.M. to 1 P.M. Monday to Saturday, also 2 to 6 P.M. Tuesday. Good seats are obtainable if the requests are made early enough. Prospective visitors should write as soon as they know when they will be in Rome, and state on which Wednesday they would like to attend an audience. They can pick up their tickets on arrival.

Requests for audience tickets may also be addressed to the American Church of Santa Susanna, 14 Via Venti Settembre, 00187 Rome (telephone: 4827510). The Paulist Fathers, in charge of the 1,600-year-old church near the U.S. Embassy, run a community center for Roman Catholic Americans in Rome. Citizens of other countries may obtain tickets for papal audiences through various ecclesiastical institutions for priests and seminarians of their nations in Rome.

General audiences last one and a half hours and longer.

The pope enters St. Peter's Square or the Audience Hall making gestures of blessing and shaking hands. When he reaches the dais he greets visiting bishops and other prelates awaiting him there and may exchange a few words with some of them. Then he addresses the audience, usually in Italian. He gives brief summaries of his remarks in a few other languages, and welcomes national delegations and various groups of pilgrims who may be present. He steps down from the dais to bless newlyweds and disabled persons and may briefly talk to other visitors in the front rows.

At the end of the audience the pope imparts his apostolic blessing to all those present. He will say that he is blessing also their "dear ones" at home as well as any religious objects, like rosaries or medals, that the visitors may have brought with them.

Procedures are similar when the pope is in his summer residence, Castelgandolfo, usually during a few weeks in August or September. He appears on a balcony of the papal palace at noon on Sundays to pray the Angelus, and he receives pilgrims and tourists on Wednesdays in a courtyard or a hall of the pontifical mansion.

Tickets to Castelgandolfo audiences are distributed in Rome. Travel organizations provide coaches for participants in the audiences who can't reach Castelgandolfo (16 miles [25 kilometers] southeast of the capital) by their own means or by public transport.

The pope occasionally receives special groups of visitors—like participants in a convention or members of church-affiliated associations—in a hall in the Apostolic Palace or in the Courtyard of St. Damasus, which is enclosed by three wings of that ancient building. He receives visiting statesmen and personal guests in individual audiences in his private library.

If a general audience is held in Nervi's modern hall,

participants walk past a somber edifice at 11 Piazza del Sant'Uffizio (now also known as Via di Papa Paolo VI) behind the left-hand colonnade of St. Peter's Square. It is the headquarters of the Sacred Congregation for the Doctrine of the Faith, the church's highest authority, next to the pope, in all matters of faith and morals. Until 1908 this body, set up in 1542 to combat heresy, was known as the Holy Inquisition. Sightseers are barred from the sprawling palace, which is considered extraterritorial although it is located outside the State of Vatican City.

THE ANGEL'S CASTLE

The broad, straight **Via della Conciliazione**, leading from the Tiber to St. Peter's Square, is a creation of Mussolini's architects. Its name recalls the "reconciliation" between the Roman Catholic Church and the Italian state, enshrined in the Lateran Treaties of 1929.

Until the 1930s the space between the river bend and St. Peter's Square was filled with old and partially decrepit buildings belonging to the Borgo district. A section of the Borghi—the word *borgo* is related to the English term *borough*—survives north of the Via della Conciliazione and the Castel Sant'Angelo.

Before the Via della Conciliazione was opened, travelers and pilgrims approaching the Vatican had to traverse a maze of narrow streets—to find themselves suddenly in the vast St. Peter's Square with the facade and the dome of the huge church in front of them. The demolition of this part of the Borgo section has been harshly criticized by art and architectural experts; it is true, nevertheless, that the ancient neighborhood could not have coped with today's mass tourism and its sightseeing coaches.

The Via della Conciliazione is lined with old palaces—
one of which was moved from its previous site and rebuilt—and with new edifices housing Vatican offices.
Cafés, banks, and souvenir stores occupy the ground floors
of many buildings. Two rows of white obelisks, topped
with lanterns, on either side of the broad avenue confer on
it a somewhat funereal character.

The **Castel Sant'Angelo** (Castle of the Holy Angel),
overlooking the Tiber on the western edge of the Borgo
section, is one of Rome's major landmarks. It is treated in
this chapter because from the early Middle Ages to the
nineteenth century it served as a papal fortress and advanced bulwark of the Vatican and was often used by the
government of the popes as a prison and place of execution.
Today it is Italian state property, containing an art museum
and military collections, and it is on occasion host to special
exhibitions and official receptions.

The imposing circular structure, 210 feet (64 meters)
in diameter, was started under Emperor Hadrian in A.D.
133 as a mausoleum for himself, his family, and his successors. He was buried in it after his death in 138, as were
several other Roman emperors and their relatives until Caracalla's death in 217. In the time of the barbarian invasions,
the mausoleum with its thick stone walls was converted
into a military citadel for the defense of river crossings.

During a plague in A.D. 590, Pope Saint Gregory the
Great reported that while presiding at a penitential procession he had seen the Archangel Michael sheathing his
sword; he interpreted the apparition to mean that the ca-
lamity would soon end. Saint Gregory erected a chapel
dedicated to the "Holy Angel" on top of the former mausoleum, where once a giant statue of Hadrian had stood. The
present bronze statue of the Archangel Michael crowning
the Castel Sant'Angelo, a work by the Flemish sculptor

Pieter Verschaffelt, was put there in 1752; it has recently been restored.

The Castel Sant'Angelo played a crucial role during the Sack of Rome in 1527, when Spanish and German troops of Emperor Charles V occupied the city and ran wild. Pope Clement VII, with thirteen cardinals and hundreds of followers, took refuge in the river fortress, hastily reaching it from the Vatican by way of a partially covered gallery that had been built in the thirteenth century.

This passageway still exists. It delimits what has remained of the Borgo section at the south side, and is in the neighborhood known as the *passetto* (little passage). The Holy See and the Italian government reached agreement in 1991 that the gallery linking the Vatican with the Castel Sant'Angelo, more than half a mile (700 meters) in length, is under Italian jurisdiction. The long-neglected relic from medieval military architecture is due to be restored and eventually opened to visitors.

During the Sack of Rome, 147 of 189 Swiss mercenaries died in defense of the pontiff. The entourage of Clement VII, a member of the Medici family of Florence, included Benvenuto Cellini. The Florentine sculptor, jeweler, and adventurer gives a vivid description in his memoirs of the anxious weeks in the besieged papal fortress; he claims personally to have shot the commander of the attacking imperial troops, the Constable Charles of Bourbon, with a harquebus (a small-caliber gun).

The castle's function as a papal prison is recalled in the third act of Puccini's *Tosca*.

The Castel Sant'Angelo (telephone: 6875036), the former outworks of which are now a public park, is open 9 A.M. to 2 P.M. Monday to Saturday, 9 A.M. to 1 P.M. Sunday, and on some afternoons during special exhibitions. The entrance is at 50 Lungotevere Castello on the

Tiber embankment. The panorama from the castle's various terraces and galleries alone is worth a visit, although
interesting parts of the complex old bulwark may be closed
for restoration or other reasons.

From the gateway a long spiral passage with mosaic
floors winds up past the sepulchral chamber of Hadrian,
where niches for the urns with the ashes of the emperor
and his family are visible. Today's visitors are directed to
bypass this *rampa circoidale* (circular ramp). They ascend
the *rampa diametrale* (diametrical ramp), a stairway with
low steps cutting across the bulwark's ground floor, past
massive Roman walls. Midway is a wooden bridge (replacing an earlier drawbridge) above the empty tomb chamber
of Hadrian.

The visitor emerges in the Courtyard of the Angel,
named after the marble statue of the Archangel Michael
by Guglielmo della Porta, which topped the Castel
Sant'Angelo for two hundred years until it was replaced
by the present bronze statue. Della Porta's angel dominates
the courtyard in which ancient stone cannonballs the size
of large grapefruit are piled up.

At the end of the lengthy courtyard is the facade of a
(usually closed) chapel designed by Michelangelo. Small
rooms on the outer rim of the fortress contain a collection
of weapons, from prehistoric times to the twentieth century, that is being reorganized and is inaccessible to visitors. The Rooms of Clement VIII (1592–1605) opening to
the Courtyard of the Angel are used for special exhibitions.
A frescoed Hall of Justice at the center, above Hadrian's
burial cell, was the courtroom in which the papal judges
issued sentences in criminal cases.

The Courtyard of Alexander VI on the side opposite
to the Courtyard of the Angel is bordered, on the outside,
by former prison cells. Famous prisoners who were held

in the papal dungeons included Beatrice Cenci, who was found guilty of having plotted the assassination of her prominent father. She was executed in 1599. The sensational affair in papal Rome was evoked by Shelley in his tragedy *The Cenci*, as well as by Stendhal and other writers; it inspired paintings by Guido Reni, among others.

The center of the castle's upper level is taken up by the Papal Apartments. Period furniture in them includes a canopied bed in the Room of Eros and Psyche (*Camera di Amore e Psiche*), named after a wall frieze representing episodes from the love story of Greek mythology. Various paintings from Italian state collections are hung in the ornate rooms on a rotation basis. The Hall of the Library, on a higher level, leads to the Treasury, a circular chamber with wooden shelves for secret archives and, in the middle, metal-covered chests in which valuables were kept. On various levels of the stronghold the visitor may see old guns and blunderbusses; storerooms for oil, grain, and other provisions; and ancient tools.

On the top level of the castle (often closed to sightseers) is a round hall where prelates in disgrace, aristocrats, and important political prisoners were held. The hall now contains Italian military memorabilia. A terrace at this level below the bronze angel commands one of the best panoramas of Rome.

The bridge in front of the Castel Sant'Angelo was for many centuries the only direct way of communication between the core of Rome and St. Peter's. Known as Ponte dell'Angelo (Bridge of the Angel), the structure goes back to Hadrian's time, and its middle arches are from antiquity. Statues of saints Peter and Paul and ten angels were placed on the bridge in the sixteenth and seventeenth centuries. Through the ages millions of pilgrims have passed the often-repaired bridge.

In 1911 the Ponte Vittorio Emanuele II, a broad bridge a few hundred yards downstream, was opened. It now bears almost all east-west traffic between the two banks in this section of the Tiber. West-east motor traffic is channeled over the modern Ponte Principe Amedeo farther downstream.

BUSINESSES AROUND THE VATICAN

Pilgrims have meant money to Rome for more than a millennium. To lodge, feed, care for, and entertain them has always kept thousands of Romans busy. Hospices for pilgrims existed near St. Peter's in the early Middle Ages. In past centuries trade flourished in authentic or spurious relics related to the Holy Land or various saints.

Today the visitor passes numerous souvenir shops and peddlers, photo stores, travel agencies, currency exchanges, cafés, taverns, and fast-food outlets in the streets and squares close to St. Peter's. The pontifical state itself derives part of its revenue from the sale of postage stamps, coins, picture postcards, souvenirs, books, brochures, museum tickets, and refreshments to sightseers.

Stamp and coin collectors are welcome to contact the Vatican's Philatelic-Numismatic Office in the Palace of the Governor in the gardens behind St. Peter's (telephone: 6982, ext. 4037). It adjoins a small stamp and coin museum that can be visited between 9 A.M. and noon Tuesday, Thursday, and Saturday.

Although sightseers who have traipsed around St. Peter's and the Vatican Museums all morning may not want to search for a cab to reach their hotel or some downtown restaurant in heavy midday traffic, they shouldn't expect to find haute cuisine anywhere near the Vatican. The best solution for lunch may be a plate of pasta, a salad or other snack, a beverage, and time enough to rest up in some simple trattoria in the Borghi section, particularly along the straight, narrow Borgo Pio, the neighborhood's main street. Between print shops and other small businesses there are half a dozen sit-down eating places that will do. The Borghi section has retained some of the flavor of old Rome; local and visiting priests and off-duty members of the Swiss Guard and Vatican Security Service may be sitting at the next table at a trattoria.

The so-called pizza sold by the refreshment wagons outside St. Peter's Square doesn't deserve that name, nor is their gelato among Rome's best. Fruits offered by stands along the Vatican walls are outrageously overpriced, and so is much of the merchandise—like T-shirts—that souvenir vendors display there.

The neighborhood's stores, filled with souvenirs of Rome and religious articles like rosaries and statuettes, are more reputable, but do some comparison shopping. Don't be shy about bargaining.

To get lire for foreign currency, turn to a regular bank; there are several near the Vatican, although their business hours may be inconvenient. Some stores near the Vatican accept foreign currency in payment, but their exchange rates are substantially below the official ones.

9.

Cosmopolitan, Aristocratic, and Plebeian Rome

EMBASSIES AND CONSULATES

ROME IS HOST to more foreign embassies than are Washington, Moscow, Tokyo, London, or Paris. Indeed, most of the world's governments maintain two separate diplomatic missions in the Italian capital—one accredited to the Quirinal (meaning the Italian Republic), the other to the Holy See.

The diplomats posted in Rome do what their colleagues in other capital cities do: they deal with officials of the host government, entertain one another, and pick up information by cultivating politicians, journalists, intellectuals, economic leaders, artists, and other outstanding or knowledgeable persons. The foreign diplomats assigned to the Vatican also get into formal dress now and then to attend some pontifical ceremony in St. Peter's.

The consulates or consular sections of the foreign embassies that are accredited to the Italian state provide various services for citizens of their country who live in Italy or are visiting it. They renew expired passports or will issue a substitute passport or travel document if the original passport has been lost or stolen; they notarize documents, register births or deaths, and furnish assistance in dealings with the local bureaucracy and judiciary system. They also issue visas, where required, to noncitizens who want to travel to their own nations.

The American Consulate in Rome furnishes on demand lists of reliable doctors, dentists, and lawyers who speak at least some English and are acquainted with American procedures. The consulate also advises on federal income tax matters, Social Security benefits, and U.S. voting rights.

If a resident or American citizen is in trouble in Rome, the American Consulate will on request inform the family back home. Don't expect any money loan or handout. If you have the misfortune of getting arrested and put in prison, the consulate cannot get you out but will see that you are represented by a lawyer and are treated according to Italian laws. Italian judiciary procedures are notoriously slow, and there is no bail in most criminal cases.

If you want to get married in Italy the American Consulate will give you a leaflet detailing how to go about it. (It's more complicated than you would expect in the capital of la dolce vita.)

Some of Rome's many foreign embassies occupy historic or stately buildings: the U.S. Embassy has its seat in the Palazzo Margherita on the Via Veneto, the French Embassy in the Palazzo Farnese, and the Spanish Embassy to the Holy See in the palace that gave its name to the Spanish Square.

Following are the addresses and telephone numbers of the embassies of the major English-speaking nations.

Embassies to the Italian Republic

United States: 119A Via Vittorio Veneto; United States Consulate, 121 Via Vittorio Veneto (telephone for both: 46741).

Great Britain: 80A Via Venti Settembre (telephone: 4755441), near the Porta Pia.

Canada: 27 Via Giovanni Battista de Rossi (telephone: 855341); Canadian Consulate, 30 Via Zara (telephone: 8441841); both near the Via Nomentana.

Ireland: 3 Largo del Nazareno (telephone: 6782541), near the Spanish Square.

Australia: 215 Via Alessandria (telephone: 832721), near the Via Nomentana.

Embassies to the Holy See

United States: 294 Via Aurelia (telephone: 6390558), on the western outskirts.

Great Britain: 91 Via Condotti (telephone: 6789462).

Canada: 4D Via della Conciliazione (telephone: 6547398), near the Vatican.

Ireland: 1 Via G. Medici (telephone: 5810777), in the Villa Spada on the Janiculum.

Australia: 27 Corso Trieste (telephone: 852792), near the Via Nomentana.

Some nations that recognize the claim to sovereignty by the Order of Malta maintain diplomatic relations with that entity also. Usually their ambassadors to the Holy See formally present their credentials to the Grand Master of the Knights of Malta as well.

Furthermore, many governments are represented at the United Nations Food and Agriculture Organization by special envoys who enjoy diplomatic status. Thus a couple of thousand or so diplomats are stationed in the Italian capital. Their offices and the private residences of some among them are protected by Italian police around the clock; their cars with CD (diplomatic corps) plates have parking privileges.

CULTURAL MISSIONS

In addition to the many ambassadors, counselors, first and second secretaries, and other embassy personnel there is a parallel semidiplomatic establishment of foreign cultural missions. These are the academies and institutions that large and small nations maintain in the Italian capital to support research projects by their own scholars. These missions enable young archeologists, historians, and artists to benefit from the cultural riches of Rome.

The **American Academy of Rome**, 5 Via Angelo Masina (telephone: 58461), near the Porta San Pancrazio, is a privately funded center for independent study and advanced research in the fields of fine arts and humanities. The institution includes a school of classical studies founded in 1895, a school of fine arts, a large library, and a photo archive.

The American Academy, with its two villalike buildings in a garden on a slope of the Janiculum, is open to visitors in May and June, when it holds its annual art exhibition with works by resident fellows on display. Visiting scholars may be authorized to use the academy's research facilities.

The British School at Rome, 61 Via Antonio Gramsci (telephone: 3213454), near the National Gallery of Modern Art, was established in 1901 as the British School of Archeology. It too holds an annual exhibition in early June.

The **French Academy**, in the Villa Medici near the top of the Spanish Stairs, plays an important role in Rome's cultural life through its periodic art exhibitions.

Austria, Belgium, Brazil, Germany, Hungary, the Netherlands, Romania, Spain, Sweden, and a few other countries maintain learned institutions in the Italian capital; they organize shows, lectures, concerts, and other events.

A network of foreign-language private schools from kindergarten to college level serves the educational needs of Rome's cosmopolitan community. For information, consult the directory of the Rome International Schools Association at the American Consulate. Several U.S. universities conduct overseas programs in the Italian capital.

A large segment of the non-Italian population of Rome is made up of several thousand foreign priests, seminarians, friars, and nuns who teach or study in church institutions, are assigned to the headquarters or establishments of their religious orders, do pastoral or humanitarian work in churches and hospitals, or belong to the Vatican staff.

WORSHIP IN ENGLISH

Rome offers many opportunities for worship in English. Following is a list of Christian churches and communities where English-language Sunday services are held.

Anglican. All Saints Anglican Church, 153C Via del Babuino (telephone: 3235493), near Piazza del Popolo.

Assemblies of God. International Christian Fellowship, 7 Lungotevere Michelangelo (telephone: 3211207), in the Mazzini section.

Baptist. Rome Baptist Church, 35 Piazza San Lorenzo in Lucina (telephone: 8926487), off the Via del Corso.

Church of Jesus Christ of Latter-Day Saints. Rome Mission, 103 Via Cimone (telephone: 898394); meetings at 20 Piazza Carnaro; both in the Monte Sacro section.

Episcopal. St. Paul American Episcopal Church, 58 Via Napoli (telephone: 4883339), also known as St. Paul's Within the Walls, near the Baths of Diocletian.

Methodist. 3 Via del Banco di Santo Spirito (telephone: 6868314), near the Ponte dell'Angelo.

Presbyterian. St. Andrew's of Scotland, 7 Via Venti Settembre (telephone: 4827627), near the Quirinal Palace.

Roman Catholic. American Church of Santa Susanna, 7 Via Venti Settembre (telephone: 4827510), near the U.S. Embassy.

Sunday masses in English are also said in the churches of Sant'Agnese in the Piazza Navona; of San Silvestro, Piazza di San Silvestro (telephone: 6797775), next to the Central Post Office, where the congregation includes many Filipinos; and in the church of the Venerable English College, 45 Via Monserrato (telephone: 6868546), near the Piazza Farnese.

There is no regular English-language synagogue service, but English-speaking interpreter-guides can be pro-

vided by the Synagogue at 15 Lungotevere dei Cenci
(telephone: 6543168).

EXPATRIATES

The foreign population of Rome includes a growing number of executives and personnel of banks, multilateral con-
cerns, industrial corporations, and other business enter-
prises that operate in Italy.

The American Chamber of Commerce, 25 Via Abruzzi
(telephone: 4814540), near the U.S. Embassy, provides
assistance for business companies, schedules monthly lun-
cheons with guest speakers, and has a library with commercial publications. Corporations and individuals may
become members.

Add to the non-Italian residents many thousands of
recent immigrants from the Third World and eastern Europe. They are all bunched together by the term *extracomunitari*, a neologism meaning newcomers from outside the
European Community. Americans and Japanese, Swiss
and Swedes, among others, would also fall into that cate-
gory, but nobody would ever refer to persons from rich
countries outside the European Community as *extracomunitari*. The word is a euphemism for poor nonwhites and
newcomers from Eastern Europe.

Extracomunitari are particularly conspicuous around the
Stazione Termini and in some neighborhoods on the city's
eastern and southern outskirts. At intersections some of
the new immigrants will try to wash car windows or sell
flowers or tissues before the traffic light changes. In subway stations and along shopping streets Senegalese and
other *extracomunitari* spread their wares on the pavement,
always watching out for the police, who may sometimes

close an eye or who may chase the peddlers off and seize their illegal merchandise.

For centuries Rome has been a place where foreign expatriates choose to live—like former Queen Christina of Sweden in the seventeenth century, and countless writers and artists during the Romantic Age. Read the names of famous or long-forgotten guests of Rome on the headstones of the Cemetery of Non-Catholics.

Today thousands of Westerners reside in Rome, writing books, giving language lessons, working in movies or in the fashion industry, earning money in other ways, or living on their savings or pensions. They meet at embassy receptions or in their own clubs—or keep away from fellow expatriates and resolutely go native, which isn't hard in Rome.

The American Club of Rome can be contacted via the American Overseas School, 811 Via Cassia (telephone: 3668531).

Many of the Italian capital's foreign residents become romanized, at least to a degree, whether they want it or not. They get used to a few cups of potent espresso every day, become addicted to pasta al dente and a glass of wine at lunch, and enjoy their siesta. They will dine late and stay up even later, and may oversleep in the morning. They will complain about the sirocco and feel buoyant when the cold tramontana blows in from the north. And they will gradually be converted to the easygoing ways that are the Eternal City's mode of coping with life. If they ever return home they will have a readjustment problem.

NOBLES AND PROLETARIANS

A class conflict between its wealthy patricians and the common people (the plebs) agitated early Rome 2,500 years ago (see page 152). Curiously, the visitor today may still hear of Roman patricians: they are the bearers of aristocratic titles bestowed on their clans by the popes of past centuries.

At the hotel bar, in a restaurant, or at some party one may meet a prince or a count, a marchesa or a baronessa. Some of them belong to families that produced pontiffs, or were otherwise prominent and influential, commissioned important works from famous artists, waged private wars, equipped and manned galleys to fight the Turks, erected baroque palaces, squandered fabulous fortunes, married American heiresses, and after World War II often made a lot of money again by selling off their estates around the capital to real estate developers.

Some members of the Roman nobility are very wealthy, still live in palatial mansions that carry their names, own works of art that rate color plates in encyclopedias and coffee-table books, and are big landowners. Others are in business as banking executives, insurance brokers, couturiers or interior designers, lend their impressive names for the marketing of fragrances, or dabble in the movie industry or in public relations. Many titled Romans are in the Italian diplomatic service. Quite a few aristocrats, however, are impoverished, hard pressed to maintain appearances. Many once-princely palaces have been converted into apartment buildings or house corporate offices, law firms, or fashion ateliers.

ORNATE HALLS AND rooms in the immense Palazzo Taverna, 36 Via di Monte Giordano (telephone: 6833785), between the Piazza Navona and the Tiber, can be rented for social affairs—working lunches, wedding receptions, and gala dinners for a dozen to a thousand guests. Princess Stefania Aldobrandini will make the arrangements; she also runs her own catering business, Le Diner, 65A Via Donatello (telephone: 3203912).

The Palazzo Taverna, now named after a noble family from Milan that bought it at the end of the nineteenth century, was for hundreds of years a fortress of the powerful Orsini clan. It rises on a hill, the Monte Giordano, which Dante mentions in the eighteenth canto of the *Inferno*. The strategic elevation, which controlled the approaches to the Vatican from the east bank of the Tiber, owes its name to Giordano Orsini, a medieval nobleman.

The building complex is not particularly noteworthy for its architecture, but you might wander into its main courtyard to marvel at the dimensions of the structure and have a look at a graceful fountain. As do many other Roman palaces, the Palazzo Taverna today houses private and corporate tenants.

MOST OF THE barons, counts, marquesses, dukes, and princes, and their female counterparts, whom one may meet at embassy parties, at the golf club, or in night spots, are not Roman patricians at all. A few derive their titles from the Holy Roman emperors, and many others from the monarchies that coexisted on Italian soil before the nation was unified. The kingdoms of Piedmont-Sardinia and Naples-Sicily in particular were lavish in conferring titles. The kings of united Italy added another layer of aristocracy, naming their own marquesses, counts, and barons.

For several decades in the late nineteenth and early twentieth centuries, Rome's high society was split between the "black" aristocracy, which owed its titles to the popes, and the "white" aristocracy, whose members professed loyalty to the kings of unified Italy. The two factions boycotted each other's parties, considered intermarriage scandalous, and snubbed each other in other ways.

The Italian Republic, voted into being in a plebiscite in 1946, declared in a constitutional law that it did not recognize any aristocratic titles, but conceded that those acquired before the advent of the Fascist dictatorship in 1922 were to be regarded as part of their bearer's name. The titles are at any rate still widely used. Through friends you may get an invitation to a cocktail party that some prince is about to throw. The card in raised print will carry a little crown and his title, but he will have crossed out both with strokes of his pen. The message: For you, distinguished foreigner, I am just plain mister. Yet you will do well to address him as *principe* and his wife as *principessa*, as everybody else does.

Some of the countesses and so forth to whom the stranger may be introduced are spurious; they invented their own nobility, or their parents did. Since aristocratic titles don't legally exist in the Italian Republic, it is not punishable to claim them unduly.

There are a few places in Rome where one can always meet a number of genuine aristocrats, and maybe some dubious ones as well. One is the Circolo della Caccia (Hunting Club) in the 400-year-old Palazzo Borghese, 19 Largo Fontanella Borghese (telephone: 6878232). Another hangout for titled or wealthy Romans is the Nuovo Circolo degli Scacchi (New Chess Club), 4 Piazza San Lorenzo in Lucina (telephone: 6871342). Both clubs are centrally located, west of the Via del Corso.

Hunting and playing chess aren't conspicuous activities today at the two exclusive clubs. Diplomats entertain guests in their halls; there may be a little card game; deals are made; and there is plenty of gossiping. To have a look at the premises, you need an invitation by some member. Joining either of the two clubs is a more complicated matter.

Members of the Italian and European aristocracy will always be found at the headquarters of the Sovereign Military Order of Malta (telephone: 6798851), 68 Via Condotti. Nobility and diplomats also favor the oldest of Rome's golf clubs, the Acquasanta Club.

The relatively large number of people in the city who are addressed by aristocratic titles are much less of a caste than is, for instance, the British peerage. The families of Rome's princes and other patricians have lived for centuries in palaces that were surrounded by the dwellings of the little people, and have shared the robust tastes in food and drink as well as the earthy idiom of the *popolino*.

The authentic Roman aristocrat will not display a high degree of sophistication but rather will affect the low-class local vernacular known as *romanesco*, although he or she may also speak public-school English and elegant French.

While a Roman may still have trouble understanding the dialects of, say, Venice or Palermo, all Italians today are familiar with the plebeian *romanesco* thanks to Rome-made films and television shows.

Foreigners, although they may have studied Italian, will encounter difficulties in grasping the unrefined flavor of Roman talk, which seems to be increasingly larded with vulgarities. At any rate, local people will address visitors from abroad in standard Italian, and often will try on them whatever English they have learned in school or picked up otherwise.

As for titles, nonaristocratic Romans fancy them too. Waiters and the man who parks your car will call you *dottore*, whether you are a university graduate or not. If you are middle-aged or elderly and wear a clean shirt, you may be addressed as *commendatore*, an honorific title that the president of Italy confers on deserving citizens. Any member of the Italian Parliament is called *onorevole* (honorable); every ambassador, elder statesman, or Roman Catholic bishop is an *eccellenza* (your excellency). A physician is often a *professore*.

It is wise to address a police officer as *ispettore* (inspector). Unless you resort to the all-purpose *senta, scusi!* call the waiter or the man behind the espresso counter *capo* (chief), although their correct job description would be *cameriere* or *barista*.

Women, on the other hand, are often addressed as just *signora* (if married) or *signorina* (miss), even though they may have earned a Ph.D. Nevertheless, it doesn't hurt to call the woman in the white smock who sells you aspirin in a pharmacy, or any woman official who seems to have some decisional power, *dottoressa* (the female form of *dottore*).

10.

Beyond Sightseeing

MUSIC IN ROME

WHILE THE TREASURES of the visual arts in Rome seem inexhaustible, the city does not offer quite as much to the music lover.

The capital's opera house, the **Teatro dell'Opera**, has a glorious past, but performances there may be problematic today. Long gone are the nights at the Rome opera when fans of Giuseppe Verdi and Richard Wagner fought memorable battles on the floor and in the galleries, and when world-famous stars from Enrico Caruso to Maria Callas sang in glittering gala performances. Lately the reputation of the Teatro dell'Opera has suffered because of artistic, managerial, and labor troubles. Top singers and conductors have been reluctant to take on Rome engagements.

The opera house at Piazza Beniamino Gigli and 72 Via Firenze (telephone: 4881755), near the Stazione Termini, was built in 1880, enlarged during the 1920s, and dressed up with a new modern facade after World War II. The square in front of the opera house is named after Beniamino

Gigli, the celebrated tenor who was immensely popular in
Rome. The operatic season normally runs from December
to the beginning of June, but in some years it is shortened.
Performances are occasionally canceled or postponed because of strikes by the orchestra, the chorus, or the stage-
hands. A night at the Teatro dell'Opera is unpredictable:
you may be lucky and enjoy a brilliant show, or the singing
and acting may be poor and the orchestra sound ragged.

For information in English on Rome Opera programs,
call 67595725; for ticket reservations, 67595721. Tickets
may be bought two days before a scheduled performance
at the box office, 9:30 A.M. to 1 P.M. and 5 to 7 P.M. Often
there is a long line; instead of joining it, the visitor with
limited time might better turn to a travel agency or hotel
concierge.

The Teatro dell'Opera has an open-air season in the
Baths of Caracalla, Viale delle Terme di Caracalla (telephone: 5758300), in July and August. The lavishly staged
performances amid the hulking ruins of the ancient thermae are a beloved feature of the Roman summer. Verdi's
Aïda, with armies of extras in Egyptian and Ethiopian
costumes and live horses on the giant stage, is the all-time
favorite.

A loudspeaker system enables the operagoers even in
the last rows of the vast audience to hear the singing and
the music, although jet noise from an airliner in a holding
pattern in the starry Roman sky may occasionally drown
out the lyrical drama. Musical purists sneer, but the action
on the stage, the costumed chorus, the dramatic voices,
the orchestra, and the remarkable lighting effects conjure
up an enchanting experience.

Rome's summer weather is normally stable until at least
mid-August, and the heat of the day will have abated,
thanks to the *ponentino*, by the time the opera in the Baths

of Caracalla starts at 9 P.M. During the last act, close to midnight, you will be glad you brought a woolen scarf or jacket with you. Plenty of taxis and public buses are waiting to take operagoers home. Tickets can be bought in travel bureaus or hotels.

Every year the Teatro dell'Opera will offer an occasional evening of ballet, with its own troupe performing. Roman ballet fans may witness more exciting dancing when a famous foreign company on an Italian tour visits the capital.

ROME HAS HAD no first-rate concert hall since 1936, when the Augusteo, which had splendid acoustics, was demolished to free the remains of the Mausoleum of Augustus of superstructures. In 1991, after long public discussions, a site for a new concert hall was selected in the city's north near the Milvian Bridge. Until it is ready, the Orchestra of the Academy of Santa Cecilia and other orchestras will continue to perform in one of two halls, both with questionable acoustics: the **Santa Cecilia Auditorium**, 4 Via della Conciliazione (telephone: 6541044), in a Vatican-owned building near St. Peter's; and the **Auditorium Foro Italico**, Piazza Lauro de Bosis (telephone: 865625), near the Olympic Stadium, which is used mainly by the Italian state broadcasting system (RAI).

Concert program changes are frequent. Watch Rome's daily newspapers for announcements of concerts and indications of where tickets can be bought, or request information from Ente Provinciale per il Turismo di Roma, 5 Via Parigi (telephone: 4883748), near the Grand Hotel.

Locally, and more frequently, visiting orchestras, choirs, and soloists can be heard (normally free of charge) in one of Rome's many churches. The offerings are not always religious works, though the ecclesiastical authorities have lately expressed displeasure about the performance of "profane" music in sacred buildings. There is usually not much publicity for church concerts; look for posters near the entrance doors of individual churches. The Vatican's Sistine Choir sings in St. Peter's during pontifical functions, such as canonizations, beatifications, and papal high masses.

ROME HAS A thriving jazz, pop, and rock scene. The Testaccio section, now the habitat of a cultural avant-garde, has lately become its center.

Live music can be heard at **Caffè Latino**, 96 Via di Monte Testaccio (telephone: 5744020); **Caruso Caffè Concerto**, 36 Via di Monte Testaccio (telephone: 5747720), and several other nearby places. For listings, consult the *Trova Roma* supplement of the newspaper *La Repubblica* every Thursday.

International pop, rock, and rap stars or groups on tour often perform in the Sport Palace (Palazzo dello Sport) in the EUR district.

THEATERS

The Italian capital is not as famous for its theater as is, for instance, London. Rome's legitimate stage may attract visitors who have learned at least some Italian and want to test themselves as to how much they understand of a Shakespeare production in that language or a Pirandello play in the original version.

Scan the Rome newspapers for what is playing at the

old **Teatro Argentina**, Largo di Torre Argentina (telephone: 6544601) or the nearby **Teatro Valle**, 23A Via Teatro Valle (telephone: 6543794), both close to the Pantheon; or the **Teatro Eliseo**, 183E Via Nazionale (telephone: 4882114) and its intimate annex, the **Piccolo Eliseo** (telephone: 4885095), both housed in a building near the Quirinal Palace.

Most of the time, except at the height of summer, the newspapers will list the programs of a dozen or so small or experimental stages in various parts of the city.

Neapolitan farce is occasionally offered by one of the Roman theaters, particularly the vernacular classics by Eduardo de Filippo. To savor the fun, familiarity with the rich idiom of Italy's third city (after Rome and Milan) is indispensable.

Repeated attempts to transplant Broadway-type musicals to Rome have so far met with little success. Local audiences instead love extravagantly produced revues with beautiful women, plenty of racy double entendres, and topical jokes aimed at political figures and other people in the news. The principal place for such music-hall entertainment is the **Teatro Sistina**, 129 Via Sistina (telephone: 4826841), near the Spanish Stairs.

The note *"riposo"* (rest) often found after the name of a theater in the newspaper listings means that no performance is scheduled.

CINEMAS AND MOVIEMAKING

Foreign films shown in Rome's movie houses are almost always dubbed in Italian; local cinemagoers hate subtitles. New American, British, Canadian, and Australian films are regularly screened in their original language only in one small theater on a hard-to-find, twisted and narrow street in the Trastevere section, near the Piazza di Santa Maria in Trastevere: the **Pasquino**, 19 Vicolo del Piede (telephone: 5803622). The latest English-language releases reach the Pasquino fairly quickly, often before the Italian-dubbed versions are shown in the other local movie theaters. On summer evenings after dark, the movable roof of the low-slung building of the Pasquino opens over an audience in which many know one another; it's like an informal club of the city's English-speaking expatriates under Rome's starry sky.

A few other movie houses in Rome, hard pressed by the competition from the little home screen, have lately become *cinema a luci rosse* (red-light cinemas), specializing in hard-core porn.

The heady years when Rome was "Hollywood on the Tiber," and teen-aged Sophia Loren made her film debut as an extra in a *Quo Vadis?* remake in the Cinecittà studios are only a memory. Cinecittà (Cinema City), on Rome's southeastern outskirts 6 miles (10 kilometers) from the center, was built during the last years before World War II because Mussolini and his sons were interested in movie production. After the roaring 1950s and 1960s it has become much quieter in the vast studios, but projects are still in the works most of the time. Italian and foreign producers keep renting the facilities and hiring their expert staff for movie, television, and publicity projects.

The entrance to the Cinecittà complex is at 1055 Via Tuscolana (telephone: 722841) at the Cinecittà stop of the subway's Line A. There are no regular studio tours, but it isn't hard to gain admission to Cinecittà if you know somebody who is somehow connected with moviemaking—quite a few Romans and foreign residents are.

NIGHT LIFE

Long, drawn-out dinners, late movies, jazz clubs, and gossiping or flirting in the piazzas and on the terraces of private apartments take care of much of Rome's night life. Like any international hub, Rome too has a galaxy of night spots catering mainly to foreigners. They cluster around the Via Veneto and the Piazza Barberini, and few Romans care to be fleeced in them. Every now and then, when a tourist complains to the police that he was charged $300 for a couple of drinks, one of the places will be closed for some time, and the management may be fined.

Young Romans populate the discotheques around town and on the outskirts. Popular ones are **Piper '90**, 9 Via Tagliamento (telephone: 8414459); **Open Gate**, 4 Via San Nicola da Tolentino (telephone: 4824464), near the Via Veneto; and **Uonna Club**, 871 Via Cassia (telephone: 3662837), in the far northwest of the city.

Swinging politicians, media personalities, aristocrats, and other well-to-do people can be seen in a number of piano bars. In addition to live entertainment some of these also offer restaurant service until after midnight: **Tartarughino** (Little Turtle), 1 Via della Scrofa (telephone: 6786037), central, near the Tiber; **Taverna Caffè degli Specchi**, 5 Via degli Specchi (telephone: 6861566), near the Largo di Torre Argentina; and **Arcadia**, 73 Via G. G. Belli (telephone: 3213290), near the Castel Sant'Angelo.

THE ROMAN YEAR

The traditional celebrations and rituals of the Roman calendar provide plenty of entertainment for residents and visitors; urban and even rural folklore lingers in the city.

For New Year's Eve many restaurants organize parties
with Pantagruelian supper menus for which tables have to
be reserved well in advance. The all-inclusive fee per person may run to the equivalent of $300.

Rome, like other Italian cities (especially Naples),
greets the new year with an amazing barrage of fireworks.
The authorities warn every December against what they
regularly condemn as the "barbarous custom" of setting
off firecrackers and launching rockets from rooftops, balconies, and windows, but to no avail. Each year a number
of persons get injured, if not killed, by inexpert handling of
pyrotechnic articles. Though throwing damaged crockery
and old pots and pans out of apartment windows at midnight on New Year's Eve has been largely abandoned, it
is still imprudent to be in the streets around that hour. Cars
parked at the curbside are often damaged by objects tossed
out of windows on New Year's Eve.

The church feast of Epiphany, January 6, is again a
legal holiday in Rome after attempts to abolish it met with
general resistance. The evening of that day marks the cli-
max and end of a toy fair in Piazza Navona.

The Roman carnival, beginning at Epiphany and end-
ing the day before Ash Wednesday, is now a far cry from
the wild revelry in the Corso that Goethe, Dickens, and
other writers of the eighteenth and early nineteenth centuries described. Children dress up in fancy costumes and
wear masks, roaming major streets and throwing confetti
at one another and on grownups. Lately a less harmless
twist of aerosol spraying has developed. Many parties are
held in private homes during the carnival period.

Saint Joseph's Day, March 19, brings fritters and cream
puffs, which the Romans call *bignè* (bin-YAIH), to the
city's pastry shops. Around the parish church of St. Joseph,
4B Via B. Telesio, in the popular Trionfale section north

of the Vatican, street vendors offer *fritelle* (fritters), and a religious procession is held.

Holy Week before Easter attracts thousands of visitors from the Italian provinces and abroad, and in effect opens the tourist season. The pope is busy performing the time-honored rites: He washes the feet of twelve men, symbolizing the apostles, in the Lateran Basilica or some other church on Maundy Thursday, and carries a wooden cross during a Stations of the Cross ceremony staged between the Palatine and the Colosseum on the evening of Good Friday. He celebrates Easter Mass in St. Peter's and at the end appears on the church's outer loggia to bless the crowd in St. Peter's Square.

The Monday after Easter, known as *Pasquetta* (Little Easter), is a legal holiday in Italy. To Romans it is traditionally a day for outings and picnics *fuori porta* (outside the city gates).

The Rome International Horse Show at the end of April and the beginning of May is held in the Piazza di Siena of the Villa Borghese gardens and is a cosmopolitan society event.

The church feast of Saint John the Baptist on June 24 is celebrated in the popular district around the Lateran, the San Giovanni section, with fireworks and outdoor conviviality. The many trattorie in the lower-middle-class neighborhood put extra tables out on the sidewalks and serve garlicky snails (*lumache*) and Frascati wine.

The Festa de Noantri starts in the Trastevere section on the feast day of Our Lady of Mount Carmel, July 16, and continues until the end of the month as a self-celebration of the populace along the right bank of the Tiber.

Rome's midsummer doldrums begin long before Ferragosto, August 15, which the Roman Catholic Church celebrates as the feast of the Virgin Mary's Assumption, and continue to the first half of September. During this time, foreigners will seem to have taken over the Italian capital.

Traffic in the city becomes hectic again after the middle of September, when school starts and most Roman families have drifted back home from their vacations. There are no particular celebrations during the *ottobrate*—just enjoy the ripe glory of Rome's October weeks.

December 8, the religious feast of the Immaculate Conception, is a legal holiday in Rome. The pope prays at the column carrying the statue of the Virgin Mary in the Spanish Square.

Weeks before Christmas, bagpipers dressed up as shepherds from the wild Abruzzi Mountains—although they may actually be jobless barbers or ice cream vendors from the suburbs—turn up in the Via dei Condotti and other shopping streets of the center. They always play the same plangent Yuletide tune and hold up their rustic hats for handouts.

The toy fair in the Piazza Navona starts several days before Christmas. On Christmas Eve all stores and virtually all restaurants close early. The pope usually celebrates midnight mass in St. Peter's, but many Romans attend the midnight rite in a church closer to their homes or in the Church of Santa Maria in Aracoeli on Capitol Hill. On Christmas Day the pope says another mass in St. Peter's and blesses the people in St. Peter's Square, where a tall Christmas tree from the Alps and a crèche with life-size figures will have been erected a few days earlier.

Many Romans visit various churches to see other crèches. Some of these are artistic, with hand-carved wooden figures that may have come from Naples, whereas others move mechanically or electronically when a coin is inserted in a slot.

December 26, the feast of Saint Stephen, is a legal

holiday in Italy and a day of rest in Rome when people recuperate from their Christmas celebrations and gather strength for the New Year's Eve merrymaking. Museums and other collections are closed December 24–25 and on New Year's Day.

SOCCER

A pervasive element in Roman folkways is soccer fever, or *tifo* (typhus). It seems to grip the entire city when an important game is played. The Olympic Stadium will be seething with *tifosi* (soccer fans—literally, "typhus patients"), and the city's streets and squares will be nearly empty for a couple of hours as hundreds of thousands watch the game on television or follow it on the radio.

Strong police forces guard the Olympic Stadium and the approaches to it long before, during, and after soccer matches, but supporters of the rival teams may clash all the same. (Even in antiquity opposing factions of the populace attending the races in the circus often caused riots.)

A victory by one of the two leading Roman soccer clubs—the Roma and the Lazio—or of the national soccer team in an international match sets off tumultuous celebrations. Honking cars with delirious fans waving the purple-and-yellow banners of the Roma or the blue-and-white ones of the Lazio careen in streets and piazzas, disrupting traffic for hours.

Big-league or international soccer games take place in the Olympic Stadium on Sunday afternoons during the championship season from September to June, and often also on Wednesday night.

Tickets for soccer games can be purchased at the headquarters of the playing clubs: Società Roma, 7 Via del

Circo Massimo (telephone: 5781441); and Società Lazio, 3 Via Col di Lana (telephone: 385141); or at the Olympic Stadium before the match. Travel agencies and hotel concierges can also get tickets.

Any visitor to Rome who understands enough Italian to figure out what people in espresso bars or barbershops talk about will realize that an astonishing number of conversations are about soccer (*calcio*) and about the soccer pools (*totocalcio*), which are in effect a lottery linked with the national spectator sport.

EXERCISE

Although most Romans—at least the male half of the population—dote on professional soccer, a growing part of the citizenry also wants to do more for their individual fitness than tossing plastic bottles onto the field after a disappointing game.

Jogging

Jogging has caught on especially quickly in Rome; foreigners setting out from their hotel in a sweatsuit or in shorts, wearing running shoes, no longer draw stares.

Some Romans jog along the Tiber embankments despite heavy motor traffic and the resulting foul air on either side of the river. Much better is one of the city's vast parks.

The Villa Borghese gardens at the upper end of the Via Veneto will be handy for many visitors because they are close to most hotels and pensions.

Another, much larger, park favored by resident joggers is the Villa Doria Pamphilj on the western outskirts. It is attractive, with its old pines and plenty of greenery, and is open from dawn to sunset. To reach it one needs a car, or takes the No. 26 bus from Largo di Torre Argentina and walks from its last stop for a few minutes to the park's entrance.

Tennis

Tennis too is gaining more popularity. Many Roman parents now consider practice of the game a part of their children's education. In addition to several hotels with tennis courts (see pages 35–42), some tennis clubs rent courts to visitors who are not members, or arrange for special guest memberships. Here are some that are not too distant from the city center:

Union Sportiva Flaminio, 6 Lungotevere Salvo d'Acquisto (telephone: 3231368), near the Milvian Bridge.

Tennis Club Nomentana, 882 Via Nomentana (telephone: 8274385), on the northeastern outskirts.

Circolo Tennis EUR, 35 Via dell'Artigianato (telephone: 5924639), in the EUR district.

For other options, inquire at Federazione Italiana Tennis, 70 Viale Tiziano (telephone: 3233807), or scan the listings under *Impianti Sportivi e Ricreativi* in the Rome Yellow Pages.

Swimming

The large outdoor pool of the Cavalieri Hilton Hotel, 101 Via Cadlolo (telephone: 31511), is accessible also to persons who are not hotel guests, but the price of admission is relatively high. Here are a few other convenient swimming pools:

Foro Italico (telephone: 393625), in the sports complex near the Olympic Stadium, with outdoor and covered pools. They are at times closed to guests because of training or competitions.

Roman Sports Center, 33 Viale del Galoppatoio (telephone: 3601667), in the Villa Borghese gardens.

Piscina delle Rose, 20 Viale America (telephone: 5926717), in the EUR district.

Oasi di Pace, 2 Via degli Eugenii (telephone: 7184550), off the Ancient Appian Way.

Golf

As elsewhere on the European continent, golf is advancing in Italy, although it is still regarded as elitist. The number of golf clubs in and around Rome has lately increased; they all extend guest privileges to members of other golf clubs who show proof of a handicap. Greens fees range from $25 to $50 at the following:

Circolo del Golf Roma, 3 Via Acquasanta (telephone: 7803407), between the ancient and new Appian ways; the oldest and most prestigious of the Roman golf courses. From the clubhouse and the rolling terrain the panorama embraces ruined Roman aqueducts and the hillside to the southeast. Founded in 1903, the Acquasanta (Holy Water) club counts aristocrats, diplomats, business executives, and the occasional churchman from English-speaking countries among its members. Mussolini's son-in-law, Count Galeazzo Ciano, favored the Acquasanta Club for his notorious dalliances.

Olgiata Golf Club, 15 Largo Olgiata (telephone: 3789141), is near a high-class residential development on the Via Cassia (National Highway No. 2), on the city's northern outskirts.

Country Club Castelgandolfo, 13 Via di Santo Spirito (telephone: 9312301), at Castelgandolfo in the Castelli Romani hills.

Parco dei Medici, km 4.5 Autostrada Roma-Fiumicino (telephone: 6553477), off the motor road to the Fiumicino Airport, near the Holiday Inn-EUR-Parco dei Medici Hotel.

Fioranello, Viale della Repubblica, Santa Maria delle Mole (telephone: 7138291), off the New Appian Way (National Highway No. 7), 10.6 miles (17 kilometers) from the city center.

Horseback Riding

During the late nineteenth and early twentieth century members of the Roman nobility, imitating the British gentry, used to ride with hounds in the Campagna Romana. While the aristocratic foxhunts in the plains around the Italian capital are a thing of the past, horse riding enjoys a renewed and growing popularity. Following is a list of riding schools and clubs of particular convenience to visitors:

Villa Borghese Sport Club, 23 Viale del Galoppatoio (telephone: 3606797), near the Via Veneto.

Rome Pony Club, 43 Via dei Campi Sportivi (telephone: 8088706), near the left bank of the Tiber in the city's north.

Circolo Ippico Olgiata, 15 Largo Olgiata (telephone: 3788043).

Centro Equestre Cinque Stelle, 191 Via Casal Selce (telephone: 6968109), off the Via Aurelia (National Highway
No. 1) after the Grande Raccordo Anulare beltway.

For information on other riding establishments, contact
the Federazione Italiana di Sport Equestri, 70 Viale Tiziano
(telephone: 3960626).

Horse races are held mostly on weekends, at the Capan-
nelle Racetrack, 1255 Via Appia Nuova (telephone:
7183143), 7 miles (about 11 kilometers) southeast of the
city center. To reach this turn-of-the-century equestrian
complex by public transport, take the subway's Line A to
its Colli Albani stop and proceed by No. 664 bus.

EMERGENCIES

Police Forces

The variety of police personnel and their uniforms astound
many first-time visitors to Italy. In Rome the guardians of
law and order are, above all, either carabinieri or state
police. The carabinieri, identifiable by the broad red stripes
along their dark blue uniform trousers, belong to an all-
male corps of the Italian army that carries out many police
functions. The state police, men and women in uniforms
of a lighter blue than those of the carabinieri, also enforce
the law. During parades or demonstrations members of the
two police organizations can be seen carrying out crowd
control side by side.

The men in gray-green uniforms with yellow collar
facings who perform customs control at the airport belong
to the finance guard, a fiscal police force that also operates
in the city; they may carry out spot checks in plain clothes.

The finance guard primarily enforces economic and currency regulations but is occasionally entrusted with other police work.

The men and women of the Roman municipal police, clad during the cold months in black uniforms and during summer in smart white tunics, try to regulate the daunting traffic. They fine undisciplined motorists, often arrive first on the scene of an accident, patrol outdoor markets, and handle administrative chores as well.

Thus the Italian capital is policed by four different forces that often act in parallel ways and are occasionally competitive.

In an emergency—an accident or a crime—one has the option to call the emergency phone number of the carabinieri (112), that of the state police (113), or an all-purpose number (115). The dispatcher will, if necessary, send an ambulance or alert the fire department.

Medical Emergencies

Medical emergency (*pronto soccorso*) and blood bank services for transfusions function around the clock in a number of major hospitals. Among them are:

Rome American Hospital, 69 Via Emilio Longoni (telephone: 25671), in the Prenestina section on the city's eastern outskirts. This modern 150-bed institution with an English-speaking staff is affiliated with the Hospital Corporation of America.

Policlinico, Viale del Policlinico (telephone: 4469909), near the Porta Pia.

Santo Spirito, 1 Lungotevere in Sassia (telephone: 6838901), near the Vatican.

San Camillo, 87 Circonvallazione Gianicolense (telephone: 58701), on the western outskirts.

San Giovanni, 8 Via Amba Aradam (telephone: 77051), near the Lateran.

Fatebenefratelli, 2 Piazza Fatebenefratelli, on the Tiber Island (telephone: 5873299).

Policlinico Gemelli, 8 Largo A. Gemelli (telephone: 30151), on a hill on the northwestern outskirts.

English-speaking residents also favor the Salvator Mundi International Hospital, 67–77 Viale delle Mura Gianicolensi (telephone: 586041), on the Janiculum, although it lacks medical emergency services. The facility has been operated since the end of World War II by the Salvatorian Sisters, a far-flung Roman Catholic order whose general house (headquarters) adjoins the hospital in a garden.

Often the person on duty in an all-night pharmacy, who must be a university graduate, will be able to advise or help you in a minor medical emergency. Don't be put off if the pharmacist speaks, takes cash, and hands out medicines through a small opening in the strong shutters: it's a precaution against robbers and drug addicts who haunt night pharmacies. Local newspapers list those pharmacies that, on a rotating basis, stay open after normal business hours and during the night. Pharmacies that are closed are obliged by law to display near their entrance doors a list of the nearest after-hours and all-night stores.

Reporting Theft or Loss

If you lose your passport or an important object, or are the victim of a robbery or another crime, you should report the fact to the carabinieri or the state police. The chances are not too good that you will eventually recover your property, but you will need a copy of the report if you claim indemnification from an insurance company or enter your loss as a deduction on your income tax return. You will also have to produce a copy of the report for the replacement of passports, credit cards, traveler's checks, and airline tickets. If your driver's license has been lost or stolen you may temporarily use the police report as a substitute.

The report to the carabinieri or the state police is known as a *denuncia*. Go to the nearest station of either law enforcement agency, preferably between 9 A.M. and 1 P.M. when it will be fully staffed, taking with you whatever identification you still may have and legal stationery for the copy of your report. The double sheet of legal stationery, known as *carta bollata* (stamped paper), carrying the seal of the fiscal authority, is on sale at any tobacconist's. (Such shops are marked by signs with a large black or white *T*.) Don't be surprised if the duty officer at the carabinieri or state police station questions you as if *you* were a suspect.

Rome's Office of Lost Property (*Ufficio Oggetti Smarriti*) is at 1 Via Nicolo Bettoni (telephone: 5816040) in the Trastevere section. The municipal streetcar-and-bus system, ATAC, has a lost-and-found office at 65 Via Volturno (telephone: 46951) near the Stazione Termini. The lost and found for the subway and ACOTRAL bus system (see page 229) is at 131 Via Ostiense (telephone: 57531), near the Porta San Paolo; that for the State Railways is at the Stazione Termini (telephone: 4669, ext. 6682).

Personal Safety

Like other European cities, Rome has lately experienced an increase in street crime. Tourists and persons easily recognizable as foreigners are prime marks for pickpockets, purse snatchers, muggers, and con artists. Visitors should leave their passports and valuables at their hotel, possibly depositing them with the management for safekeeping. Take only as much money with you on strolls and sightseeing trips as you think you will need, and don't wear showy jewelry.

Be particularly watchful on public transport. Pickpockets often operate in pairs: one jostles you as the other is getting hold of your wallet; while a young woman on a crowded bus engages the attention of a foreign male, the bored-looking elderly gentleman who ostensibly is watching the street scene through a window has one hand in the stranger's back pocket. In warm weather quite a few tourists who wear no jackets can be seen with their passports conspicuous in their bulging shirt or trouser pockets—an invitation to thieves.

Be on your guard especially when leaving a bank or money exchange with a sizable sum. Robbers who have been watching may be following you on foot or a motorscooter, waiting for their best chance to pounce. If a motorized purse snatcher grabs your shoulder-strap bag or camera, it's dangerous to try to hold on to it at any price. Robbery victims are often thrown to the ground and dragged along on the sidewalk, suffering injuries.

If a pack of gypsy children closes in on you, holding pieces of cardboard or a newspaper in your face, they will try to empty your pockets or snatch your bag or camera. Don't be shy about pushing or even kicking them away and shouting for help. The police say that kids who are too young to be prosecuted are trained by their elders to prey on tourists.

While you are enjoying your dinner at the outdoor table of some restaurant, a furtive hand may lift your handbag that you have put on an empty chair next to you.

Thieves disguised as pious friars or nuns have been known to steal purses placed on a church pew.

At the Stazione Termini a suitcase that a traveler has put on the floor briefly while buying a newspaper may vanish.

If you pay for the entrance ticket to a museum or buy a souvenir from a street vendor, always count your change.

Young women tourists ought to be careful about embarking on what may look like the start of a romantic adventure. That pair of flirtatious, good-looking men in a fancy car who offer to show you the sights of Rome may not be as harmlessly playful as they seem. Every summer the police have to investigate complaints by foreign women that they were molested or raped by supposed Roman Romeos—sometimes also robbed in the bargain.

Unescorted women should also shun certain neighborhoods at night to avoid being mistaken for prostitutes. Such areas are the environs of the Stazione Termini, Via Veneto, the Villa Borghese gardens, the Tiber embankments (except at the very center of the old town), Viale Tiziano in the Flaminio section, the approaches to the Colosseum, the vicinity of the Baths of Caracalla, and the entire EUR district.

Caution is also advisable for male visitors in the abovementioned neighborhoods at night. Turf wars among prostitutes, transvestites, and other night people are frequent.

SERVICES

Like most museums in Rome, many administrative agencies, police stations, and post offices close at 1 or 2 P.M. for the day. The central post office and the telephone office

next door, both on the Piazza San Silvestro off the Via del
Corso, are open 8 A.M. to 9 P.M. Monday to Friday, 8 A.M.
to noon on Saturday. A few major outlying post offices
also have afternoon service. Banks may or may not reopen
for an hour or ninety minutes in the afternoon. Money
exchanges have longer office hours than banks, but their
commissions are usually higher. It pays to convert one's
foreign currency into lire at a legitimate bank during the
morning hours, Monday to Friday. Cash machines outside
banks—if you can access them at all—are often out of
order or out of funds. Watch out for who may be around
while you get money from the machine.

Following is a random list of services that a visitor to
Rome may require:

Alcoholics Anonymous. Information in English:
6780320. English-language meetings are held at the
churches of San Silvestro, 1 Piazza San Silvestro, adjoining
the central post office; St. Paul's Within the Walls, 58 Via
Napoli; and St. Andrew's, 7 Via Venti Settembre on various days and at various times.

Babysitters. Hotel concierges can often recommend experienced persons. Inquire at the churches with English-
language services (see page 194), or look at the bulletin
board at Lion Bookshop, 181 Via del Babuino/3 Via della
Fontanella. The Rome Yellow Pages have listings under
Baby Sitters and *Nidi d'Infanzia*, including English-language
services.

Dentists. Ask for the American Consulate's list of recommended English-speaking practitioners.

Lawyers. The American Consulate has a list of attorneys
who speak English and are familiar with foreign legal
systems.

Physicians. English-speaking general practitioners and specialists examine and treat outpatients at the Rome American Hospital and Salvator Mundi International Hospital (see pages 219–20). The American Consulate has a list of English-speaking doctors.

Toilets. Outside the airports and the railroad terminals (Stazione Termini and suburban stations) public toilets, especially for women, are scarce in Rome. Where the facilities exist (for instance, in the Spanish Square and in the Piazza San Silvestro, in front of the central post office), they are often closed. The Vatican, which is used to handling large crowds, is well equipped with restroom facilities on either side of St. Peter's Square, at the right side of the portico of St. Peter's Basilica, and in the Vatican Museums.

All restaurants and espresso bars are by law obliged to maintain public toilets, but such laws aren't always practicable, and managements tend to restrict their facilities to patrons. When asking where the facilities are, say *"Per favore, dove è il bagno?"* (Pehr fa-VOH-ray DOH-vayh ayh il BAHN-yoh?).

A small fee is required for use of the restrooms in the two surviving *alberghi diurni* (day hotels) in the city. These establishments also offer showers, barber and hairdresser services, shoeshine, and other amenities. One *albergo diurno* is at the Stazione Termini, lower level (it also has a few rooms where the weary traveler can take a nap); the other one is at 136 Via Cola di Rienzo, the main shopping street in the Prati section.

Tourist Information. Brochures and other materials on Rome and environs, plus information on forthcoming events, can be had for the asking from Ente Provinciale per il Turismo (EPT), 5 Via Parigi (telephone: 4881851), near the Grand Hotel; branch offices are at Fiumicino Airport and Stazione Termini. Many nations, including all of Italy's neighbors, maintain tourist information offices in Rome. Look them up in the Rome Yellow Pages under *Enti Turistici*.

Travel Agencies. A great number of these operate in the Italian capital, and some act also as ticket agents for the State Railways. Travel agencies are listed in the Rome Yellow Pages under *Agenzie Viaggi e Turismo*.

United Service Organization (USO), 2 Via della Conciliazione (telephone: 6864232), near St. Peter's Square, assists U.S. armed services members and their families, offering a lounge, showers, American newspapers, and magazines; it also arranges tours and visits to the Vatican.

SHOPPING

Rome's historical core is also the city's main shopping area, although savvy residents will favor stores in outlying sections for many of their purchases because prices are often lower there. Some of the most elegant shops and boutiques are on the Via dei Condotti and the parallel streets to the south, Via Borgognona and Via Frattina. The famous fashion houses cluster around the Spanish Square, particularly in the Via Gregoriana and Via Sistina.

For shoes, leatherware, and casual wear, try Via del Corso and, at a right angle to it, Via del Tritone. A great variety of merchandise at reasonable prices will be found in stores along the Via Nazionale and Corso Vittorio Emanuele II.

Rome's biggest department store, La Rinascente, Piazza Fiume (telephone: 8841231), is east of the Villa Borghese gardens, not too far from the upper end of Via Veneto. Another, older, La Rinascente store at the corner of Via del Corso and Via del Tritone (telephone: 6797691) now sells mainly apparel.

The first few blocks of the Via Salaria, which starts at Piazza Fiume, are also a good shopping area. So are the broad, straight Via Cola di Rienzo in the Prati section; the Via Ottaviano, a few blocks north of the Vatican (Ottaviano terminal of the subway's Line A); and the nearby Via Candia.

The main neighborhoods for art and antiques shops are the Via del Babuino and Via dei Coronari, and nearby streets and squares. Browse in the little bookshops in a wide radius around the Pantheon for old prints. Outdoor stands display ancient books and prints on weekdays in the Piazza Borghese outside the palace of the same name.

For fun or to pick up some oddity, a trip to Rome's flea market may be a diversion on a slow Sunday morning. It is held along the Lungotevere Portuense on the right Tiber embankment south of the Porta Portese, a gateway from the baroque era, and is known as the Porta Portese market. During the week it is a place for buying car and bicycle tires and spare parts. On Sundays scores of stands offer scratchy records with the voice of Enrico Caruso, blue jeans and other garments with phony (and usually misspelled) American labels, new Japanese cameras, fake Swiss watches, Russian icons, mountain bikes, Ethiopian silver coins, and countless other items. Hard bargaining is the rule at the Porta Portese market, which always attracts Romans from faraway parts of the city. City Hall would like to transfer the flea market to some area on the eastern outskirts, but the vendors and habitués are reluctant to leave the Porta Portese neighborhood, so close to the Trastevere section and the city center.

It is also good shopping policy to bargain in apparel and appliance stores anywhere in Rome. Ask, *"Mi fa lo sconto?"* (Do you give me a discount?) At worst the salesperson may point to a sign reading *Prezzi Fissi* (Fixed Prices), but often you will get a few thousand lire knocked off the initial price.

Best buys in Rome are shoes and leatherware, as well as casual clothing. Men's dress shirts, neckties, and suits are generally overpriced, as is much of the jewelry. Famous Italian designer labels can often be had cheaper in department stores and shopping malls in the United States than in and around the Via Condotti in Rome. Attractive ceramics made in various parts of Italy are excellent souvenirs if properly packaged.

If you purchase a work of art, insist on getting an invoice. You may also need an export license, which the seller should obtain. Hands off presumed Etruscan vases, Roman sculptures, or other antiquities! They will almost always be fakes; if they are not, they will be considered a part of Italy's artistic-cultural patrimony and cannot legally be taken out of the country unless covered by a hard-to-get special permit from the government's Ministry of Cultural Affairs.

11.

Side Trips

LOCAL AND INTERNATIONAL travel organizations conduct convenient package excursions by coach from Rome to places of interest in the immediate environs as well as to Pompeii (possibly with a boat trip to the Isle of Capri), the hill towns of Umbria and Tuscany, and other destinations. Visitors who would rather fend for themselves while sparing time from sightseeing in Rome should not find it difficult to undertake some sortie on their own and thus learn a little more about the country and the people than will the passengers on a tour bus.

Virtually all the towns and major villages around Rome can be reached by railroad or by the public coaches of the Latium Transport Consortium (ACOTRAL). For schedule and fare information, call 5915551. The blue ACOTRAL "extraurban buses" leave from various terminal areas in Rome, which are indicated case by case in the following pages.

ACOTRAL bus lines to the Alban Hills (see page 239) and other destinations converge at a well-functioning terminal adjoining the last stop (Anagnina) of the subway's

Line A on Rome's southeastern outskirts. In a sunken patio of the bus terminal an old blue car of the long-defunct tramway that plied between Rome and Fiuggi, a spa 51 miles (82 kilometers) to the southeast, sits on a length of track. The antique is a reminder of bygone days when much of the traffic between the capital and the southeastern hills was by rail.

If you want to explore the surroundings of the Italian capital by rented car, do it preferably on a weekday. Beginning in the afternoon hours on Sundays thousands of Romans in their cars scramble back home from their weekend outings, causing traffic jams at the approaches to the city.

This guidebook's suggestions for side trips from Rome that can be pleasantly made in half a day or a day are by no means exhaustive. For other possible visits to the hinterlands of the Italian capital—to attractive spots like Anzio, Orvieto, Perugia, Tarquinia, Viterbo, and others—see my book *Cento Città: A Guide to the "Hundred Cities and Towns" of Italy*.

OSTIA ANTICA

A half-day's outing is barely sufficient for a visit to the impressive remains of ancient Rome's seaport and biggest suburb, Ostia. The ruins convey a vivid idea of how workers and the middle classes lived two thousand years ago. It is better not to be rushed and to combine the trip with a picnic in the extensive archeological park of Ostia Antica.

A cosmopolitan population of up to eighty thousand had their homes near their jobs in ancient Ostia, where the seashore and the mouths of the Tiber delta were close by. (*Ostia* is Latin for "mouths.") There were boat builders, dockers, sailors of the merchant fleet and of the imperial navy, foreign seamen and shipping agents, traders, warehouse personnel, customs and supply officials, and laborers.

Old Ostia was both an important naval base and an emporium through which Rome imported grain from Sicily and Egypt as well as many other provisions from around the Mediterranean. Since then the Tiber has silted up: today the coastline is more than 1.5 miles (2.5 kilometers) distant, and the principal mouth of the Tiber is more than 3 miles (5 kilometers) southwest of Ostia Antica.

The ancient sea and river port can be reached by rail in thirty to forty-five minutes. Take the subway's Line B to the Magliana stop, changing there to the Rome-Ostia railroad; its trains run at thirty-minute intervals. Get out at the Ostia Antica station, which is close to the entrance of the archeological park. If you prefer to travel by boat, *acquabus* riverboats leave from the Lungotevere Ripa (on the right bank of the Tiber, in the southern part of the Trastevere section) and the Marconi Bridge (near St. Paul's Outside the Walls) to Ostia Antica and back. A special gate of the archeological park is opened whenever an *acquabus* boat arrives at the nearby landing stage. For schedules, call 6869068. By car, take the Via del Mare from the Porta San Paolo to the Ostia Antica turnoff. Parking lots are near the ticket office of the archeological park and near the museum.

The excavation area of Ostia Antica (telephone: 5650022) is open from 9 A.M. to an hour before sunset daily; its museum from 9 A.M. to 1 P.M. daily. The entrance ticket to the archeological park entitles one to visit the museum.

With its well-preserved ruins amid cypresses and pines, Ostia Antica is a haunting archeological site. It is silent and restful, although in its day the seaport town must have been a bustling, rackety place.

Visitors who don't arrive by boat enter the archeological area from the former town's east side and main gateway, the Porta Romana (Roman Gate). A huge statue of Minerva the Victorious from the first century A.D., which probably once decorated the principal gate, stands on a square to the left. Opposite are the remains of warehouses. The east-west main street of the ancient town, paved with flagstones that are hard on one's feet, starts here. It is three-fourths of a mile (1.2 kilometers) long, passing baths, a firefighters' barracks, temples, a theater, the porticoed forum, a market, and a Christian basilica.

There are some—but not a great many—explanatory signs in Italian and English. Visitors who want detailed comments on what they see can make a deal with one of the licensed guides at the entrance gate. Garbage cans for the benefit of picnickers are provided; the park is reasonably tidy.

The oft-restored theater from the second century A.D. had space for 2,700 spectators. At present theatrical performances and concerts take place in it occasionally. The front of the theater houses an espresso and snack shop and a bookstore.

Behind the theater, toward the river, is the large, so-called Square of the Guilds (Piazzale delle Corporazioni) with the remains of seventy offices of workers' associations and agencies of foreign shippers. Black-and-white floor mosaics identify the groups that were using the chambers by their logos—ships with square sails, bushels of grain, dolphins, elephants, and a swastika. Corporations of shipowners in Carthage, Alexandria, Narbo (the modern French Narbonne), and other seaports are mentioned in inscriptions.

The central forum is delimited toward the Tiber by the brick ruins of the Capitol, ancient Ostia's most important temple, which was dedicated to three major deities, Jupiter, Juno, and Minerva. Opposite was the temple of the goddess of Rome and the deified Augustus, and adjacent was a vast, comfortable bathing establishment. Several other public baths once existed in the town, and their mosaics and pipes for water and vapor have been partially preserved.

On the western outskirts of the ancient town, close to the old seacoast, the remains of a Jewish synagogue, identified by ritual symbols, were dug up during the 1960s. According to scholars the synagogue was used between the first and fifth centuries A.D.

Ostia Antica is of paramount importance in our understanding of ancient Roman civilization. The town presents well-preserved examples of residential buildings for the middle and lower classes that in all likelihood once abounded in Rome as well, but which have vanished there almost completely.

Most of the people in ancient Ostia lived in apartment houses, up to four stories high, that were grouped in blocks called *insulae* (islands). Apartments came in various sizes, a few with terraces or balconies. Windows of mica or some other translucent mineral—traces of which have been found—let daylight into the rooms. The ground floors often contained shops and taverns.

The upper class of ancient Ostia, including high officials and rich traders, lived in low villalike houses reminiscent of those that have been preserved in Pompeii (which, unlike the densely populated seaport of Rome, was a well-to-do country town and resort).

The **Museum of Ostia Antica (Museo Ostiense)**, close to the Tiber, contains a dozen showrooms in a building that goes back to the sixteenth century, with a neoclassical facade erected on orders from Pope Pius IX in 1864. It holds reliefs, mosaics, sculptures, vases, and other objects found in the area. Noteworthy are detached wall paintings with various portraits, statues of Roman emperors, and a black headless Isis in dramatic movement, her vestments billowing, with the fragments of a large snake; the Egyptian goddess was widely worshipped in Rome as well.

East of the archeological park, a few minutes' walk from the ticket office or the railroad station, is the present-day village of Ostia Antica, home to a few thousand people, many of whom commute to jobs in Rome. It is dominated by a fifteenth-century fortress with stout brick walls that the pugnacious Cardinal Giuliano della Rovere, who was to become Pope Julius II, built to protect the seaport, which was then still nearby, and to intercept seaborne raiders who might try to assault Rome.

Minor sculptures and other local finds, for which the museum had no space, are stored in the fortress. The structure, also known as the Castello (Castle), needs repairs and has been closed to visitors for some time. A sign says that the office of the Superintendent of the Antiquities of Ostia Antica cannot grant any special permits to visit the Castle.

Facing the fortress is the little Church of St. Aurea, with a rose window. It was designed by Cardinal della Rovere's architect, the Florentine Baccio Pontelli. Next to it is an arcaded bishop's residence. Ostia Antica is the see of the Cardinal Bishop of Ostia (who lives in Rome). Well-maintained old houses, some adorned with flowers, huddle within the village's walls. New buildings are found outside the walls.

When you get hungry for simple fare, try Ristorante Monumento, 8 Piazza Umberto I (telephone: 5650021); or Allo Sbarco di Enea, 675 Via dei Romagnoli (telephone: 5650253), with garden.

Air passengers who look out of the windows during

takeoff from Leonardo da Vinci International Airport at Fiumicino, northwest of Ostia Antica, see a hexagonal pond about 3 miles (5 kilometers) from the seashore. The artificial lake is a harbor basin constructed under Emperor Trajan in A.D. 103 as an alternative to Ostia. Trajan's harbor soon took away much commerce from the older seaport.

SEASIDE TOWNS AND BEACHES

The seaside community of **Lido di Ostia**, also known as Lido di Roma, almost 2 miles (a little more than 3 kilometers) from Ostia Antica and about 19 miles (30 kilometers) from the center of Rome, extends along the bathing beach closest to the capital. An abandoned and malarial stretch of the coastline until the beginning of the twentieth century, the area was developed after World War I. It borrowed its ambitious name from the fashionable resort island that separates Venice's lagoon from the Adriatic Sea, the Lido.

The construction of the electric railroad from Rome to Ostia, which originally started near the Pyramid of C. Cestius, and the two motorways—the Via del Mare (National Highway No. 8) and the Via Cristoforo Colombo—resulted in a construction boom along the shore. Today Lido di Ostia is a seaside suburb 3 miles (5 kilometers) long and up to ten city blocks deep. Many Romans own second homes here; others rent apartments for the summer months. Many thousands, including recent immigrants to Italy, also live in Lido di Ostia in winter.

On summer weekends more than 100,000 people may crowd the many bathing concessions that take up almost all the dark gray, iron-rich sand, leaving precious little space to persons who don't feel like paying for access to the sea. Bathing off Lido di Ostia is not recommended because the water is heavily polluted from the nearby Tiber delta. Some beach concessions offer their patrons freshwater pools. Several beach establishments have restaurants; other eating places abound along the waterfront and in the adjacent streets. Don't expect memorable culinary experiences.

Campsites (see page 45) and "free" beaches, unencumbered by concessions, are to be found southeast of Lido di Ostia, beyond the last stop of the Rome-Ostia railroad at Via Cristoforo Colombo. All beaches near Rome are overrun by ambulant vendors from African countries peddling cheap rugs, sunglasses, leather goods, and other merchandise.

Fiumicino, which has lent its name to the nearby international airport, is a harbor village at the northern mouth of the Tiber, nearly 4 miles (6 kilometers) northwest of Lido di Ostia and 17.5 miles (28 kilometers) from Rome's center. ACOTRAL buses to "Fiumicino Paese" (Village of Fiumicino, as distinct from Fiumicino Airport) leave from the Pyramid of C. Cestius.

Fiumicino looks scruffy, but quite a few Romans like to drive out to the village for an alfresco meal in one of a score of seafood restaurants. There is a project for the construction of a large marina.

Fregene, 5.5 miles (nearly 9 kilometers) northwest of Fiumicino and 24 miles (38 kilometers) from the center of Rome, is the choicest beach resort near the capital. ACOTRAL buses for Fregene leave from Via Lepanto in the Prati section (Lepanto stop of the subway's Line A). By car, take the Via Aurelia (National Highway No. 1) or the A-12 Motorway to Civitavecchia as far as the Maccarese-Fregene exit.

A vast pine grove and a beach of fine sand that isn't as dark as Ostia's are Fregene's main attractions. The water is described as relatively clean, but some of the bathing concessions have freshwater swimming pools. Many Roman middle-class families own villas in Fregene, and their breadwinners commute to businesses or professional offices in Rome during the hot months.

There are a few restaurants, cafés, pizzerias, and discotheques, but on weekdays the place is quiet; less so on weekends. Visitors wanting to stay overnight may try to get accommodation at the La Conchiglia Hotel (telephone: 6460235, fax: 6460229), which is open all year and has a pleasant garden restaurant.

An Etruscan-Roman settlement, Fregenae, existed in the area more than two thousand years ago. The name was revived in 1925 when the beach resort was started after the marshland in its rear had been reclaimed. What once was Fregenae is now the village of Maccarese, the center of model farms that supply Rome with dairy products and vegetables.

Farther to the northwest, at 32 miles (51 kilometers) from Rome and 3 miles (about 5 kilometers) from the popular beach of Ladispoli, is the very ancient town of **Cerveteri** (cher-VAYH-ta-ree), which the ancient Romans called Caere. Some 2,500 years ago it was one of the wealthiest and most powerful Etruscan cities, and its ships sailed far and wide. Rome annexed Caere in the fourth century B.C. In the Middle Ages the town became a possession of aristocratic families, first the Orsinis, then the Ruspolis.

Cerveteri's fame rests on the vast Etruscan cemeteries in its vicinity. The tombs, systematically excavated since the early nineteenth century, have yielded Greek and Etruscan vases, other pottery, sculptures, and sundry objects

that are on view today in the Etruscan museums of the
Vatican and the Valle Giulia in Rome, as well as in institutions abroad.

Archeological poachers known as *tombaroli* (roughly,
grave robbers) have looted the Etruscan tombs for generations and are still active in the area. Clandestine diggings
are said to result in valuable finds from time to time even
now. Italian officials assert that precious articles unearthed
near Cerveteri have recently been spirited out of the country and sold to museums and private collectors in the
United States and elsewhere.

ACOTRAL buses leave for Cerveteri from Via Lepanto (see page 236, under Fregene). By car, take the Via
Aurelia (National Highway No. 1) or the A-16 Motorway to Civitavecchia as far as the Cerveteri-Ladispoli exit.
Trains from the Stazione Termini in Rome reach the
Cerveteri-Ladispoli station in about forty minutes; there is
bus service from the station to Cerveteri.

The cemetery most easily visited is the Necropolis of
the Banditaccia, on a tufa hill 1.25 miles (2 kilometers)
north of Cerveteri. It is open 9 A.M. to 1 P.M. and 4 to 7
P.M. Tuesday to Sunday (10 A.M. to 4 P.M. from September
30 to April 30).

The vast burial site includes open graves and underground chambers. Tombs from the seventh and sixth centuries B.C., some decorated with stuccoes and reliefs,
imitate the dwellings of people who were living at that
time.

The National Museum of Cerveteri in the Palazzo Ruspoli (the former Orsini castle) in the town (telephone:
9941354) is open 9 A.M. to 1 P.M. and 4 to 7 P.M. Tuesday
to Sunday. Sarcophagi, ceramics, including vases that the
Etruscans had imported from Greece, and other items
found in the tombs are on display.

THE ALBAN HILLS

Romans of past generations loved to spend summer vacations in the picturesque and salubrious hillside to the southeast of their city, which still supplies much of the wine that is drunk in the capital all year round. More recently the Alban Hills have slipped out of fashion because city dwellers, especially the younger ones, now prefer the seaside for relaxation and vacations.

Visitors to Rome who can spare half a day or a day will nevertheless enjoy a trip to one of the hill towns. These have been known as the **Castelli Romani** (Roman Castles) since the Middle Ages, when the ever-feuding aristocratic clans built their strongholds there.

Geologically, the hills in which the wine-growing towns nestle are parts of a volcanic system that was extinct already at the dawn of history. The vines that early settlers planted throve in the volcanic soil. The rim of a giant crater, 36 miles (nearly 57 kilometers) in circumference, can be discerned in circular ridges. Two subcraters are filled with water, forming Lake Albano and the delightful Lake Nemi.

The most worthwhile excursions are to the town of Frascati, the papal summer residence of Castelgandolfo, Lake Nemi with its Museum of Roman ships, and the summit of Monte Cavo. All Castelli Romani are linked with the capital by public buses, and some can be reached by rail.

Frascati

Frequent trains depart for Frascati from the Stazione Termini, platforms 23–26 (a quarter-mile or 400-meter walk from the front gallery); the trip takes about thirty minutes.

ACOTRAL buses for Frascati leave from the Anagnina
stop at the southeastern end of the subway's Line A.
By car, take the Via Appia Nuova from the Lateran and
turn off, left, into the Via Tuscolana (National Highway
No. 215).

More than 1,000 feet (300 meters) above the level of
Rome, Frascati's vast main square, the Piazza G. Marconi,
is like a balcony looking out on the capital. The view is
best in the late afternoon and evening. Turn around toward
the hillside to view Villa Aldobrandini, the most magnificent of the aristocratic mansions in and near Frascati. It
was designed around 1600 by Giacomo della Porta, the
architect who succeeded Michelangelo in directing the giant building project of St. Peter's.

In 1943–44 the princely residence was the seat of the
Nazi High Command in Italy, a circumstance that
prompted heavy Allied air attacks. The Villa Aldobrandini
was gravely damaged, and four-fifths of Frascati was
bombed into rubble. The town was quickly rebuilt; most
of the houses in the narrow streets and little squares are
new. The Villa Aldobrandini too was completely restored,
but it cannot be visited.

A large section of the gardens of the Villa Aldobrandini
is now a public park, with an entrance from the right side
of the Piazza G. Marconi. Statuary, artificial grottoes and
ruins, ponds and fountains combine with natural rocks
and old trees into the quintessential baroque pleasure
garden.

The spacious Aldobrandini mansion and its park contrast with the compactness of the town proper. Note the
exuberant baroque facade of the cathedral, which survived
the air raids. Inside, left, is a plaque commemorating
Charles Edward Stuart, the "Young Pretender" who, after

failing to win the English throne, lived in Rome; his brother Henry, Duke of York, was cardinal of Frascati. Follow the yellow street signs to the Jesuit Church, remarkable for its interior with a painted cupola that is an optical trick, a trompe l'oeil. The nearby bishop's palace was built in the Middle Ages as a castle. A Romanesque bell tower, the Campanile di San Rocco, also signposted, belongs to a rebuilt church; it is leaning slightly.

A lively market is held every weekday morning in a hall and nearby square on the eastern edge of Frascati. Fresh country bread, cold cuts, and cheeses on sale there make excellent sandwiches for outings to the other Castelli Romani. Several plain trattorie and a couple of more pretentious eating places in and around Frascati tend to be crowded on weekends. None is exceptional, but one or the other has a pleasant terrace.

One possible hike is to the ruins of ancient **Tusculum** (in Italian: Tuscolo) on a slope about 1,000 feet (300 meters) higher than Frascati, southeast of the town. A road and eventually a footpath through oak and chestnut forests lead to the site in an hour. In classical times Tusculum was a fashionable resort favored by Cicero, Lucullus, Maecenas, and other Roman notables who had villas there.

In the early Middle Ages the counts of Tusculum were for a time the overlords of Rome, and they appointed the popes. Then the Romans revolted, destroying the hilltop castle of the bothersome counts and all of Tusculum with it. Only an ancient amphitheater, which accommodated 3,000 spectators, and a few other ruins have remained.

Buses for the other towns in the Alban Hills leave Frascati from the Piazza G. Marconi. The Tourist Information Office, 1 Via Marconi (telephone: 9420331) at the lower left side of the main square, offers advice on what

to see and do in and around Frascati and elsewhere in the
Castelli Romani.

Castelgandolfo

When the pope is staying in his summer residence, travel
organizations in Rome conduct coach trips to Castelgandolfo on Wednesday, the day of his general audience for
pilgrims and tourists. A visit to the little town on the rim
of a prehistoric crater, with vistas of Lake Albano below,
is also worthwhile when the pontiff is not in residence.

The ridge on which Castelgandolfo sits was the site of
the very ancient town of Alba Longa, which gave its name
to nearby Albano and to the Alban Hills. The Romans
destroyed Alba Longa around 600 B.C.

ACOTRAL buses for Castelgandolfo leave from the
Anagnina terminal of the subway's Line A (see page 240,
under Frascati). Trains from the Stazione Termini, platforms 23–26, leave for Castelgandolfo and Albano every
one or two hours. The Castelgandolfo railroad station is
about halfway between the lake and the town; a road and
a footpath lead up the north end of Castelgandolfo near
the papal palace. The walk takes ten to fifteen minutes.

By car, take the Via Appia Nuova (National Highway
No. 7) from the Lateran to a turnoff at the left side soon
after Ciampino Airport, and proceed on the Via dei Laghi
(Road of the Lakes, National Highway No. 217), which
rises to Castelgandolfo.

The papal palace was erected in the early seventeenth
century by Carlo Maderna, with a simple facade looking
at what is now the Piazza del Plebiscito. The pontifical
estate is legally a dependency of the State of Vatican City
and therefore extraterritorial. It includes vast walled gardens and an astronomical observatory, staffed by Jesuit

scientists, which was transferred to Castelgandolfo from the Vatican in 1936. There is also a modern audience hall for rainy days, a model farm, and a covered swimming pool built on orders from Pope John Paul II.

Lake Albano, fed by underground springs, is 436 feet (133 meters) below Castelgandolfo and 960 feet (293 meters) above sea level; its circumference is 6.25 miles (10 kilometers), its maximum depth 558 feet (170 meters). The lake is kept always at the same level by a drain that ancient Rome's engineers built by boring a tunnel 8,200 feet (2,500 meters) in length through the crater rim. A point near the drain's opening (in Latin: *emissarium*) can be reached by a footpath descending to the lake from the Castelgandolfo railroad station. The water from Lake Albano, which is at present badly polluted, eventually flows into the Tiber.

Two roads bordered by evergreens, Galleria di Sopra and Galleria di Sotto (Upper and Lower Gallery), lead from Castelgandolfo to **Albano Laziale**. The town still commands fine views from some spots, but its entire area is vastly overbuilt. Traffic in Albano, which straddles National Highway No. 7 (Via Appia), is at times as hectic as in Rome, especially on weekends.

Castelgandolfo has a few plain restaurants with views of Lake Albano. Run-of-the-mill eating places abound in Albano.

Lake Nemi

One of the principal beauty spots of the Alban Hills, Lake Nemi is much smaller than Lake Albano: its circumference is 3.5 miles (5.6 kilometers), its maximum depth only 112 feet (34 meters). It too is drained by an ancient underground canal.

To reach Lake Nemi, take the ACOTRAL bus to the

town of Genzano from the Anagnina terminal of the subway's Line A, then walk to the lake by a steep footpath. By car, drive to Genzano, southeast of Albano, on National Highway No. 7 (Via Appia), proceeding on the road to Nemi, which skirts the south side of the lake.

The Nemi Museum of the Roman Ships, at the north side of the lake, contains scale models of two large galleys built during the reign of Emperor Caligula (A.D. 37–41) and sunk a few years later. It was long known that the two boats were on the bottom of the lake, and in 1928–31 they were recovered after the lake was partially drained.

The salvaged state galleys astonished naval engineers by their size—the larger one was 239 feet by 79 feet (73 meters by 24 meters)—and by their nautical equipment. A special museum to house the ships was built on the lakeshore. A fire destroyed the two galleys and a portion of the building during the German army's retreat from the Alban Hills in June 1944.

The rebuilt museum was reopened in the late 1980s with scale models of the galleys, constructed on the basis of detailed plans that had been drawn up during the 1930s. Also on view are bronze decorations of the original ships that survived the fire and materials related to ancient shipbuilding. The museum, Museo delle Navi (telephone: 9368140), is open 9 A.M. to 2 P.M. daily.

Genzano di Roma

Often choked by traffic on the Via Appia, Genzano carpets its sloping main street, Via Italo Berardi, with flowers in various colors and artistic patterns on the Sunday after the Roman Catholic church feast of Corpus Christi. The spring flower festival, known as the *infiorata*, brings many guests to the town's simple trattorie.

Nemi

At 1,709 feet (521 meters) of altitude, Nemi is nearly 700 feet (205 meters) above the lake that bears its name. June is the time to sample Nemi's famous wild strawberries; a strawberry festival is held on one Sunday in that month, when young local women dressed in the region's traditional costumes serve the delicate fruit to visitors.

ACOTRAL buses for Nemi leave from the Anagnina terminal of the subway's Line A. By car drive either by way of Genzano (see page 244) or by National Highway No. 217, the Road of the Lakes.

Monte Cavo

An ascent of this historic mountain takes the visitor to the loftiest of the Castelli Romani, **Rocca di Papa**, at 2,247 feet (685 meters) altitude. The town, rising scenically on the northern slope of the Monte Cavo, was a well-liked resort to which middle-class Roman families fled from the summer heat until the late 1930s. Evenings in Rocca di Papa in fact are remarkably cool even in July and August. But fashions in summer vacations are fickle, and today the town looks stagnant, its once-fancy hotels long closed.

Take the ACOTRAL bus to Rocca di Papa from the Anagnina terminal of the subway's Line A, or drive by way of National Highway No. 7 (Via Appia) and Road of the Lakes as far as the turnoff at Ponte di Nemi, then less than 2 miles (2.8 kilometers) to Rocca di Papa.

Monte Cavo, 3,113 feet (949 meters) high, is not the most elevated of the Alban Hills; Monte Faete, 1.25 miles (2 kilometers) to the southeast, is 50 feet (7 meters) higher. Yet to the ancient tribes of Latium (the region around Rome), the summit of Monte Cavo, dedicated to Jupiter, was a sacred spot on which their leaders used to meet periodically. A steep, well-preserved Via Sacra (Sacred Road), paved with basalt blocks, climbs the mountain.

More comfortably, a private toll road, starting south of Rocca di Papa, close to the Road of the Lakes, reaches the summit in a series of bends. Hikers ascend the mountain in about an hour on an old mule track, which traverses a dense chestnut and oak forest and allows views of the Sacred Road from some stretches.

The top of Mount Cavo is occupied by a forest of antennas and booster masts put up by various television networks. The exact site of the ancient sanctuary is controversial. An old building on the summit was once a convent of Passionist monks, founded in 1783 by the Duke of York; in the more recent past it served as a hotel. A promenade, a little lower, permits one to take in a panorama embracing the city of Rome, the Tyrrhenian Sea, the Alban Hills, and the mountains south and east of them.

PALESTRINA

Picturesquely rising on a foothill of the Apennine Mountains, this town, 24 miles (38 kilometers) east of Rome, is a showcase of its long history. From many points the visitor sees in the foreground present-day Palestrina, which looks old enough, surmounted by five levels of imposing ruins of an ancient sanctuary, topped by palaces from the seventeenth century.

World War II painfully and bizarrely made Palestrina a major archeological monument. Heavy Allied bombings destroyed many medieval houses, which, when the rubble was cleared, appeared to have been built over the remains of what may well have been the largest temple complex in all of Italy. Even before the immense ancient structures came to light, the National Archeological Museum of Palestrina had been famous for its collection of pre-Roman, Hellenistic, and Roman finds.

ACOTRAL buses for Palestrina leave from the Rebibbia terminal of the subway's Line B.

By car, take the Via Prenestina, a provincial highway starting from Piazza di Porta Maggiore, southeast of the Stazione Termini. Or take the Via Casilina (National Highway No. 6), also starting from Piazza di Porta Maggiore, and National Highway No. 155 from a turnoff near the village of San Cesareo. Either route traverses an area of unattractive suburban sprawl with heavy commercial traffic.

Praeneste, as the ancient Romans called what is today Palestrina, was a fortified settlement of a pre-Roman people 2,700 years ago. Remains of a prehistoric stronghold, with walls of large irregular stones put together without mortar, can be seen high on the slope on which the town rises.

That Praeneste's pre-Roman inhabitants had a remarkable degree of refinement is proved by, among other things, finely worked toiletry boxes in beaten bronze, some of which are on display in the Palestrina museum. Few such cosmetic cases, apparently a must for the elegant Praeneste lady, have been found elsewhere; scholars call these sophisticated artifacts *cistae*.

A scale model of the Praeneste sanctuary, worked up by archeologists, can be viewed in the museum. It shows various sacred buildings supported by huge walls, surrounded by stairways, porches, colonnades, courtyards and fountains. Since earliest times the cluster of temples was dedicated to the goddess of Fate (Fortuna Primigenia), considered the mother and nurse of all the divinities of the

Greek-Roman pantheon. In the imperial era this sacred complex covered nearly the entire area of the present town of Palestrina.

The sanctuary was also the seat of a widely renowned oracle to which Roman emperors, foreign potentates, and other important personages turned for advice. Scholars have identified a "Cave of the Lots" in the courtyard of a former seminary adjoining the cathedral of Palestrina, where the responses of the oracles could be picked up. These pronouncements were apparently written on small tablets and—as was the usual way with all oracles—allowed various interpretations. The questions submitted to the oracle had to be handed to priestly attendants.

Sculptural representations of the goddess of Fate, including fragments of a large marble statue, are displayed in the museum.

A top-floor room of the museum holds the so-called Barberini Mosaic, a first-century B.C. work that adorned one of the temples. It alone is worth a trip to Palestrina. The large tableau, in brilliant colors and in designs one is tempted to describe as witty, represents an Egyptian scene during one of the periodic Nile floods. There are oarsmen navigating the swollen river in basket and papyrus boats, Roman legionnaires and archers, revelers at a banquet on the river shore, and crocodiles, rhinoceroses, snakes, ibises, and ducks. Some of the animals are identified by labels in Greek lettering.

The National Archeological Museum of Palestrina occupies a palace that the Barberini family erected in the seventeenth century on the site of a medieval baronial building, which in its turn had incorporated structures topping the ancient sanctuary. To reach the museum's entrance door the visitor climbs the rows of a ruined Roman amphitheater. The museum, in Piazza della Cortina (telephone: 9558100), is open 9 A.M. to 1:30 P.M. Tuesday to Saturday, 9 A.M. to 12:30 P.M. Sunday.

Most of Palestrina is built on sloping ground, with some lanes consisting entirely of stairs. One of these is marked Via Thomas Mann: the German writer and future Nobel laureate and his brother Heinrich Mann, also an author, stayed in Palestrina in 1897. Thomas Mann put the town into his 1948 novel *Doctor Faustus*.

Palestrina's greatest native son was Giovanni Pierluigi da Palestrina, the sixteenth-century conductor of papal choirs and composer who pioneered polyphonic music. A modern monument praises him in an inscription as "Prince of Music"; it stands in the square next to the cathedral. The town's main street is fittingly named Corso Pier Luigi da Palestrina.

TIVOLI AND HADRIAN'S VILLA

Tivoli

The Latin motto of the hill town 19.5 miles (31 kilometers) northeast of Rome is *Tibur Superbum* (Proud Tivoli). Situated near a dramatic ravine where the Aniene River breaks out of the Sabine Mountains to cascade into the Roman plains, Tivoli is centuries older than the Eternal City. During the imperial era it was a resort where rich Romans relaxed in their sumptuous villas.

Today Tivoli is a cramped, bustling city of fifty-thousand inhabitants that has virtually become a congested suburb of Rome. The visitor has to do some exploring to detect what remains of its once-vaunted charm.

ACOTRAL buses for Tivoli leave at intervals of ten to twenty minutes from the Rebibbia terminal of the sub-

way's Line B. Trains from the Stazione Termini or the
Tiburtina Station take forty to fifty minutes to reach Tivoli, climbing the hillside in a wide loop. The view from
the right-hand windows as the train approaches Tivoli is
not to be missed: after a few tunnels the traveler suddenly
sees the town spreading out below, the Aniene waterfalls
in the foreground.

By car, take the Via Tiburtina (National Highway No.
5) from the Campo Verano cemetery. The road is heavily
traveled and is flanked by machine shops, chemical and
pharmaceutical plants, and other light industry. An alternative is the A-24 Motorway from the GRA beltway to the
Tivoli exit. From there it is almost 7 miles (11 kilometers)
to the town of Tivoli, past the Villa Adriana (see page 252).

Visitors traveling by road arrive in the Piazza Garibaldi,
a vast square where the Via Tiburtina enters the town. The
square is some 700 feet (about 200 meters) above what was
once the Campagna Romana. From the edge of the Piazza
Garibaldi one sees Rome reaching out toward Tivoli with
housing developments, industrial agglomerations, and
busy roads. On the right are two hills topped by two small
towns, Montecelio and Palombara Sabina.

The Tivoli Tourist Office is on the Piazza Garibaldi
(telephone: 0774-21249). A short walk to the north, past
souvenir stands, leads to what tour operators appear to
regard as the city's principal sight, the **Villa d'Este**, a
large, terraced garden with bizarre waterworks amid baroque statuary, tall cypresses, and other evergreens. The
hydraulic wonders include an "Avenue of Hundred Fountains," a "Water Organ," and a "Dragon Fountain." The
effect of the aquatic pleasure park is heightened by its panorama—the old town of Tivoli above and the Roman
plains below, with the capital on the horizon.

The curious gardens with their ornamental fountains

were laid out around the middle of the sixteenth century at the site of a former Benedictine monastery for Ippolito II, Cardinal d'Este, an aristocratic and rich prelate. The park remained a property of the Este family, which once ruled the dukedom of Ferrara, through the centuries. The last private owner was Archduke Franz Ferdinand of Austria-Este, heir apparent to the Habsburg throne, whose assassination in Sarajevo in 1914 unleashed World War I. At the end of that war, in 1918, Italy claimed the Villa d'Este as a part of the national patrimony.

The Villa d'Este is open from 9 A.M. to an hour before sunset Tuesday to Sunday. From the beginning of May to the end of September the gardens are floodlit from 9 to 11:30 P.M. Tuesday to Sunday and are open during these hours. Sound and light performances take place on some summer evenings. Information: 0774-22070.

The waterworks are fed by the Aniene River. In 1990 the water of that river was found to be so polluted in Tivoli as to represent a health hazard if sprayed by the fountains of the Villa d'Este. A new aqueduct, opened in 1991, channels relatively clean water from upstream into the gardens.

Another large park, the **Villa Gregoriana** on the northwestern side of Tivoli, permits a close look at the cascades by which the Aniene plunges from a double tunnel a total of 355 feet (108 meters) into the valley. The park is named after Pope Gregory XVI, who had the tunnels pierced in 1826–35 to end floods that had frequently plagued the area.

A terrace looks out on the ruins of two ancient Roman temples on a cliff, one circular and the other rectangular. Both sanctuaries were thought at one time or another to have been dedicated to the Sibyl, a mythical prophetess. The round temple, which retains ten of its eighteen original Corinthian columns, may actually have been a shrine of

Vesta, the goddess of hearth and home. The rectangular
temple is the one that scholars believe may have been raised
in honor of the Sibyl. The Villa Gregoriana is open daily,
from 9:30 A.M. to an hour before sunset.

A few restaurants have terraces overlooking the Aniene
ravine and the waterfalls; they are often crowded on weekends. Among them is Sibilla, 50 Via della Sibilla (telephone: 0774-20281).

A citadel with towers and battlements near the Piazza
Garibaldi is known as the Rocca Pia (Rock of Pius) because
Pope Pius II had it built in the second half of the fifteenth
century to reassert papal rule of "proud Tivoli." Behind
the stronghold are the remains of a Roman amphitheater.

The vast medieval quarter in the north of Tivoli is a
maze of sloping streets, stairways, and old houses, many
of them dilapidated. The overall impression is gloomy.
The cathedral (Duomo) in a northern neighborhood is very
old; it was rebuilt in the baroque style during the sixteenth
century and today looks musty.

The best views of Tivoli and its cascades are from the
Via delle Cascatelle, a curving road turning off from the
Villa Gregoriana (see above), leading to the Palombara
Sabina-Marcellina railroad station, about 5 miles (8 kilome-
ters) to the northwest.

Hadrian's Villa

A trip to Tivoli can be combined with a visit to the ruined
imperial pleasure grounds of Hadrian's Villa, 3 miles
(nearly 5 kilometers) southwest of the town.

Buses for Villa Adriana (Hadrian's Villa) leave from
the Tivoli bus terminal at Viale delle Nazioni Unite near
Piazza Garibaldi. Sightseers wanting to reach Hadrian's
Villa directly from Rome take the ACOTRAL bus for

Tivoli, getting out at the Bivio Villa Adriana (turnoff for Hadrian's Villa) stop, and proceed on the local bus. From the turnoff it is about a mile (1.6 kilometers) to the entrance.

By car, take the Via Tiburtina or the A-24 Motorway to the Bivio Villa Adriana and proceed to the parking lot past the ticket office. Private travel organizations in Rome conduct coach trips to Hadrian's Villa.

A scale model in the hall adjacent to the coffee bar gives an idea of how the vast imperial estate was laid out. Hadrian, emperor from A.D. 117 to 138, had it developed in a bowl of the terrain southwest of Tibur (Tivoli) toward the end of his reign. His villa spread over 180 acres (73 hectares), not quite the size of one-fourth of Central Park in New York. In addition to a large imperial palace there were many other structures, including quarters for bodyguards, firemen, and slaves, as well as artificial lakes and splendid gardens.

When Hadrian's incessant journeys all over the Roman world were nearly ended, he ordered his architects to fill the vast grounds with replicas of colonnades, sanctuaries, amphitheaters, baths, and other sights that had struck his fancy in Greece, Egypt, and elsewhere. A circular building containing a pond and an artificial island is signposted as Teatro Marittimo (Naval Theater), but it may have served other purposes.

A copy of the temple of the Greek god Serapis, healer of the sick, in the town of Canopus, near Alexandria, may have been built to stage Egyptian-rite celebrations, then fashionable in Rome. The vast reproduction of an Egyptian landmark in the north of the villa, with a canal cut into a tufa hill, was probably meant to commemorate Hadrian's unforgotten favorite Antinoüs, who had been drowned in the Nile in A.D. 130.

Near the Canopus site is the museum containing statues and other objects found in a continuing series of excavations begun in 1950. Many of the sculptures that were dug up in Hadrian's Villa earlier—since the Renaissance era—are on view in the Vatican Museums, in other collections in Rome, and in institutions from London to St. Petersburg.

Visitors are not allowed to enter any of the many underground passages in Hadrian's Villa. These formed an intricate network enabling service personnel to reach most points of the estate without being seen, but they also may have been used by the emperor, who had become something of a recluse, and his guests.

Hadrian's Villa (telephone: 0774-20281) is open from 9 A.M. to about an hour before sunset Tuesday to Sunday. Licensed guides are usually to be found near the entrance. To inspect it thoroughly, half a day is barely sufficient. It's a good place for a picnic; otherwise, outside the Villa Adriana is the pleasant Ristorante Adriano (telephone: 0774-529174).

LAKE BRACCIANO

The Renaissance fortress at Bracciano on the southwestern shore of large, circular Lake Bracciano looks real even today. With five round towers over battlements, and ramparts in gray-brown tufa stone, it scowls and seems to menace as in the days of old.

The somber structure is still known as the **Orsini Castle** in memory of the princely Roman family that built it toward the end of the fifteenth century and held it for more than two hundred years. Eventually the Orsinis sold the stronghold to another aristocratic clan, the Odescalchis of Rome, for 386,300 scudi, equivalent to $2 million today.

Guided half-hour tours of the Orsini Castle (telephone: 9024050) start from the doorway in Piazza Mazzini every hour, from 9 A.M. to noon and 3 to 5 P.M. Thursday, Saturday, Sunday, and public holidays. Visitors are shown magnificent halls on two levels with beamed and stuccoed ceilings, frescoes and paintings by minor masters of the fourteenth and fifteenth centuries, and Renaissance furniture.

Many windows and the terraces of the castle command a vast panorama of the lake, with Mount Soracte (Monte Soratte) as a backdrop in the northeast. Virgil and Horace praised that isolated limestone ridge; Byron likened the Soracte to a "long-swept wave about to break."

The town of Bracciano, interesting in itself, is also a good starting point for exploring the other communities around the lake. With a maximum depth of 525 feet (160 meters) and a circumference of 19 miles (30 kilometers), Lake Bracciano fills the crater of a long-extinct volcano.

ACOTRAL buses for Bracciano and two other towns on the lakeshore, Trevignano and Anguillara (see below), depart from the Lepanto stop of the subway's Line A at Viale Giulio Cesare and Via Lepanto. Trains to Bracciano leave from the Stazione Termini or the San Pietro Station, south of St. Peter's Square, taking seventy-five minutes for the trip, with many intermediate stops.

By car, take the Via Cassia (National Highway No. 2) from the Flaminio Bridge to the suburb of La Storta, turning left there to proceed on National Highway No. 493. The road distance from Rome to Bracciano is 24 miles (39 kilometers).

Bracciano's tourist information office is at 72 Via Claudia (telephone: 9024451).

The medieval district of Bracciano (Borgo Medioevale) huddles on a slope descending from what once was the castle's drawbridge and is now a bridge in masonry over a moat to an outer wall at the foot of the castle hill. The highest part of the old town is occupied by an undistinguished church with a Baroque facade. Nearby is the "Sentry," a lookout with a splendid view of the lake.

The modern section of Bracciano, where many Roman families own second homes, extends between the medieval town and the railroad station, also on a slope. The north side of the castle hill is a walled private park whose tall palms are evidence of the lakeside's mild climate. A road descends to the lakeshore, where a few cafés and a bathing beach can be found.

The restaurant and hotel Casina del Lago, 11 Lungolago Argenti (telephone: 9024025), on the lakefront about half a mile (1 kilometer) from the town center is plain but satisfactory.

Bracciano is linked by a bus service with **Trevignano Romano**, 7 miles (11 kilometers) to the northeast. This overgrown village, which hugs the northern lakeshore for more than a mile, has lately become a favorite weekend retreat and summer resort both with Romans and with expatriates living in the Italian capital. English and other foreign languages can often be heard in Trevignano's espresso bars and simple trattorie. A ruined medieval castle tops a hill overlooking the village.

On the opposite (south) shore of the lake, 8.5 miles (14 kilometers) from Bracciano, is **Anguillara Sabázia**, a picturesque town on a high promontory. The name *Anguillara* may or may not be derived from the Italian word for eel, *anguilla*. Lake Bracciano was indeed famed since antiquity for its eels and other fish. Today the lake is badly polluted.

The word *Sabázia* in the town's official name is a reminder of the lost Etruscan town of Sabate, which supposedly was located somewhere around the lake, maybe at the site of Trevignano Romano. What today is Lake Bracciano was to the ancients the Lake of Sabate (Lacus Sabatinus). Recent excavations have found evidence that prehistoric settlers were dwelling on the lakeshore long before the Etruscans.

Lake Bracciano is popular with camping enthusiasts. Various campsites occupy the lakefront near Trevignano and Anguillara.

Index